The Everyday Political Economy of Southeast Asia

In this empirically rich collection of chapters, a team of leading international scholars explore the way that economic policy making is sustained and challenged by everyday practices across Southeast Asia. Drawing together a body of interdisciplinary scholarship, the authors explore how the emergence of more marketized forms of economic policy making in Southeast Asia impacts everyday life. The book's twelve chapters address topics such as domestic migration; trade union politics in Myanmar; mining in the Philippines; halal food in Singapore; Islamic finance in Malaysia; education reform in Indonesia; street vending in Malaysia; regional migration between Malaysia, Indonesia, and Cambodia; and Southeast Asian domestic workers in Hong Kong. This collection not only enhances understandings of the everyday political economies at work in specific Southeast Asian sites, but makes a major theoretical contribution to the development of an Everyday Political Economy approach in which perspectives from developing economies and non-Western actors are taken seriously.

JUANITA ELIAS is Associate Professor of International Political Economy at the University of Warwick.

LENA RETHEL is Associate Professor of International Political Economy at the University of Warwick.

The Everyday Political Economy of Southeast Asia

Edited by

Juanita Elias

and

Lena Rethel

CAMBRIDGE
UNIVERSITY PRESS

CAMBRIDGE
UNIVERSITY PRESS

University Printing House, Cambridge CB2 8BS, United Kingdom

Cambridge University Press is part of the University of Cambridge.

It furthers the University's mission by disseminating knowledge in the pursuit of
education, learning and research at the highest international levels of excellence.

www.cambridge.org
Information on this title: www.cambridge.org/9781107122338

© Cambridge University Press 2016

First published 2016

A catalogue record for this publication is available from the British Library

Library of Congress Cataloguing in Publication data
Names: Elias, Juanita, editor. | Rethel, Lena, editor.
Title: The everyday political economy of Southeast Asia / edited by
Juanita Elias and Lena Rethel.
Description: Cambridge, England : Cambridge University Press, [2016] |
Includes bibliographical references and index.
Identifiers: LCCN 2015042944 | ISBN 9781107122338 (hardback)
Subjects: LCSH: Southeast Asia – Economic conditions. |
Economic development – Social aspects – Southeast Asia.
Classification: LCC HC441.E946 2016 | DDC 330.959–dc23
LC record available at http://lccn.loc.gov/2015042944

ISBN 978-1-107-12233-8 Hardback

Such was the love of this grandson for his grandmother that two years after the death of his mother, when she herself fell gravely ill, he vowed to her that someday he would try to tell the world her life story.

'But why?' she asked humbly. 'I'm no one, just a girl from the coast.'

'But you are everyone, Grandma', the young Pramoedya told her. 'You are all the people who have ever had to fight to make this life their own.'

Pramoedya Ananta Toer, *The Girl from the Coast*

Contents

Figures and Map

Figures

Map

Tables

Notes on Contributors

ALVIN A. CAMBA is a PhD student in sociology at Johns Hopkins University.

JUANITA ELIAS is Associate Professor in International Political Economy at the University of Warwick.

JOHAN FISCHER is Associate Professor in the Department of Society and Globalization, Roskilde University.

ANJA K. FRANCK is Senior Lecturer and researcher at the School of Global Studies at the University of Gothenburg.

NICHOLAS HENRY is Lecturer in International Relations at Deakin University.

JOHN M. HOBSON is Professor of Politics and International Relations at the University of Sheffield.

JONATHON LOUTH is a Visiting Research Fellow at the University of Adelaide, where he is also an associate of the Indo-Pacific Governance Research Centre.

JEWELLORD T. NEM SINGH is a Japan Society for the Promotion of Science International Research Fellow at the University of Tokyo.

LENA RETHEL is Associate Professor of International Political Economy at the University of Warwick.

JONATHAN RIGG is a development geographer and Professor at the National University Singapore.

ANDREW ROSSER is Associate Professor of Development Studies and an Australian Research Council Future Fellow at the University of Adelaide.

LEONARD SEABROOKE is Professor of International Political Economy in the Department of Business and Politics, Copenhagen Business School.

CAROL G. S. TAN is Professor of Law and former Chair of the Centre of Southeast Asian Studies at SOAS, University of London.

ADAM TYSON is Lecturer in Southeast Asian Politics at the University of Leeds.

Acknowledgements

This book has its origins in the workshop 'The Everyday Political Economy of Southeast Asia' held in 2012 at the University of Warwick. The event was co-sponsored by Warwick's Department of Politics and International Studies and the Griffith Asia Institute, Griffith University. We thank both Andrew O'Neill at Griffith and Chris Hughes at Warwick for their support for the initial workshop project. Many of the chapters in this book (Nem Singh and Camba, Franck, Rethel, Tyson, Tan, Elias and Louth) were presented in some form as part of this workshop, but we are also grateful to the authors who came on board with this project at later dates (Rosser, Fischer, Rigg, Henry, Hobson and Seabrooke).

There are numerous other people whose support we would like to acknowledge. For his comments on the initial book proposal, we thank Jason Sharman. We are grateful to André Broome, Shahar Hamieri, Carolin Liss, Jewellord Nem Singh, Andrew Rosser, Lisa Tilley, Lauren Tooker, Matthew Watson and Wesley Widmaier for their comments on the introductory chapter. We also thank the two anonymous reviewers whose comments and criticisms on the initial manuscript have greatly strengthened the book. We are thankful to Patrick Allington for editing the first draft of the manuscript and to Tadgh O'Sullivan for the compilation of the index. We are also extremely grateful to Lucy Rhymer at CUP for her support for this project.

Part I

Introduction

1   Southeast Asia and Everyday Political Economy

Juanita Elias and Lena Rethel

Introduction

Southeast Asia is an increasingly interdependent, globalized and urbanized region of the world. The eleven countries that are generally understood as comprising modern-day Southeast Asia are now ever more closely linked together via flows of trade, investment and migration, in addition to traditional state-led processes of regional integration – most notably the emergence of the Association of Southeast Asian Nations (ASEAN) – as well as ever closer, and overlapping, bilateral economic and security ties.[1] In the nearly two decades since Thailand floated the baht, an event commonly held to mark the outbreak of the Asian financial crisis of 1997–8, the region has become more closely integrated than ever before. The launch of the ASEAN Economic Community marks – at least rhetorically – the high point of a period of state-led economic development, market reform and regional integration. Indeed today, we see a region that while not unified is certainly deeply interconnected. In the shadow of Asia's two giants, India and China, the Southeast Asian region has been somewhat sidelined within debates about and discussions of the looming 'Asian Century'.

Much analytical effort has been put into understanding the respective influences of state and market forces in driving the region's economic transformation. Nonetheless, Southeast Asia provides an important site for considering how processes of economic transformation are refashioning – and refashioned by – the lives and daily routines of ordinary people: their decisions to migrate across borders; their experiences of growing affluence as well as of inequality, poverty and associated forms of violence and destitution; their activities as activists, citizens and workers; and the ways in which economic and social relations, responsibilities and activities are being transformed. Southeast Asia is, and will remain, a heterogeneous region of the world. And yet, this very diversity of culture, politics, religion, society and economics – intersecting

---

[1] These are Myanmar, Cambodia, Laos, Vietnam, Thailand, the Philippines, Malaysia, Indonesia, Brunei Darussalam, Singapore and East Timor. With the exception of East Timor, all of these states are ASEAN members.

with divisions of race, class, gender and even age – provides important insights into how economic transformation takes shape. If we are entering an Asian Century, then we need to remain attentive to how this transformation is taking shape in the lives of Asia's people and their engagement in changing economic practices, with Southeast Asia providing an important terrain for initiating this focus.

Accordingly, this book brings an Everyday Political Economy (EPE) perspective to the fore. In this perspective, we consider not only the ways in which economic transformations 'touch down' within the lives of ordinary people but also how the emergence of more marketized forms of economic policy making is sustained and challenged through everyday practices of economic engagement. We use the term 'Everyday Political Economy' in a broad and inclusive sense, as a mechanism for generating interdisciplinary conversations across a range of theoretical traditions. As we outline later (and also in our conclusion), our use of EPE draws upon a broad extant literature on 'the everyday', 'everyday life' and 'everyday politics'. In certain respects we embrace the fuzziness of the term, in large part because it serves to open up interdisciplinary dialogue as well as to challenge what Hobson and Seabrooke (2007) have referred to as a 'regulatory' bias in studies of the International Political Economy (IPE). It should be noted, however, that while this book seeks to engage with work on the everyday in IPE (see following sections), we explicitly refer to EPE rather than use Hobson and Seabrooke's term 'Everyday IPE' (EPIE). This is in large part because we seek to develop an interdisciplinary and inclusive approach that reaches beyond the intellectual confines of IPE. Nonetheless, we recognize the significance of IPE works that highlight the role of non-elite local actors in constituting political economic transformations (notable here is Hobson and Seabrooke's engagement of the work of everyday politics scholars such as Scott 1985 and Kerkvliet 1990) or works that engage more of an 'everyday life' perspective emphasizing both the 'mundane' everyday of economic practices (Enloe 2013) and how these practices are underpinned by wider logics of discipline and/or governmentality (Amoore 2002; Paterson 2007; Langley 2008) (see also our concluding chapter in which we elucidate this distinction between an everyday politics and an everyday life perspective in more detail).

In this volume, we seek to present the EPE of Southeast Asia in ways that combine an understanding of both everyday politics and everyday life in order to understand how the reach of the market is being extended into the lives of ordinary people across this economically, culturally and politically diverse region. In this endeavour, charting the voices and actions of the socially marginalized certainly matters – and many of the chapters in this volume do chart these struggles. But it is just as important to examine 'the praxis that organizes' these accounts of everyday life (de Certeau 1986, cited in Joan Scott 1991: 777), in particular how actors' knowledges and accounts of the world take shape within broader processes of state and capitalist transformation. In a Southeast Asian context, this widening and deepening of market relations includes things such as the rise of new commodity trading and consumption regimes (e.g., around Islamic finance and halal products or the turn of former factory workers to street vending), as well as new forms of intra-regional migrations (such as the expansion of markets for migrant domestic work or flows of 'talent'). Ordinary people are situated in and constitute these economic processes and yet also seek to resist, subvert and challenge them. At the same time, however, resistance itself often takes shape within state-led attempts to accommodate dissent by creating spaces for 'market friendly' and regime maintaining civil society engagement (Gerard 2014; Rodan and Hughes 2014; Elias 2015).

In the years since the 1997–8 Asian financial crisis that hit many of the region's economies exceptionally hard, we have seen a consolidation of the political economy literature on Southeast Asia with analyses of the crisis and its impacts providing a fertile ground for advancing political economy scholarship on the region ever since. Much early post-crisis work focused on the responses of elites – generating important insights regarding the tensions that emerged between different groupings of state elites in the aftermath of the crisis. But alongside this work, we can also observe an emerging consensus around the need to focus on the significant roles of non-elite actors and their daily practices of economic engagement. Indeed, this is a theme that has become increasingly important in recent years. Furthermore, as will be detailed later, the emergence of these more 'everyday' perspectives has also generated discussion over the development of a less Western-centric approach to the study of IPE. Such an IPE should recognize that economic transformations outside of the West be understood not in terms of a top-down modernization narrative but instead as enacted, embedded and resisted at the points of intersection with local practices and economic cultures. In so doing, such an approach offers an important point of departure for 'rethinking' Southeast Asian political economy.

This empirically rich book draws together a body of research in Southeast Asian studies spread across a range of disciplinary areas. The authors included in this volume are both established and emerging scholars working on the empirical study of Southeast Asian political economy, and the chapters draw upon original fieldwork conducted in Southeast Asia or among Southeast Asian diasporas. At its core, this research develops a focus on everyday practices of economic engagement that have transformed – and are being transformed by – the region's embrace of market-led developmentalism. In so doing, this volume draws attention not only to a wide range of non-elite actors whose actions are not necessarily considered in studies of the region's economic transformation but also to their practices and routines of daily economic life that play an important role in understanding economic, political and cultural change in

Southeast Asia. Thus, we aim to contribute both to an enhanced understanding of the everyday political economies at work in specific Southeast Asian sites and to the theoretical development of an EPE approach more generally, in which perspectives from emerging economies and non-Western actors are taken seriously. In so doing, we strive to develop the deeply influential literature on everyday politics in Southeast Asia, in particular with regard to the work of Scott (1985) and Kerkvliet (1990), by employing a global political economy lens in which the 'everyday' is seen not only as a site of political struggle and resistance but also as a site within which the ongoing marketization and economic transformation of the region play out in variegated ways.

Rethinking Southeast Asian Political Economy

In thinking about the everyday politics of Southeast Asia's economic transformation, we aim to embrace (i) the mounting interest in moving beyond elite-centric studies of neoliberal developmentalism and towards a growing recognition of everyday economic actors and practices within a range of interdisciplinary studies of the political economy of Southeast Asia; (ii) the rise of an influential everyday perspective in IPE in which attention is drawn to the need to bring in non-Western, specifically Asian, perspectives; and (iii) the fact that Southeast Asia has traditionally served as a major reference point for those interested in everyday politics. Importantly, the Southeast Asian case enables a sharper focus on how the everyday does not exist as an autonomous space separate from the regulatory or elite level. Indeed, one of our central concerns is to show how the developmental ambitions of elites intersect with local social relations of gender, race, class and even age, producing distinctive political-economic outcomes, and how capitalist processes of marketization intersect with everyday lived experiences on the ground.

Social Conflict and the Political Economy of Neoliberal Developmentalism in Southeast Asia

In the wake of the Asian crisis, the work of a number of influential political economists served to define the study of the Southeast Asian region in important ways. This literature – often country-based – sought to emphasize the rise of neoliberal or more regulatory forms of state rule that served to replace the attachment to ideas of state developmentalism (Jayasuriya 2005; Hewison and Robison 2006). It has long been argued that the model of the Asian developmental state that emerged from the writings of Chalmers Johnson (1982) and others was never wholeheartedly reproduced within capitalist Southeast Asia. But with the crises in state governance that emerged out of the Asian crisis, social conflict approaches sought to emphasize the fracturing of elite rule as neoliberal reform moved apace within the region's regulatory states (Robison and Rosser 1998; Hewison 2000, 2005; Khoo 2000; Jayasuriya and Hewison 2004; Case 2005, 2009; Hadiz and Robison 2005; Robison and Hewison 2005). The emphasis on elite fracturing and class tensions in this post-crisis wave of writings must be contrasted with the deeply undersocialized, highly technocratic accounts of Southeast Asia's economic transformation that are perhaps best exemplified by the World Bank's report, *The East Asian Miracle* (1993). And, of course, as we argue in more detail later, the emphasis on elites was not to deny the significance of non-elites in the transformation of the state. In particular, attention has been drawn to how political systems have sought to accommodate a range of social forces such as the region's rising middle classes (Robison and Goodman 1996; Hilley 2001), as well as the strategies and dilemmas faced by organized labour in ever more capitalist-oriented states (Hadiz 1997; Bello *et al.* 1998; Hutchinson and Brown 2002; Brown 2004; Hutchinson 2012). It is worth restating that scholarship mainly associated with the social conflict or 'Murdoch school' of critical political economy has developed grounded understanding of how capitalism and class politics operate within particular nation-states in the Southeast Asian region.

Interestingly, although this research has focused considerable attention on conflicts within the social elite in order to understand the nature of transformations in state rule in the region, the detailed empirical research that underpinned these accounts does open up further space for the discussion of a more 'everyday' political economy – for example, in terms of accounts of the rise of precarious, low-paid work (including migrant work) that have accompanied the region's neoliberal transition (Hewison 2006; Hewison and Kalleberg 2013); or more specifically in terms of thinking about and theorizing the agency (and lack of agency) of civil society actors and organized labour; see Rodan and Hughes's (2012) work on anti-corruption activism in the Philippines and Cambodia. While this work tends to depict labour and civil society activism rather cynically emphasizing the limited possibilities for resistance (and, moreover, democratization), one must take into account the endurance of authoritarian systems of rule, oligarchic capitalism and political violence in the region that place significant limits on the ability of everyday actors to enact a transformatory politics (Jayasuriya and Rodan 2007). Moreover, this greater openness to non-elite agency – and recognition of an expanding number of non-elite actors – has been reinforced by the increasing attention that disciplines such as sociology and social anthropology paid to the everyday economic and political cultures within which middle-class groupings and other social actors are embedded (see, e.g., Chua 2003 on Singaporean patterns of consumption, and Sen and Stiven's 1998 edited volume on women and the new rich in Asia).

We would suggest that in recent years an important shift is afoot in studies of Southeast Asian political economy. On the one hand, we have already charted the increased attention to the everyday that has emerged in Southeast Asian political economy scholarship. But, on the other hand, it is also important to consider the move within studies of the social anthropology (a discipline traditionally focused on the realm of everyday life) of the region to take political economy seriously (notably Tsing 2005; Li 2007; Nevins and Peluso 2008; Rudnyckyj 2010). In seeking to represent the emergence of EPE in Southeast Asian studies, it is essential then to recognize the work of social anthropologists who have sought to connect ethnographies of everyday life to global political-economic restructuring. This work emphasizes the associated processes of enclosure, commodification and proletarianization that contribute to the ever-widening reach of the market into the lives of Southeast Asians (a position articulated most concisely in Nevins and Peluso 2008). Economic change is, nonetheless, overseen by forms of state rule that seek to promote ideals of the neoliberal citizen-subject while simultaneously ensuring that such ideas rest upon (deeply racialized and gendered) practices of exclusion – particularly of the region's indigenous, migrant and refugee populations (Ong 2006). Of course, we should also recognize the rise of more everyday accounts of the political economy of the region from geographers highlighting the everyday spatial organization of economic development both inside and outside the cities of Southeast Asia (Clammer 2003; Rigg 2003; Bunnell 2004), as well as the (re) location of neoliberal development within previously non-capitalist places such as the household (Brickell 2011). We identify this interdisciplinary consensus around the need to take *both* political economy *and* the everyday seriously as an important analytical shift in the study of the region. The chapters in this volume seek to showcase this emergent approach and, in doing so, reveal how the EPE exists in relation to complex configurations of classed, gendered, racialized and other sets of social relations.

The Everyday Turn in IPE and the Significance of Non-Western Contexts

The development of a more everyday perspective on Southeast Asian political economy also mirrors wider trends within IPE – namely a significant body of literature that points to the role of everyday practices, cultures and relationships in understanding the social sources of the global political economy (Amoore 2002; Aitken 2007; Hobson and Seabrooke 2007; Langley 2008; Best and Paterson 2009; LeBaron 2010; Seabrooke and Elias 2010). Hobson and Seabrooke's edited volume, *Everyday Politics of the World Economy* (2007), seeks to identify how broader processes of global political economic change are rooted within particular forms of everyday activity. The arguments put forward by Hobson and Seabrooke are important for a number of reasons. First, they rightly identify the problematic reification of regulatory elites and actors across a spectrum of IPE writings – be they state policy-makers, international financial institutions and other organizations engaged in global economic governance; elite groupings tied to international business interests; or so-called global civil society actors. Second, the final section of Hobson and Seabrooke's volume makes important points regarding the need to recognize how the EPE takes shape in non-Western contexts. Hobson (2007), thus, argues that we need to not only bring Eastern agents back in but also recognize how everyday practices of capitalist transformation that took shape in Asia are intimately bound up with the processes of capitalist transformation experienced in the West. As the chapters in this volume attest, an EPE approach can serve to highlight the inadequacies of much IPE scholarship rooted in the study of Western(ized) elites.

We build upon these two important insights – seeking to illustrate how IPE is enacted and performed at the very local (non-elite) level and also how the Asian region needs to be recognized as an important site within which political economic identities and behaviours are (re)produced. Conventional accounts of the incorporation of Southeast Asia into the global political economy emphasize the role of (both Western and Japanese) imperialism in the establishment of both states and markets in the region and the post-independence trajectories of states pursuing economic 'development' (Berger 2009). This economic history of the region is frequently overlaid with social constructivist accounts of the emergence of the idea of Southeast Asia as a region – a hallmark of the literature on economic regionalism within ASEAN and the so-called ASEAN-Way (Acharya 1998). Ordinary people have been profoundly affected by the politics of development pursued by states across the region – be it via the impact of large-scale development projects funded by international financial institutions such as the Asian Development Bank or the World Bank on indigenous communities, through the incorporation of large numbers of young women into export sector industries and systems of return migration, or through the increased commercialization and marketization of everyday life. But what we also see is that practices of capitalist developmentalism in Southeast Asia are themselves serving to generate newly marketized spaces, products and modes of work. In other words, everyday capitalist practices are not simply imposed on local communities in Southeast Asia but work within, and are embedded within, patterns of everyday social relations (Brenner et al. 2010). Accordingly, it is wrong to present Southeast Asia as just another site of capitalist expansion, without recognizing the distinct ways in which capitalist expansion takes shape locally.

Building on the recognition by Hobson and Seabrooke of the need for an Asian focus in the development of EPE, we demonstrate how a focus on the

Southeast Asian region serves to generate an important shift in how the concept of the everyday is articulated in political economy scholarship. Namely, this shift entails placing problem(s) of development more centrally within the analysis while also highlighting the embedded forms of gendered and racialized identities and inequalities that are so central to the functioning of markets. Although we acknowledge that most of the contributors to this volume are of the 'West', be it in terms of their nationality and/or their education/scholarly training, we seek to develop an understanding of Southeast Asia as a region in which new ways of theorizing and understanding the world can emerge. To this end, we draw upon the literature on the everyday advanced within IPE, seeking not to 'impose' this concept onto the Southeast Asian space but to ask how the study of Southeast Asia brings new and unique insights into how we understand the functioning of the global political economy from an everyday perspective. It is in this sense that we intend to take Hobson's call for the development of a non-Western IPE more seriously.

The Everyday Politics of Southeast Asia's Economic Transformation

The EPE perspective in the studies of Southeast Asia builds upon an important, widely cited and deeply Southeast Asia-centric body of work concerning the contentious nature of everyday politics within agrarian societies undergoing social transformation in the name of 'modernity' (Scott 1985; Ong 1987; Evans 1990; Kerkvliet 1990, 2005; Stivens 1996). Scott's work, for example, examines the often unconscious tactics of the socially marginalized Malaysian peasantry whose livelihoods and traditional social structures were ever more eroded in the face of agricultural modernization and mechanization. Scott asks what can happen when modernization leads to 'a gradual bulldozing of the sites where class conflict has historically occurred' (p. 243), suggesting that alternative manifestations of class politics would emerge – resistances such as foot-dragging, small acts of non-compliance or ridicule that evade direct confrontation with elites. These 'weapons of the weak' represent 'the tenacity of self-preservation ... the steady, grinding efforts to hold one's own against overwhelming odds – a spirit and practice that prevents the worst and promises something better' (p. 350). Similarly, situated against the backdrop of the decline of small-scale cash-cropping in Malaysia, Aihwa Ong's (1987) study of women migrating to take up work in export processing makes comparable observations about everyday resistance but also provides an interesting point of contrast to Scott's. Here class struggles are not simply being undermined by modernization but are completely reconstituted as peasant women manage their incorporation into new modes of capitalist discipline that take shape alongside recompositions of patriarchal gender relations within the factory setting. The evocative focus on incidents of spirit possession, alongside more mundane forms of protest such as crying and requests for prayer breaks, represents women's engagement of 'an idiom of protest against labour discipline and male control' (p. 207). And yet, these weapons of the weak are approached with rather less optimism than Scott's account, serving as they do to reinforce traditional gender roles and stereotypes[2] (see also Hart 1991).

This literature serves to highlight the multiple visions of 'modernity' that exist within a region characterized by diverse experiences of colonialism and Cold War politics that fundamentally shaped the conditions within which resistances and even revolutionary struggles took shape. More importantly, it points to how everyday politics – that is, struggles that marginalized and subaltern groups engage in, often outside of formal political arenas – is shaped by experiences of poverty and destitution and is mediated by gender, ethnic, class and religious identities, as well as age.

The chapters in this volume certainly illustrate the many and varied manifestations of capitalist modernity in select Southeast Asian sites. At the same time, however, we should not ignore the important economic, political and cultural transformations that have taken place since the heydays of the (peasant-centric) everyday politics scholarship – transformations that have contributed to a fracturing of identities and the emergence of new sites of everyday resistance. We can also observe a growing range of non-elite actors engaged in forms of everyday politics as the boundaries between rural and urban living become ever more blurred (Thompson 2007). Strategies for everyday political action have also transformed – chapters by Nem Singh and Camba and Henry in the volume, for example, situate everyday politics within broader, more formalized resistance campaigns. Moreover, new, more formalized pathways for resistance have opened up for non-elite actors (see the discussion by Rosser and Tan on the courts in Indonesia and Hong Kong and the discussion by Henry on the formation of trade unions in Myanmar in this volume), which may well serve to transform the nature of everyday resistance politics.

The EPE of Southeast Asia

With these comments in mind, we propose that an EPE of Southeast Asia is about more than simply bringing the voices and experiences of the region's ordinary people into our analysis. Rather, it is through a focus on everyday life of the people, their daily routines and their ordinary – and at times extraordinary – actions that we come to see how economic transformation is manifested in relation to three important processes around which we have structured the chapters in this volume. These are: (i) the variegated pathways towards

---

[2] See the concluding chapter of this volume for more details on the everyday politics approach, specifically in terms of how it is utilized in the work of Benedict Kerklviet.

economic modernization – that is, how market building and development processes take shape and are resisted through an engagement with local social relations (gender, class, nationality, and so on); (ii) the widening and deepening of the market into everyday spaces – that is, how economic development projects and programmes increasingly specify the need for a politics of competitiveness in which new spaces (such as the household, religious practices or school education) are seen as prime sites for processes of marketization; and, finally, (iii) the production and performance of the economic subjectivities of worker and/or migrant and how these forms of commodification are challenged and resisted from below – that is, how the EPE intersects with individual and collective struggles and practices of contestation. Accordingly, the empirical chapters in this volume are organized into three analytically distinct sections to highlight key ways in which EPE matters.

Each of the chapters individually draws out the importance of an EPE perspective for understanding the specific case that it explores. However, in so doing, we are keen to allow for theoretical diversity and methodological pluralism. Indeed, one of the core aims of this volume is to show that there are various ways of 'doing' an EPE approach, especially as this volume brings together scholars working in a range of different disciplinary fields, including economic geography, law, political economy and social anthropology. Collectively, the chapters in this volume explore how economic change gets enacted in Southeast Asian political economies through a combination of top-down and bottom-up agency, how economic practices are being embedded in specific sociocultural contexts and institutional settings, and how processes of economic transformation embody conflicting subjectivities/contested rationalities which are sources of both acquiescence and resistance to these processes. In so doing, the contributions to this volume throw a new light on the ongoing political, economic and cultural transformation of Southeast Asia at a time where market relations are both widening and deepening. At the same time, taking Southeast Asia seriously offers a lens through which to question assumptions of mainstream IPE that the periphery is simply reactive to trends within the core.

From Developmentalism to Multiple Modernities

What is by now clear is that rather than following a set path to modernity and a 'developed' economy, Southeast Asia has been a site of multiple experiences and where 'economic development' has found variegated manifestations. A focus on the everyday recasts commonly held understandings of these processes. In so doing, it allows for the probing and ultimate rearticulation of a number of binary understandings: states versus markets as agents of economic development; the traditional and the modern as the opposite ends of the development process; and inclusion and exclusion as different modalities of progress and transformation. We will discuss these three dynamics in turn.

First, in the political economy literature on Southeast Asia, there has been considerable emphasis on studying state-led development projects and economic policy frameworks at the cost of more in-depth studies of the emergence and changing nature of the region's market societies (e.g., Rasiah and Dragsbaek Schmidt 2010; Slater 2010; Kuhonta 2011). Not only do there remain pertinent questions about the capacity of Southeast Asian states to devise, implement and manage development strategies in a way similar to the paths taken by their counterparts in Asia's industrialized north, but these accounts might also have fallen prey to providing 'too ordered' an account of development in the region. Thus, Jonathan Rigg (2012) questions teleological understandings of development, drawing attention to its contingencies and chance. In this context, we suggest that the ways that markets have unfolded and how market relations have become entrenched in various parts of the region play a significant but underexplored role. Indeed, as the contributions to this volume will show, centrally emplacing the EPE of Southeast Asia fosters an analytical shift from old-style developmentalism to embracing various forms of marketization, be they developmental in character or predatory or a combination thereof, and be they the result of top-down or bottom-up agency (see also Nevins and Peluso 2008).

Second, moving from a focus on developmentalism towards a need to better understand and theorize the various processes of marketization that are underway in the region and their effects also puts into question a dichotomous conceptualization of the traditional and the modern as markers of the region's developmental process. Instead, the Southeast Asian experience has given rise to 'multiple modernities', each enacted in its specific way and in return transforming the 'premises, symbols and institutions of modernity' itself (Eisenstadt 2000: 14). The result is a transformative dynamic where Southeast Asian societies selectively incorporate, adapt to and resist processes of marketization. This is as a result of both top-down and bottom-up agency, as the contributions in this volume will show. It includes the marketization of religious practice as we will discuss later, but also more general attempts at invoking traditional values and practices in both advancing and resisting economic modernization and nation-building agendas – be it calls for a 'sufficiency economy' in Thailand, or ongoing debates about vernacular education and global competitiveness in Malaysia (see, e.g., Ritchie 2005; Hewison 2008).

Third, embracing the notion of 'multiple modernities' must not desensitize us to the politics of exclusion that are engendered by Southeast Asia's transformation. Indeed, as Hall *et al.* (2011: 7) argue, this entails moving from a binary of inclusion/exclusion to the broader questioning of 'ways in which people are prevented from benefiting from things'. This is especially clear if we look at the treatment of citizens and non-citizens in the region (Aguilar 1999). It also manifests itself in the region's changing urban spaces (Clammer 2003). Taking the politics of exclusion seriously will make more visible the everyday and political struggles and contestation that have underpinned the processes of economic, political and cultural transformation in the region. Along these lines, the complex relations between the state and civil society in Southeast Asia need to be understood as taking shape within and alongside the widening and deepening of markets. On the one hand, studies of civil society activism in the region have pointed to the forms of repressive state rule that have been enacted against groups seeking to oppose statist development projects that impinge upon the lives of ordinary citizens (Li 2007). But at the same time, a more consensual characterization of state–civil society relations is emphasized in Gramscian readings of the Southeast Asian state as embedded in the relative interests and ideologies of civil society (Hilley 2001; Ramasamy 2004; Hedman 2006; Sim 2006; Nair 2007). Thus, for example, Rodan and Hughes (2014) point out how the interests of civil society groups are harnessed for state development and accountability programmes via a selective engagement with liberal and moral agendas. Moreover, as the important writings of James C. Scott remind us, resistances are not confined to the workings of organized civil society groups.

How this has come about and how it has given rise to specific politics of economic (non-) belonging is a core interest of the first group of chapters in this collection (Rigg, Nem Singh and Camba and Henry). Jonathan Rigg kicks off this collection by questioning our understandings of development and modernity as they can be applied to the contexts of Thailand and Vietnam. Exploring the interstices of 'development-as-project' and 'development-as-practice', he adopts an EPE perspective to look at how the everyday actions of urban migrants in Vietnam and rural dwellers in Thailand give new meanings to local development policies and the modernization project as a whole. Rigg's chapter draws attention to the ways in which state policies 'do not operate in the ways that they are intended' and where 'modernities are re-worked in ways that rhyme with local customs'. This is followed by a chapter by Jewellord Nem Singh and Alvin Camba on the emergence of the anti-mining movement in the Philippines. They provide an intriguing account of how the most recent commodity boom has led to new forms of civil society mobilization and politics of resistance in the Philippines. However, theirs is not just a story about how global capitalism is confronted by local everyday politics. Competing visions of development exist not only between state and civil society actors but also between the two major civil society coalitions that have emerged to contest the foreign investment-led mining regime in the Philippines. Nicholas Henry then turns his gaze towards trade union activism in Myanmar. In showing how labour norms are locally enacted against the background of the country's rapidly changing political environment, he demonstrates the impor- tance of both transnational and local actors in bringing about change and how they selectively engage global normative frameworks. As Myanmar has turned to seeking integration with the world economy, new spaces are opening up for everyday actors to affirm their rights and to develop their own agential capacities.

Widening and Deepening Markets

In looking at specific processes of market deepening and widening that are underway in contemporary Southeast Asian sites, we will draw attention to three relationships in particular: the various forms of engagement between transnational and domestic elites and everyday actors such as NGOs, small businesses, ordinary consumers and savers; the relationship between a 'faith in markets' (Hopgood and Vinjamuri 2012) and the region's deeply ingrained spirituality, including the growing invocation of religion in everyday processes of work, finance and consumption; and the dynamic interplay between local economic cultures, practices and understandings and global circuits of capital, including aid, foreign direct investment and portfolio finance. Taken together, these relationships shape and format the region's economic, political and cul- tural transformation.

First, the dynamic interactions between domestic and transnational market and policy elites and everyday actors need to be subjected to careful scrutiny. The fracturing of developmental processes and the emergence of variegated modernities has been accompanied by a deepening and widening of market relations as elites have sought to increasingly incorporate alternative forms of exchange and new socioeconomic groupings into their marketized and increas- ingly outward-oriented – if not global – developmental ambitions. In various ways, these elite efforts are shaped by local realities and, in so doing, sustained, resisted and transformed by everyday actors. This includes, for example, the growing popularity of halal-certified products and services or the introduction of a competitive education market.

Second and related, more attention has to be paid to the relationship between secular development and the persistent, if not growing, influence of religion in public and market life in the region (see also Kong 2010). Attention can be drawn here to renewed interest in issues such as the impact of Catholicism on economic and political development in the Philippines (Hedman 2001); the effect of Pentecostal and other forms of Christianity on Singapore's development model (Pereira 2005; Goh 2009; Chong 2011); or the role of Buddhist monks in affirming and resisting globalizing tendencies – for example, in the contestation of statist development projects in the Mekong Region (Hughes 2011). In this regard and as the work of influential scholars such as Clifford Geertz and Robert Hefner attests, Muslim Southeast Asia has long been an important research site, giving access to both the world's biggest Muslim majority country (Indonesia) and perhaps the most successful early Muslim modernizer (Malaysia). At the same time, new work focuses much more explicitly on the intimate links between local forms of what Rudnyckyj (2009) terms 'market Islam' and the increasingly global ambitions of countries in the region. Thus, a number of scholars of the region have turned their gaze to the role of Islam in facilitating regional economic development and national competitiveness agendas. This includes Rudnyckyj's (2010) work on the harnessing of 'spiritual economies' for Indonesia's privatization drive and modernizing business practices; Jones's (2010) and Fischer's (2011) studies of halal (literally: permissible) consumption; and Sloane-White's (2011) work on the 'Sharia-ization' of the workplace. Importantly, many of these developments are fraught with tensions which in themselves create new opportunities to at least contest processes of market deepening and widening. Thus, for example, in his recent work on Islamic finance, Rudnyckyj (2014: 112) illustrates 'how differently positioned Islamic finance experts see Islamic finance as either a means of furthering the extension of the market or providing an alternative to it'.

Third, and following on from the above, analyzing the EPE of Southeast Asia requires looking into the relationship between local economic cultures, practices and understandings and how they interact with global circuits of capital, including foreign direct investment and portfolio finance. Indeed, this relationship is multidirectional. Stephen J. Collier and Aihwa Ong (2005: 12) have developed the notion of 'global assemblages' to draw attention to 'inherent tensions' as 'global implies broadly encompassing, seamless and mobile; assemblage implies heterogeneous, contingent, unstable, partial and situated'. This is especially so as elites' ambitions to insert their economies in global circuits of capital in specific ways – be it through globalizing markets for halal products and services, or by the increasing marketization of education and the production of a 'competitive' workforce – are both promoted and challenged by everyday actors.

Together, these themes are taken up more explicitly in the second group of chapters (Fischer, Rethel and Rosser). The importance of religiously informed economic practices as a site of elite politics fostering global competitiveness agendas is interrogated in the two chapters by Fischer and Rethel. Johan Fischer's chapter examines the proliferation of halal certification in Singapore. He looks in particular at how this had led to the emergence of a political economy of standardization with important implications for the practices of economic factors such as retail supermarkets, their employees and consumers. Continuing this investigation in the relationship between the secular and the spiritual at times of state-led marketization, Lena Rethel looks at the case of Islamic finance as an instance where an elite-driven logic of competitiveness that leads Malaysia to market itself as an international Islamic financial centre meets local realities such as a significant increase in household debt. It also highlights the difficulties experienced in reconciling a diversity of Islamic practices with Malaysia's global and developmental ambitions. The final chapter in this section, by Andrew Rosser, explores how ordinary citizens resist the creeping marketization of schooling by contesting the introduction of user fee regimes in Indonesia. In so doing, he considers the scope and possibilities for civil society challenges to both state-led marketization agendas and the particular forms of predatory capitalism that continue to characterize Indonesia's low-quality democratic polity.

People, Mobilities and Work

The last thematic section addresses more squarely the question of how marketization entails ongoing processes of labour commodification as new types of work emerge and new groups are identified as workers, as well as the aligned forms of worker resistance and acquiescence (for a classic discussion of these processes, see Ong 1987). Two dimensions are central to the discussion here: the persistence of poverty and its importance in shaping economic flows; and gendered and racialized forms of inequality and oppression. Furthermore, these two dimensions are taking shape within the context of attempts to build markets or deepen the processes of marketization that serve to adversely incorporate some of society's most marginalized groups ever further into the market economy (Carroll 2010; Hughes and Hutchison 2012).

First, capitalist developmentalism is taking shape within an economically diverse region in which large pockets of poverty persist. Many Southeast Asian states (or regions of particular states) suffer high levels of poverty and unemployment and have been subjected to the imposition of large-scale development projects that often fail to bring about economic advancement to society's poorest. Many parts of the region remain locked into systems of return contract migration that serve to exacerbate intra-regional inequalities and generally fail to generate long-term economic growth and poverty alleviation. The EPE of Southeast Asia is thus characterized in Nevins and Peluso's (2008) work as reflecting more, to use Scheper-Hughes's (1993) phrase, 'the violence of everyday life' than the rather benign focus on the sources of social change in the global political economy that characterizes much of Hobson and Seabrooke's approach.

Second, Southeast Asia has long been recognized as an important site for the emergence of studies of employment, with regard to both factory work under conditions of export expansion as discussed by Franck in this volume (see also Ong 1987; Wolf 1992; Elias 2004; Caraway 2007; Pangsapa 2007) as well as the expanding market for migrant domestic work (Huang and Yeoh 1996; Chin 1998; Williams 2007; Briones 2009; Rodriguez 2010). While these studies certainly serve to highlight the possibilities and opportunities that engagement in the market economy opens up for marginalized groups (such as young women from some of the most economically marginalized regions of Southeast Asia), they also highlight the structural (and at times more direct) forms of violence so central to the expansion of markets that uphold systems of low-wage labour. Most importantly, these studies demonstrate the need to take gender and gendered social relations (i.e., how gender inequalities are cross-cut with inequalities based on race, nationality, class and age) into account. Waylen (2010), for example, has criticized the rather ungendered conceptualization of the everyday actor in Hobson and Seabrooke (2007), and Lebaron (2010) has called on EPE perspectives to incorporate a focus on the household economy – not least the way in which processes of neoliberal restructuring entail specific impacts on household relations (see also Gunawardana and Elias 2013; Elias and Louth, this volume).

The issue of people, mobilities and workers' agency is more specifically taken up by the chapters in the final thematic section (Franck, Tyson, Elias and Louth, and Tan). Anja Franck explores domestic–global dynamics by investigating the puzzle of 'missing women' in Malaysia's labour force. Her research, conducted among female workers in the state of Penang, shows that women, rather than leaving the labour market completely when exiting the export-oriented manufacturing sector, take on other forms of informal employment that need to be taken more seriously to understand contemporary socioeconomic change in the region. Adam Tyson's chapter explores how elites within the Malaysian government harness the language of 'talent' as part of their ambitious economic transformation programme. Economic planners' efforts to stop the 'brain drain' of well-educated Chinese and urban Malay elites, however, are confronted with their growing scepticism if not outright rejection of the racialized politics that have become the core feature of Malaysia's EPE. This is followed by a chapter by Juanita Elias and Jonathon Louth, who explore the foreign policy implications of the transnationalization of domestic work. Using the recent spats between Malaysia, Indonesia and Cambodia, the authors provide a persuasive account of this instance where the high politics of foreign policy making meet with the highly gendered everyday realities that domestic workers are confronted with in Malaysia. Carol Tan concludes this section by taking the discussion outside of the region and focusing on the plight of domestic workers, predominantly from the less developed countries of Southeast Asia, in Hong Kong. By exploring the factors that lead domestic workers to seek legal redress against employer abuse, she makes an important contribution to a better understanding of the everyday experiences and agency of Southeast Asian diasporas.

What becomes clear from looking at the diverse empirical cases discussed in this volume is that the ongoing economic transformation of the region has not only given rise to new forms of everyday politics and resistance but has had profound implications for everyday economic life. This point is taken up more explicitly in the concluding chapter, a collaborative effort of the editors of this volume, Juanita Elias and Lena Rethel, and John Hobson and Leonard Seabrooke. Indeed, in this concluding chapter, we trace two analytical traditions which are developed through the EPE perspectives that are employed in this volume – an 'everyday politics' approach that seeks to draw out the politics of non-elite actors' acquiescence, contestation and resistance to economic transformation, as well as an 'everyday life' approach that more squarely focuses on the routines of daily life that shape, and are shaped by, economic transformation. The chapters in this volume will be discussed against this backdrop. However, it is important to emphasize that much of what takes place is situated at the interstices of everyday politics and everyday life. EPE thus emerges as an approach uniquely suited to connect analyses of developmental agendas with how processes of economic, political and cultural transformation are sustained, resisted and transformed on the ground.

Conclusion

This book seeks to illustrate how processes of market building unfold on the ground involving non-elite, even marginalized or vulnerable groups in a non-Western setting while demonstrating, in turn, how such lived everyday experiences are shaping – and shaped by – the processes of marketization. Drawing on original fieldwork in Southeast Asian countries or among Southeast Asian diasporas, the contributors to this book demonstrate, rather than simply assert, that everyday actors and their daily actions and routines have significant implications for top-down neoliberal and other market-centric development agendas. In so doing, they can lead to unanticipated outcomes and economic, political and cultural transformations that are distinct to local and/or regional settings. Thus, the contributions to this volume show either how an EPE perspective adds value to more common elite-centred analyses of economic transformation or how an everyday approach unmasks tensions, subjectivities and behaviours otherwise hidden from scholarly eyes that are very much focused on (state) elites.

Importantly, however, this volume does not reject the role of elites; rather it seeks to reveal how elite plans and programmes are intricately bound up with the various responses of non-elites as well as their daily routines of economic life, often in unexpected and seemingly non-rational ways. Thereby, they are complicating, perhaps even *frustrating* as Jonathan Rigg suggests in the next chapter, top-down, elite-dominated agendas. Indeed, Rigg uses the distinction between 'development-as-policy' and 'development-as-practice' to draw attention to the lived experiences and changing livelihoods underpinning the economic transformation of countries such as Thailand and Vietnam with the result that official policies 'do not operate as intended'. However, as the chapters in this volume collectively show, there is the capacity of everyday actors to find spaces for creative responses to official policies and structural conditions beyond the simple dichotomy of acceptance/acquiescence or rejection/resistance. By confirming the complexities of the social world and its diverse sources of variability, the following chapters draw attention to the myriad forms of agency exerted by a wide range of elite but also – and perhaps increasingly so – non-elite actors which make up local political economies and feed into national political economic outcomes.

References

Acharya, A. (1998) 'Culture, Security, Multilateralism: The "ASEAN Way" and Regional Order', *Contemporary Security Policy* 19(1): 55–84.

Aguilar, F. V. (1999) 'The Triumph of Instrumental Citizenship? Migrations, Identities and the Nation-State in Southeast Asia', *Asian Studies Review* 23(3): 307–336.

Aitken, R. (2007) *Performing Capital: Toward a Cultural Economy of Popular and Global Finance*. New York: Palgrave.

Amoore, L. (2002) *Globalization Contested: An International Political Economy of Work*. Manchester: Manchester University Press.

Bello, W., Cunningham, S. and Li, K. P. (1998) *A Siamese Tragedy: Development and Disintegration in Modern Thailand*. London: Zed.

Berger, M. T. (2009) 'The End of Empire and the Cold War', in Mark Beeson (ed.) *Contemporary Southeast Asia*, Second Edition. Basingstoke: Palgrave MacMillan, pp. 29–45

Best, J. and Paterson, M. (eds.) (2009) *Cultural Political Economy*. London: Routledge.

Brenner, N., Peck, J. and Theodore, N. (2010) 'Variegated Neoliberalization: Geographies, Modalities, Pathways', *Global Networks* 10(2): 182–222.

Brickell, K. (2011) 'The "Stubborn Stain" on Development: Gendered Meanings of Housework (Non-)Participation in Cambodia', *Journal of Development* 47(9): 1353–1370.

Briones, L. (2009) *Empowering Migrant Women: Why Agency and Rights Are Not Enough*. Aldershot: Ashgate.

Brown, A. (2004) *Labour, Politics and the State in Industrializing Thailand*. London: Routledge.

Bunnell, T. G. (2004) *Malaysia, Modernity and the Multimedia Super Corridor: A Critical Geography of Intelligent Landscapes*. London: Routledge.

Caraway, T. L. (2007) *Assembling Women: The Feminization of Global Manufacturing*. Ithaca and London: Cornell University Press.

Carroll, T. (2010) *Delusions of Development: The World Bank and the Post-Washington Consensus in Southeast Asia*. Basingstoke: Palgrave.

Case, W. (2005) 'Malaysia: New Reforms, Old Continuities, Tense Ambiguities', *Journal of Development Studies* 41(2): 284–309.

(2009) 'After the Crisis: Capital and Regime Resilience in the ASEAN Three', *Journal of Contemporary Asia* 39(4): 649–672.

Chin, C. B. N. (1998) *In Service and Servitude: Foreign Female Domestic Workers and the Malaysian 'Modernity' Project*. New York: Columbia University Press.

Chong, T. (2011) 'Filling the Moral Void: The Christian Right in Singapore', *Journal of Contemporary Asia* 41(4): 566–583.

Chua, B. H. (2003) *Life Is Not Complete without Shopping: Consumption Culture in Singapore*. Singapore: Singapore University Press.

Clammer, J. (2003) 'Globalisation, Class, Consumption and Civil Society in South-East Asian Cities', *Urban Studies* 40(2): 403–419.

Collier, S. J. and Ong, A. (2005) 'Global Assemblages, Anthropological Problems', in Aihwa Ong and Stephen J. Collier (eds.) *Global Assemblages: Technology, Politics and Ethics as Anthropological Problems*. Oxford: Wiley-Blackwell, pp. 3–21.

de Certeau, Michel. (1986) 'History Science and Fiction' in de Certeau's *Heterologies: Discourse on the Other*, trans. Brian Massumi. University of Minnesota Press.

Eisenstadt, S. N. (2000) 'Multiple Modernities', *Daedalus* 129(1): 1–29.

Elias, J. (2004) *Fashioning Inequality: The Multinational Corporation and Gendered Employment in a Globalizing World*. Aldershot: Ashgate.

(2015) 'Civil Society and the Gender Politics of Economic Competitiveness in Malaysia', *Globalizations* 12(3): 347–364.

Enloe, C. (2013) *Seriously! Investigating Crashes and Crises as if Women Mattered*, Berkley: University of California Press.

Evans, G. (1990) *Lao Peasants under Socialism*. New Haven: Yale University Press.

Fischer, J. (2011) *The Halal Frontier. Muslim Consumers in a Globalized Market*. Basingstoke: Palgrave.

Gerard, K. (2014) *ASEAN's Engagement of Civil Society: Regulating Dissent*. Basingstoke: Palgrave MacMillan.

Goh, R. B. H. (2009) 'Christian Identities in Singapore: Religion, Race and Culture between State Controls and Transnational Flows', *Journal of Cultural Geography* 26(1): 1–23.

Gunawardana, S. J. and Elias, J. (2013) 'Conclusion: The Significance of the Household to Asia's Transformation and to Studies of the Global Political Economy', in Juanita Elias and Samanthi J. Gunawardana (eds.) *The Global Political Economy of the Household in Asia*. London: Palgrave MacMillan, pp. 227–231.

Hadiz, V. (1997) *Workers and the State in New Order Indonesia*. London: Routledge.

Hadiz, V. and Robison, R. (2005) 'Neo-liberal Reforms and Illiberal Consolidations: The Indonesian Paradox', *Journal of Development Studies* 41(2): 220–241.

Hall, D., Hirsch, P. and Li, T. (2011) *Powers of Exclusion: Land Dilemmas in Southeast Asia*. Singapore: NUS Press.

Hart, G. (1991) 'Engendering Everyday Resistance: Gender, Patronage and Production Politics in Rural Malaysia' *Journal of Peasant Studies* 19(1): 93–121.

Hedman, E.-L. (2001) 'Contesting State and Civil Society: Southeast Asian Trajectories', *Modern Asian Studies* 35(4): 921–951.

(2006) *In the Name of Civil Society: From Free Election Movements to People Power in the Philippines*. Honolulu: University of Hawaii Press.

Hewison, K. (2000) 'Thailand's Capitalism before and after the Economic Crisis', in Richard Robison, Mark Beeson, Kanishka Jayasuria and Hyuk-Rae Kim (eds.)

Politics and Markets in the Wake of the Asian Crisis. London: Routledge, pp. 194–213.

(2005) 'Neo-liberalism and Domestic Capital: The Political Outcomes of the Economic Crisis in Thailand', *Journal of Development Studies* 41(2): 310–330.

(2006) 'Thai Workers in Hong Kong', in Kevin Hewison and Ken Young (eds.) *Transnational Migration and Work in Asia*. London: Routledge, pp. 90–109.

Hewison, K. and Kalleberg, A. L. (2013) 'Precarious Work and Flexibilization in South and Southeast Asia', *American Behavioral Scientist* 57(4): 395–402.

(2008) 'Review of Thailand Human Development Report, Sufficiency Economy and Human Development UNDP', *Journal of Contemporary Asia* 38(1): 212–215.

Hewison, K. and Robison, R. (eds.) (2006) *East Asia and the Trials of Neo-Liberalism*. London and New York: Routledge.

Hilley, J. (2001) *Malaysia: Mahathirism, Hegemony and the New Opposition*. London: Zed Books.

Hobson, J. M. (2007) 'Eastern Agents and Globalisation: Oriental Globalisation in the Rise of Western Capitalism', in John M. Hobson and Leonard Seabrooke (eds) *Everyday Politics of the World Economy*. Cambridge: Cambridge University Press, pp. 141–159.

Hobson, J. M. and Seabrooke, L. (eds.) (2007) *Everyday Politics of the World Economy*. Cambridge: Cambridge University Press.

Hopgood, S. and Vinjamuri, L. (2012) 'Faith in Markets', in Michael Barnett and Janice Gross Stein (eds.) *Sacred Aid: Faith and Humanitarianism*, Oxford: Oxford University Press, pp. 37–63.

Huang, S. and Yeoh, B. S. A. (1996) 'Ties that Bind: State Policy and Migrant Female Domestic Helpers in Singapore', *Geoforum* 27(4): 479–493.

Hughes, C. (2011) 'Soldiers, Monks, Borders: Violence and Contestation in the Greater Mekong Sub-region', *Journal of Contemporary Asia* 41(2): 181–205.

Hughes, C. and Hutchison, J. (2012) 'Development Effectiveness and the Politics of Commitment', *Third World Quarterly* 33(1): 17–33.

Hutchinson, J. (2012) 'Labour Politics in Southeast Asia: The Philippines in Context', in Richard Robison (ed.) *Routledge Handbook of Southeast Asian Politics*. Abingdon: Routledge, pp. 40–52.

Hutchinson, J. and Brown, A. (2002) *Organizaing Labour in Globalizing Asia*. London: Routledge.

Jayasuria, K. (2005) 'Beyond Institutional Fetishism: From the Developmental to the Regulatory State', *New Political Economy* 10(3): 381–387.

Jayasuriya, K. and Hewison, K. (2004) 'The Antipolitics of Good Governance', *Critical Asian Studies* 36(4): 571–590.

Jayasuriya, K. and Rodan, G. (2007) 'Beyond Hybrid Regimes: More Participation, Less Contestation in Southeast Asia', *Democractization* 14(5): 773–794.

Johnson, Chalmers. (1982) *MITI and the Japanese Miracle: The Growth of Industrial Policy, 1925-1975* (Stanford: Stanford University Press).

Jones, C. (2010) 'Materializing Piety: Gendered Anxieties about Faithful Consumption in Contemporary Urban Indonesia', *American Ethnologist* 37(4): 617–637.

Kerkvliet, B. (1990) *Everyday Politics in the Philippines: Class and Status Relations in a Central Luzon Village*. Berkeley: University of California Press.

(2005) *The Power of Everyday Politics: How Vietnamese Peasants Transformed National Policy*. Ithaca: Cornell University Press.

Khoo B. T. (2000) 'Economic Nationalism and its Discontents: Malaysian Political Economy after July 1997', in Richard Robison, Mark Beeson, Kanishka Jayasuria and Hyuk-Rae Kim (eds.) *Politics and Markets in the Wake of the Asian Crisis*. London: Routledge, pp. 214–240.

Kong, L. (2010) 'Global Shifts, Theoretical Shifts: Changing Geographies of Religion', *Progress in Human Geography* 34(6): 755–776.

Kuhonta, E. M. (2011) *The Institutional Imperative: The Politics of Equitable Development in Southeast Asia*. Stanford: Stanford University Press.

Langley, P. (2008) *The Everyday Life of Global Finance: Saving and Borrowing in Anglo America*. Oxford: Oxford University Press.

LeBaron, G. (2010) 'The Political Economy of the Household: Neoliberal Restructuring, Enclosures, and Daily Life', *Review of International Political Economy* 17(5): 889–912.

Li, T. M. (2007) *The Will to Improve: Governmentality, Development, and the Practice of Politics*. Durham: Duke University Press.

Nair, S. (2007) 'The Limits of Protest and Prospects for Political Reform in Malaysia', *Critical Asian Studies* 39(3): 339–368.

Nevins, J. and Peluso, N. L. (eds.) (2008) *Taking Southeast Asia to Market: Commodities, Nature, and People in the Neoliberal Age*. Ithaca: Cornell University Press.

Ong, A. (1987) *Spirits of Resistance and Capitalist Discipline: Factory Women in Malaysia*. New York: SUNY Press.

(2006) *Neoliberalism as Exception: Mutations in Citizenship and Sovereignty*. Durham: Duke University Press.

Pangsapa, P. (2007) *Textures of Struggle: The Emergence of Resistance among Garment Workers in Thailand*. Ithaca and London: Cornell University Press.

Paterson, M (2007) *Automobile Politics: Ecology and the Cultural Political Economy*. Cambridge: Cambridge University Press.

Pereira, A. A. (2005) 'Religiosity and Economic Development in Singapore', *Journal of Contemporary Religion* 20(2): 161–177.

Ramasamy, P. (2004) 'Civil Society in Malaysia: An Arena of Contestations?', in Lee Hock Guan (ed.) *Civil Society in Southeast Asia*, Singapore: Institute for Southeast Asian Studies, pp. 198–216.

Rasiah, R. and Dragsbaek Schmidt, J. (eds.) (2010) *The New Political Economy of Southeast Asia*. Cheltenham: Edward Elgar.

Rigg, J. D. (2003) *Southeast Asia: The Human Landscape of Modernisation and Development*. London: Routledge.

(2012) *Unplanned Development*. London: Zed Books.

Ritchie, B. K. (2005) 'Coalitional Politics, Economic Reform, and Technological Upgrading in Malaysia', *World Development* 33(5): 745–761.

Robison, R. and Goodman, D. S. G. (eds.) (1996) *The New Rich in Asia: Mobile Phones, McDonald's and Middle-Class Revolution*. London: Routledge.

Robison, R. and Hewison, K. (2005) 'Introduction: East Asia and the Trials of Neoliberalism', *Journal of Development Studies* 41(2): 183–196.

Robison, R. and Rosser, A. (1998) 'Contesting Reform: Indonesia's New Order and the IMF', *World Development* 26(8): 1593–1609.

Rodan, G. and Hughes, C. (2012) 'Ideological Coalitions and the International Promotion of Social Accountability: The Philippines and Cambodia Compared', *International Studies Quarterly* 56(2): 368–380.

(2014) *The Politics of Accountability in Southeast Asia. The Dominance of Moral Ideologies*. Oxford: Oxford University Press.

Rodriguez, R. M. (2010) *Migrants for Export: How the Philippine State Brokers Labour to the World*. Minneapolis: University of Minnesota Press.

Rudnyckyj, D. (2009) 'Market Islam in Indonesia', *Journal of the Royal Anthropological Institute* 15(s1): S183–S201.

(2010) *Spiritual Economies: Islam, Globalization and the Afterlife of Development*. Ithaca: Cornell University Press.

(2014) 'Economy in Practice: Islamic Finance and the Problem of Market Reason', *American Ethnologist* 41(1): 110–127.

Seabrooke, L. and Elias, J. (2010) 'From Multilateralism to Microcosms in the World Economy: The Sociological Turn in Australian International Political Economy Scholarship', *Australian Journal of International Affairs* 64(1): 1–12.

Scheper-Hughes, N. (1993) *Death without Weeping: The Violence of Everyday Life in Brazil*. Berkley: University of California Press.

Scott, J. (1985) *Weapons of the Weak: Everyday Forms of Peasant Resistance*. New Haven: Yale University Press.

Scott, J. W. (1991) 'The Evidence of Experience', *Critical Inquiry* 17(4): 773–797.

Sen, K. and Stivens, M. (eds.) (1998) *Gender and Power in Affluent Asia*. London: Routledge.

Sim, S.-F. (2006) 'Hegemonic Authoritarianism and Singapore: Economics, Ideology and the Asian Economic Crisis', *Journal of Contemporary Asia* 36(2): 143–159.

Slater, D. (2010) *Ordering Power: Contentious Politics and Authoritarian Leviathans in Southeast Asia*. New York: Cambridge University Press.

Sloane-White, P. (2011) 'Working in the Islamic Economy: Malaysia and the "Sharia-Ization" of the workplace', *Sojourn: Journal of Social Issues in Southeast Asia* 26(2): 304–334.

Stivens, M. (1996) *Matrilinity and Modernity: Sexual Politics and Social Change in Rural Malaysia*. Sydney: Allen and Unwin.

Thompson, E. C. (2007) *Unsettling Absences: Urbanism in Rural Malaysia*. Singapore: National University of Singapore Press.

Tsing, A. L. (2005) *Friction: An Ethnography of Global Connection*. Princeton: Princeton University Press.

Waylen, G. (2010) 'Book Review', *Signs* 36(1): 237–244.

Williams, C. P. (2007) *Maiden Voyages: Eastern Indonesian Women on the Move*. Singapore: ISEAS Press.

Wolf, D. (1994) *Factory Daughters: Gender, Household Dynamics and Rural Industrialization in Java*. Berkeley and Los Angeles: University of California Press.

World Bank (1993) *The East Asian Miracle: Economic Growth and Public Policy*. New York: Oxford University Press.

Part II

From Development to Multiple Modernities

2 Policies and Negotiated Everyday Living: A View from the Margins of Development in Thailand and Vietnam

Jonathan Rigg

Introduction: Vernacular Modernities and Directional Goals

This chapter explores, through the everyday lives of urban migrants in Vietnam and rural dwellers in Thailand, a puzzle when it comes to understanding the intersection between modernization as a project and modernization as a practice. It is evident that most of the populations of Southeast Asia subscribe, in broad terms, to modernization ends. Their personal sacrifices to achieve material prosperity are both remarkable and humbling. At the same time, detailed investigation shows that they embrace and orchestrate this process of social and economic transformation in ways that run counter to and sometimes against both state-led intentions and simplistic views as to the path that is followed. So, on the one hand, we see in the everyday actions of ordinary people an undoubted, irrepressible enthusiasm for modernization. But in the details of how they go about achieving this, we discern not a resistance to modernization but rather a resistance to the modernization project.

This illustrates a point highlighted by the political economist Dani Rodrik, who suggests that the 'central economic paradox of our time is that "development" is working while "development policy" is not ... [and] we are [therefore] faced with the confluence of two seemingly contradictory trends' (2007: 85). To address this paradox, Rodrik makes a case for heterodoxy in understanding international development achievements and failure. This chapter will seek to address the paradox/puzzle in another way: by looking at the explanatory gap between development as policy as envisioned and orchestrated by states and development as practice as pursued and given meaning by people in their everyday actions.

To provide some structure to the empirical evidence and discussion that follows, a simplified two-by-two matrix provides a starting point (Table 2.1). This

This chapter was written while the author was a Professor-at-Large in the Institute for Advanced Studies (IAS) at the University of Western Australia. He would like to acknowledge and thank Susan Takao of the IAS and Matthew Tonts of the School of Earth and Environment for their encouragement and support.

27

Table 2.1 *Looking for space between the state and the everyday*

	Everyday practices	State intentionalities
Directional history	Consumerism and material progress; migration and mobilities; new divisions of labour	Neoliberalism; developmental state; territorialization
Vernacular modernities	Participatory modernities; community cultures; counter-territorializations	Asian values; sufficiency economy (Thailand); Islamic modernity (Malaysia)

highlights two binaries: between directional history and vernacular modernities, on the one hand, and everyday practices and state intentionalities, on the
other. The four resulting categories inevitably bleed into each other; they are
not viewed as neat and tightly bordered but permeable. Indeed, it is at the margins – at the points of contact – where much of interest lies. The matrix serves
a purpose in highlighting the intersections and tensions with which the chapter
is concerned:

- between state-sanctioned alternative modernities and modernity-as-
  practiced; and
- between the transition paths that are inscribed by the state in planning documents and policies and those that are enacted by the population.

The term 'directional history' is taken from Francis Fukuyama's 1995 essay,
written in response to the many critics of his book *The End of History and the
Last Man*:

The logic of this development process is determined by the progressive nature of scientific knowledge and its embodiment in technology through research and development.... It is now clear ... that there are a variety of paths to modernity, and that not all
societies will resemble England or the United States in their development histories ...
But the broad outlines of the process – urbanization, rational authority, bureaucratiza-
tion, an ever-ramified and complex division of labour – can be found in all developing
cultures.... What is remarkable about the process of economic modernization is its
universality as a goal. (1995: 32)

This quote clearly opens up just such a space between the broad movement
of societies towards the goal of modernity and the detailed paths that the individuals that comprise societies actually take. In large part arising from dissatisfaction with the universalizing tendencies of modernization theory, scholars
across the social sciences have embarked on attempts to suggest that what we
really see in populations' everyday engagement with development processes is
the emergence of vernacular, alternative, multiple or 'other' modernities. Dove

and Kammen, in their analysis of vernacular development in Indonesia, define the concept as follows:

The concept of a vernacular model of development provides a way to make sense of the informal, norm-driven, diverse, and even conflicting practices that dominate the real versus imagined landscape of development. The vernacular model is more than simply a description of what happens as opposed to what is supposed to happen, however. It encompasses a description of how official and vernacular realities articulate with one another, how the boundaries between the two are defined, maintained, and renegotiated. The modern development project cannot be understood, indeed, in terms of one or the other but only the relationship between them. (2001: 621)

This chapter views everyday political economy as providing a means of connecting vernacular modernity with state-orchestrated modernization and, in so doing, making a bridge between modernization theory and modernization practice. The argument is not that the everyday provides an alternative view of transformation, but that it permits us to connect individual capabilities and volitions, national policies and socioeconomic processes, and societal structures.

Thailand and Vietnam: Research Contexts and Themes

The empirical discussion that follows draws on two separate field research projects, in Thailand and Vietnam (Map 2.1). Briefly, the Thai research was undertaken between late 2012 and early 2013 with the intention of 'personalizing' the middle income trap through an investigation of first- and second-generation migrants in three villages in the province of Khon Kaen in Thailand's poor northeastern region (see Rigg et al. 2014a; Le Mare et al. 2015).[1] The work included a survey questionnaire, interviews with migrants and various community discussions and activities. The Vietnam research was undertaken in late 2010 and early 2011 and sought to reveal how migrants from the countryside to Hanoi have insinuated their way into the urban fabric and, in that way, made the transition from migrants to denizens and, finally, to citizens of the city (see Nguyen et al. 2012; Rigg et al. 2014b).[2] This second piece of research was based on interviews with migrants in Hanoi and with their families in rural source settlements.

Vietnam's recent development, like China's, has been strongly influenced by the household registration system or, in Vietnamese, *ho khau*. Introduced in the north of the country soon after the achievement of self-government in 1954, it

---

[1] This research was undertaken in collaboration with Dr Buapun Promphaking of Khon Kaen University and Dr Ann Le Mare of Durham University and was funded by the British Academy.

[2] This research was carried out in collaboration with Nguyen Tuan Anh and Luong Thi Thu Huong of Vietnam National University and was funded by the Social Sciences and Humanities Research Council of Canada.

Map 2.1 Field sites (Rigg et al. 2014).

tied access to state services to residency. In time, the 'link between identification and access to rights and services was all embracing' and 'to live without a *ho khau* was to live without the rights granted to Vietnamese citizens under the law' (Hardy 2001: 192). Vietnam's household registration system, until the late 1980s, effectively 'fixed' people in space. Mobility was all but impossible, because access to state services and therefore to a livelihood under Vietnam's socialist model depended on living where one was registered. Furthermore, changing one's registration was hard if not, for many ordinary people, impossible. This meant that the urbanization that was such a feature of other countries in the region was not evident in Vietnam. With the introduction and then extension of economic reform or *doi moi* from 1986, however, the logic of the household registration system was eroded: Vietnam's new development model depended on people becoming mobile if the needs of a growing industrial sector, concentrated in and around urban centres, were to be met. At the same time, the relative importance of state transfers in sustaining livelihoods was declining. The reform of the household registration system to meet this changing context has, however, been slow, with the result that from the 1990s a gap emerged and widened between the legislation, on the one hand, and people's actions and the realities of living, on the other (UNDP 2010: 5).[3]

We can see this gap reflected in a growing mismatch between population figures and employment data. Between 2002 and 2005, the increase in Ho Chi Minh City's population was recorded as 7.5 per cent. Over the same period, the number of workers employed in enterprises in the city grew by 39 per cent (Dapice et al. 2010: 3). Other widely cited surveys also seem to consistently overlook and, therefore, undercount migrants. It has been estimated that the 2006 Vietnam Household Living Standards Survey (VHLLS)[4] underestimated employment in manufacturing in Vietnam by around 22 per cent (World Bank 2008). Overall, it has been suggested that Vietnam's 'floating' population in 2010 numbered some 12 to 16 million, or between 13 and 18 per cent of the country's total population (UNDP 2010: 5). These are very large numbers indeed.

The Thailand case provides another insight into how development leads to an explanatory space opening up between policy and action. In Thailand, the development debate appeared to take a novel turn when the *sethakit phorpiang*, or 'sufficiency economy', was embraced from the late 1990s. The significance of the sufficiency economy turn can be seen reflected in the central place it has occupied in successive national development plans. Since the Eighth Plan (1997–2001), the sufficiency economy has been both the organizing principle and the inspiration for the Thai state's normative view of what form development should take (see Unger 2009: 140; UNDP 2007; NESDB 2011; http://eng.nesdb.go.th/). The 2007 Constitution even embraces the sufficiency economy.

There is no single, simple definition of the sufficiency economy (see Hewison 2008). However, the Eleventh Five-Year National Development Plan (2012–16) states that the 'heart of this Philosophy is "human development" toward well-being based on sufficiency, moderation, reasonableness, and resilience' (NESDB 2011: a). The *2007 Thailand Human Development Report* (UNDP 2007) – also inspired by the sufficiency economy – takes it to mean 'an approach to life and conduct which … promotes a middle path, especially in developing the economy to keep up with the world in the era of globalization' (xv). Critics of the sufficiency economy (see, e.g., Dayley 2011; Walker 2012) have tended to focus on what they see as an incongruity between the approach and the policies that have been developed, on the one hand, and the experience – on the

---

[3] The same has been true of the Chinese experience where a household registration system (the *hukou* system) is also in place, but increasingly out of kilter with development processes and priorities.

[4] The latest VHLSS can be downloaded from the General Statistics Office of Vietnam: www.gso .gov.vn/.

ground – of development in the country, on the other. Thus, Walker sees the sufficiency economy as 'delightfully vague' (2012: 152) and believes that it promotes an unrealistic vision of rural change in which 'rural communities should prioritize subsistence production and localized exchange in order to develop sustainable livelihoods that are not overly exposed to the hazardous excesses of the market' (182). For Dayley, this amounts to a 'myth' reconstituted as policy in the 'general belief that small-scale, subsistence farming is the most desirable form of community life for Thai rural families' (2011: 343). The sufficiency economy, it seems, is everywhere from national development plans, to publications from commercial organizations hoping to curry favour with the nation's elites (Thai Chamber of Commerce 2010), to NGOs (see Dayley 2011). It also plays a role in the political turmoil that followed former Prime Minster Thaksin Shinawatra's ousting from power in a coup d'état in 2006. As Hewison, in his review of the UNDP's sufficiency economy report, writes, 'the UNDP has produced a report that purports to address critical development issues but which does little more than add to the policy nonsense that passes for the military-backed government's development strategy' (2008: 251). What, though, of rural people? Do such visions find traction and resonance in the actions of rural people?

This chapter does not aim directly to assess or critique either Vietnam's household registration system or Thailand's sufficiency economy. Rather, attention here is paid to the ways in which people contest, ignore or rework the policies that they face. This then becomes the means to illuminate the explanatory and experiential gap between the instrumentalities of governments, reflected in the policies that are enacted, and the actions and activities of ordinary people.

Negotiating the Household Registration System in Vietnam

Whether Vietnam can be regarded as a strong state or a weak state, or indeed whether that distinction remains in any sense meaningful, is a continuing source of debate (see Painter 2003, 2005; Gainsborough 2009, 2010). Arguably in no other arena has the state, historically, been more controlling than when it comes to personal mobility. The state has been both the architect of resettlement policies (Hardy 2003) and also instrumental, through the household registration system, in enacting policies that produced immobility. The *ho khau* system consists of four registration categories (Leaf 1999: 305; GSO 2006b):

- KT1: a person registered in the district where he/she resides
- KT2: a person not registered in the district where he/she resides, but registered in another district of the same province/city[5]

---

[5] There are two forms of KT2 registration – KT2 'arrived' (or KT2 *đến*) and KT2 'left' (or KT2 *đi*) – the latter held by the authorities in the migrant's place of departure and the former in their place of arrival.

- KT3: a person from another province/city who has temporary registration in their place of destination for a period of one year, after which the KT3 registration has to be re-issued. (Since July 2007 the requirement to re-register has been lifted.)
- KT4: a person from another province/city who has temporary registration in their place of destination for a period of six months, after which the KT4 registration has to be re-issued. (Since July 2007 the requirement to re-register has been lifted.)

There are two key points to note about the *ho khau* system. First, historically it was hard to change one's *ho khau* unless this fitted with the ambitions of the state. Complex procedures existed, but in practice they were hard to navigate unless one held an urban *ho khau* and wished to move to the countryside, or held a lowland *ho khau* and desired to move to the uplands. As Hardy says, 'household registration was used as a tool of Vietnam's socialist vision of regional planning' and 'involved the restriction of urban growth, deemed detrimental to economic progress, and the development of upland areas, carried out by migrants from the plains to state farms, forestry enterprises and agricultural co-operatives known as new economic zones' (2001: 192–3). Rural folk hoping to move to the city faced almost insurmountable barriers to their relocation. The second point to note is that these policies had traction because one's *ho khau* was a form of social insurance. It was the means by which a person accessed education and health care, obtained employment and secured an existence. These former restrictions have loosened with the progressive extension of *doi moi* from the mid-1980s. Nonetheless, even in the late 1990s, Hardy reports that people without a local *ho khau* were being denied employment (2001: 206). More recently still, a significant proportion of Vietnam's large population without health insurance are migrants without an urban *ho khau* (Ekman et al. 2008: 260). Lacking such registration, they are denied access to social protection, leaving them institutionally vulnerable (Le 2009; Le et al. 2011).

Table 2.2 provides a summary of the registration status of the migrants interviewed for the study undertaken in Hanoi in late 2010. The main point to note is the proportion of respondents who have temporary status in Hanoi even after more than ten years of living in the capital. 'Temporary' registration seems, on the face of it, to have considerable longevity. Traditionally, three explanations have been proposed to account for this: the household registration system no longer has any great significance and is, therefore, largely ignored by migrants who see little benefit accruing from achieving permanent residency (e.g., Chan and Wang 2004; GSO 2006a; World Bank 2010); that changing one's registration is bureaucratically troublesome and convoluted and is avoided on these grounds (e.g., World Bank 2003; Zhang et al. 2006; Nguyen et al. 2008); and

Table 2.2 *Residency classification of interviewees, Hanoi, Vietnam (2010)*

Residency classification	Number of interviewees	Percentage of sample	Average length of time in Hanoi (years)
KT1	6	20	20
KT2	3	10	20
KT3	7	23	14
KT4	9	30	13
No registration	2	7	9
Unknown	3	10	6
Total	30	100	14

that there are real risks of revealing one's temporary status, with the result that migrants maintain a low profile (e.g., Niimi et al. 2009). The last of these seems no longer to apply, but studies continue to debate the actual influence of the *ho khau* system. Demonstrating the concerns that some agencies still have regarding the operation of the household registration legislation, the UNDP concluded in a report that:

Viet Nam's household registration system presents a systemic institutional barrier for internal migrants in accessing both basic and specialized Government services, contrary to the rights provided to them and all other citizens under the Constitution of Viet Nam. Reform of this system is needed so that the registration status of citizens is decoupled from their access to social services, giving equal access to everyone. (UNDP 2010: 7)

Since the mid-1990s, the controlling influence of Vietnam's *ho khau* system has been progressively relaxed so that movement has become easier with each year. Chan and Wang (2004), for example, in their study of factory employment in Hanoi and Ho Chi Minh City (and also in China), found no evidence of the *ho khau* system, despite its continuing legislative presence, playing any significant role in constraining workers in Taiwanese-invested factories.[6] They effectively discount the policy as important – and contrast it with the *hukou* system in China. But while Chan and Wang's research might lead us to discount household registration as significant in shaping migration or migrant decisions, Niimi et al.'s (2009) analysis of migration data leads them to a rather different conclusion. They find that there are clear links between registration status and remittance behaviour and conclude that the 'temporary and uncertain nature of [residency] status encourages migrants to retain strong links with

---

[6] Chan and Wang write, 'interviews in Vietnam with workers, officials, Taiwanese managers, foreign labour-standard monitoring agencies and the Vietnamese news media revealed no evidence that the household registration system has caused any withholding of personal documents, restrictions in job and geographical mobility, or harassment by police due to absence of documents' (2004: 638).

the origin household to insure against the risk of forced expulsion from the host destination' (2009: 35). Chan and Wang (2004: 636, 638, 645) 'contrast' the systems in Vietnam and China, but Niimi et al. (2009: 35) find that the Vietnam experience is 'resonant' with findings from China. It is in trying to reconcile this difference in view that we begin to discern the interface between policies and the everyday a little more clearly.

The migration of young people (particularly) has become crucial to the success of Vietnam's industrialization policies. Even so, the *ho khau* system remains in place. Rather than being rescinded, it has been relaxed. It may no longer stop people moving from the countryside to urban and peri-urban areas, but it does play a role – and an important one – in influencing *how* they engage with both their sites of origin and their places of destination. The argument here is not so much that the policy does, or does not, matter but rather that policies matter – or have traction – in ways that are not foreseen or antici-pated. Rather than disappearing (or not yet), the household registration system in Vietnam is being responded to in new ways. The surprises lie in two over-lapping fields. First are the effects of the *ho khau* policy, and second are the everyday responses to these effects.

Many of the migrants from rural areas who we interviewed in Hanoi in late 2010 and early 2011 took the first opportunity they could to challenge the household registration system by moving to Hanoi. This was not driven by the *ho khau* policy itself, but was due to the effects of other policies and broader economic processes that led to household registration becoming pressured from below.[7] The introduction of *doi moi* from the mid-1980s and the expan-sion of opportunities in urban and peri-urban areas connected with the opening of the economy to foreign investment; the erosion of Vietnam's iron rice bowl and the de facto privatization of farming; the declining terms of trade between farming and non-farming; and the widening in disparities between services and amenities provided in rural and urban areas – all of these social and economic processes and the policies that shaped them (but not deterministically) played a role in leading villagers tacitly to challenge the household registration system.

But these migrant villagers did not simply abandon the countryside. It is in the details of their lives that we see the untidy points of connections between policies and the everyday. In the literature it is often the surveillance element of the *ho khau* system and the policing of residency which attract most attention – the ability of the (strong) state to control its population. This, to be sure, has largely disappeared, as Chan and Wang (2004) note. None of our respondents felt that they were dangerously flouting the law and that this might bring state

---

[7] This is similar to the argument developed by Kerkvliet regarding the emergence of de facto family farming in north Vietnam and the consequent undermining of the collective system (see Kerkvliet 2005).

retribution. Some did comment on the bureaucratic hassle of changing residency. But more significantly, they dwelled on the myriad other effects of household registration, both positive and negative.

Buying a house without Hanoi residency was more difficult. Getting children into the best schools was trickier still as the children of permanent residents received priority, and places at the better schools were often unavailable. And accessing health care was also problematic. It was in these seemingly small, low-visibility ways that the *ho khau* continued to influence what people did and how and why they acted in the ways that they did. Schooling was a particular concern given the growing importance of education for building sustainable futures: getting into a good secondary school meant a much greater chance of getting a place at a good university – and a degree from a good university was much more likely to lead to secure and well-paid employment. All this, though, raises another puzzle. If the state no longer punishes people for moving to Hanoi and if the attractions of achieving permanent KT1 residency status in the city are seemingly so clear, why, even after ten years or more of working in Hanoi, do the migrants in question remain temporary residents (see Table 2.2) – denizens rather than citizens of the city? To understand this, we need to raise our line of sight from the city as destination to the countryside as place of origin.

Mrs Hong illustrated the complex calculations that migrants to the city were making when it came to deciding on whether to change their registration.[8] She travelled to Hanoi in 1988 to join her husband who had already moved to the city and was working as a *xe om* (motorcycle taxi) driver. On her arrival, Mrs Hong took on a range of different jobs: vegetable trader in Phong Khoang market, lottery ticket seller, and tea stallholder at the gates of the Security Academy. To begin with, her sojourn was just that – a temporary relocation to Hanoi. In light of this, Mrs Hong and her husband kept their house and land in Nam Dinh (Figure 2.1), ninety kilometres from the capital, wishing to keep a foot in the countryside even while they built a livelihood in Hanoi. As time went by, however, their lives became increasingly embedded in the city and their concerns shifted from 'getting by' to 'looking ahead' and, in this regard, ensuring the best education possible for their son and daughter: the attractions of permanent residency began to outweigh those of having a bolt-hole in the countryside. In the end, Mrs Hong and her husband decided to relinquish the rights to their land in Nam Dinh, trading security in terms of land in their homeland to access a better education and, therefore, a brighter future for their children – and, by extension, for themselves in a context where social protection in old age is limited.

[8] Interviews #022 and #022b, conducted on 30 September 2010 and 10 November 2010, respectively.

Most of the migrants we interviewed, however, were not willing to give up the security that comes from owning land 'at home' while also feeling a certain obligation to maintain substantive links with their places of origin. While from our interviews it seemed that local officials in source areas did not always interpret legislation in the same way, a recurring theme was the risk that reregistration might lead to the reallocation of their land. Given that land in Hanoi had increased in value to such a degree that it was out of reach to all but the most wealthy, sacrificing land in the countryside to secure residency in the city was, for many of our respondents, simply a step too far. In the late 1980s, land was selling in central Hanoi for around 1–2 million Vietnamese Dong (VND) per square metre; in 2010 it was changing hands for 100–200 million VND per square metre, a hundred-fold increase in three decades.

There was not only a livelihood calculation in play as our migrants juggled relative security, returns and prospects against the attractions of changing their registration. There was also the emotional pull of the countryside and a strong sense of obligation to a migrant's rural origins. This was partly material – as explained above, the countryside provided security. But the importance of 'home' and 'homeland' was made yet more important because in Vietnam a patriline is recorded, confirmed and celebrated in genealogies inscribed in ancestral altars in the village (Bryant 2002; Friedman et al. 2003; Rydstrom et al. 2008; see Figure 2.1). The eldest son has certain ritual obligations, and while migration can disrupt such familial connections and obligations, it also creates a social and cultural context where continuing contact and the likelihood of final return become important. Mr Viet illustrated the power of such familial connection.[9] When we interviewed him, he was fifty-seven years old and had been a *cyclo* and *xe om* driver in Hanoi for twenty years. As the eldest son, he felt a strong sense of obligation in maintaining the family patriline and returned to the village for all major and many minor celebrations, festivities and events. Partly in consequence, he also remained a temporary migrant in the city.

Mr Thinh, originally from Thanh Hoa around 150 kilometres south of Hanoi (Figure 2.1), perhaps summed up best for us the ambivalent views that migrants entertained regarding the city and the countryside and the attractions of each. He told us:

I love my homeland. However, I do not love agricultural production. Agricultural production is a hard job. ... I was even a good farmer. But I do not like farming. The homeland is where I was born. The homeland brought me up. The homeland is in my heart.... The young and capable people should choose cities, the old should live in the countryside. When you are of working age, you should live in cities. When you retire you should live in the countryside.[10]

---

[9] Interview #018, conducted on 28 September 2010.
[10] Interview #026, conducted on 7 October 2010.

Figure 2.1 Keeping people attached to the countryside: land and ancestral houses in Xuan Truong.

It was evident in the research among migrants in Hanoi that national-level policies continued to exert an important influence on people's actions and activities. *Doi moi*, the *ho khau* registration system, the erosion of the collective economy, privatization and the encouragement of foreign investment played an important role in our respondents' lives and livelihoods. The details of people's lives – from eighteen-year-old Ms Bich's employment in a garment factory to Mr Huu's setting up of a small restaurant in Cau Giay to Ms Duyen's small beauty salon – can only be understood when set against broader political and economic processes.[11] But this is evidently not enough to appreciate the *texture* of everyday living, only its broad contours. In our recent paper (Rigg et al. 2014b), we explain this with reference to three disturbing factors. First, the role of idiosyncratic events in determining the life course of individuals and their families. This is necessary to avoid aggregating and averaging highly individualized experiences where an illness, a serendipitous meeting or a traffic accident can turn lives upside down. As Krishna writes, we need 'microscopic inquiries, [that trace] events on the ground [. . .] in order to ascertain who

---

[11] Interviews #0013, #0002 and #0024, conducted on 22 September 2010, on 6 September 2010 and on 7 October 2010, respectively.

gains, who loses, and how' (2010: 11). Second, while the Vietnamese state has, to be sure, played a role in marking out the possibilities open to migrants, we need to pay equal attention and accord equal weight to how, for example, people navigate the household registration system. Lastly, occasionally these individual acts gain wider traction and can, in their collectivity, change policy. This is just Kerkvliet's (2005, 2009) point (footnote 7) when he set out the forces that led to the Vietnamese leadership dismantling collective farming from the mid-1980s.

Thailand: Building the Sufficiency Economy?

The sufficiency economy – or *sethakit phorpiang* – emerged out of a three-fold concern with the direction and nature of modernization in Thailand that began to take hold in the early 1990s and then intensified at the end of that decade.[12] First, and this was given credence and purchase in the wake of the Thai economic crisis in 1997–8, there emerged a concern for the risks and dependencies associated with the reliance on export-oriented, foreign direct investment–fuelled and debt-driven industrialization. As the UNDP's report on the sufficiency economy explains, stories of overambitious national projects, personal indebtedness and overstretched companies 'served as parable[s] for the country's vulnerability to the 1997 crisis' (2007: 25). Resilience had been lost in the race to modernity. The second concern focused on the effects of Thailand's modernization on society and environment. The UNDP observed that the country had made the transition from 'being one of the most resource-abundant areas of the planet to being resource constrained over the space of one generation' while the 'basic building blocks of local society have taken a terrible beating [as] the income from agriculture declined … families are scattered by migration … [and] … village populations are hollowed out' (2007: 24). The third area of concern focused on the ways in which Thai society had lost sight of and connection with its cultural roots, in particular with Buddhism and the principle of moderation: 'the country had clearly ignored moderation by indulging in over-consumption' (UNDP 2007: 32).

There can be scarcely a Thai person past primary school who does not know of the King of Thailand's sufficiency economy. As with Vietnam's household registration system, however, there is a considerable gap between the vision offered by the *sethakit phorpiang* (which pays attention to local knowledge, in situ living and livelihoods, traditional lifestyles, production for consumption and not for sale, and communitarian values) and the modes of living that

---

[12] There are evident links between the Community Culture movement led by the Thai economic historian Chatthip Nartuspha and the sufficiency economy (see Reynolds 2013: 14; Elinoff 2014).

most villagers actually embrace (modern technology, reliance on migration and remittances, non-farm livelihoods and cash for consumption). There is, once again, a separation between the policy (or, in this instance, more of an approach underpinned by a raft of policies and programmes) and everyday responses. This is not because the rural population of Thailand necessarily disagree with the ideals of the sufficiency economy; rather, they put them into practice in ways that are not those that were necessarily intended.

The three villages of Ban Don, Ban Na and Ban Mai are situated, respectively, fifty-eight, forty-five and twenty-three kilometres from the provincial capital of Khon Kaen province, in Thailand's northeast region (Figure 2.1). Across the three villages, we surveyed 105 households (28 per cent of the total) and followed this up with separate, semi-structured interviews with a sub-sample of households from which we collected information on the migration histories of 54 first-generation migrants and 97 second-generation migrants, 151 in total. This then led us to conduct forty-five unstructured interviews with current and past migrants. In sum, then, this approach provided us with three discrete but interlinked sets of data and information – a quantitative household data set (n = 105), a quantitative migrant data set (n = 151) and transcribed interviews with migrants (n = 45). Finally, we undertook a number of community discussions. Table 2.3 shows a handful of broad indicators that link to the sufficiency economy debate: the distribution of land ownership, consumption patterns, debt and migration practices. The table shows a mixed, seemingly contradictory insight into the villages. Some eight out of ten households still had access to and farmed land, the large portion of it riceland.[13] The village remained the geographical locus and focus of the household, and interviews showed the degree to which the inhabitants still identified themselves as villagers and valued the village community and the cultural practices – such as Buddhism and the role of the *wat* (monastery) – that have historically been such an important part of *the* village. In all these senses, the villages as a geographical, social, cultural and economic unit appeared resilient in the face of modernization. The sufficiency economy in these terms appeared built on firm foundations.

But Table 2.3 and interviews with villagers can also be used to construct a rather different development narrative. The table shows that eight out of ten households were in debt, to an average of more than 100,000 baht ($3,500); three-quarters of household heads, at some point, have had to leave the village to find work; at the time of the survey, on average, each household had at least one member absent; and almost every household owned a TV and a motorbike, and approaching one-half of households also owned a vehicle. Alongside the village as resilient, then, where traditions remain important, there is another

---

[13] This is defined as households with more than 1 *rai* of land. (For those with less than 1 *rai*, this mainly related to their house plots.)

Table 2.3 *Indicators of household livelihoods and living – Ban Don, Ban Na and Ban Mai, Khon Kaen, Thailand (2012) (n = 105)*

Percentage of households with agricultural land	81
Average area of land owned	11.8 *rai*
Average area of riceland owned	10.7 *rai*
Average number of household members living in the village	3.9
Average number of household members living away from the village	1.2
Percentage of household heads with migration experience	75
Percentage of households owning a car or pickup	47
Percentage of households owning a motorbike	93
Percentage of households owning a TV	100
Percentage of households in debt	82
Average size of debt	105,000 baht

Note: US$1 = 29 baht; 1 hectare = 6.25 *rai*.

village that has become reliant on migrant work, where consumer goods define success, and where the great majority of households are in significant debt.

We can bring some clarity to the puzzle of this dual-narrative village story in much the same way as with migrants to Hanoi – by exploring a set of questions that lie at the interface between state intentionalities – reflected in policies – and everyday practices. What do policies do, in practice and on the ground? How do people respond to policies, whether by avoiding, reworking or embracing them? What do policies mean, at an experiential level? Asking these questions enables us to begin to understand the everyday political economy of change in rural Thailand and begin to view the disjuncture between policies and practice not as a contradiction but as a puzzle and, moreover, as one that can be reconciled.

An example of this everyday space lies in the evolving role of Buddhism and the *wat* in life in Thailand. Both Buddhism as a religion and the monastery as a social and physical presence in the village remain highly important, and monks are respected. But the practice of Buddhism has changed, none too surprisingly given the changing patterns of life and living in the village. In a group discussion with villagers from one of the villages, the deputy head of the Tambon (sub-district) Administrative Organisation (TAO, or *Or-Bor-Tor*) highlighted the *wat* as a village institution that was still strong and evidence of the continuing strength of the village. But the discussion then turned to *how* people engaged with the monastery, and it was observed that while villagers still went to the *wat*, '*they now go quickly*'. Similarly, farming remains an important part of village life and many households still own and cultivate land. But farming occurs in new ways: rather than being cultivated and stored in rice barns for later home consumption, rice is now mostly sold and then bought back when needed; the buffalo has become almost extinct as a village animal, and machines are used to prepare the land and harvest the rice crop; reciprocal labour exchange (*long khaek*) is no longer possible when people work for cash and the supply of and demand for labour by households are so out of kilter. The deputy of the TAO remarked that people do not get together, as a community, in the way that they once did, and farming is no longer a topic of common concern and interest. We should not, therefore, read continuity of past practices into the ongoing and pervasive presence of farming and role of the *wat*; much has changed.

In broader terms, the *sethakit phorpiang* debate – and the policies and programmes that have developed from it – raises questions about how we think about *the* local when it comes to change. The local as commonly viewed is both a statement of the location of development processes and a comment on their tenor. What this brief discussion highlights is that the sufficiency economy is hard to situate in either of these respects. It emerges, arguably, from an urban (elite) interpretation of local practices, is extended to rural contexts, whereupon it is practiced in novel ways, and, in the process, takes on new meanings. The World Bank's evaluation of participatory development experience concludes that 'Local development policy occurs at the intersection of market, government, and civil society failures; interactions are deeply conditioned by culture, politics, and social structure, and they vary from place to place. Context matters, at both the national and the local level.... History matters.... The social, economic, demographic, and cultural contexts matter.... Geography matters.... Politics matters' (Mansuri and Rao 2012: 288–90). In writing this, the report's authors pay attention to the important point that development interventions are shaped by and in local contexts. They are conditioned by the nexus of interrelationships that exist in all local places. It is also worth noting, however, that policies are often framed in other political and geographical spaces, separate from the local, opening up a rather different separation between their meaning-as-policy and their meaning-as-practice. Ferguson (2010, 2011: 66) observed that neoliberal mechanisms of government can be appropriated in fresh ways. This point is not limited to neoliberal mechanisms, however, and, as we see here, is also relevant to how endogenous programmes shaped at the centre find purchase in 'local' spaces.

The greatest puzzle in the three villages is that, notwithstanding households' thoroughgoing engagement with non-farm work and the world beyond the village, few have abandoned the village, sold their land or given up farming. Sufficiency economy theorists might be tempted to interpret this as evidence of the resilience of the village ideal. Our conjecture, however, is rather different: that it relates to the precariousness of non-farm work. Between 1980 and 2000, the size of the informal sector in Thailand declined from 77 to 58 per cent of total employment. Since 2000, however, this trend has reversed, and in 2012 the figure stood at 63 per cent (Hewison and Tularak 2013: 450;

NSO 2013). This has been explained by the growing informalization of the formal sector, and with it growing precarity. In light of this, the reason for villagers' continuing commitment to the land and their communities is to be found in the ex situ employment context.

We can, on the basis of this discussion from Thailand, add a fourth complicating factor to the three noted at the end of the Vietnam discussion: geography matters. The geographical context within which policies are transmitted and enacted can play a large role in shaping their outcomes. The sufficiency economy may depict a particular vision of a desirable economy and society, but in practice it goes little further than rhetoric, notwithstanding scores of sufficiency economy projects and initiatives. Often this is depicted as an outcome of the 'material desires of poor citizens' and the 'problematic results of immoderation' (Elinoff 2014: 90). The rural poor are poor because they are not righteous:

Thai social critics who have taken up the sufficiency discourse have rephrased the economic and political desires of the rural and urban poor as simple greed, which itself was a product of capitalism. (Elinoff 2014: 92)

Much of the sufficiency economy debate has focused either on the practical question of whether it reflects the needs and priorities of Thailand's rural population (most of whom are *not* poor in the absolute sense) or on the politics of the sufficiency economy. Regarding the latter, it is seen by some (e.g., Unger 2009) as a means to indigenize capitalism according to the norms of the urban elite. Here the argument is that villagers take little de facto notice of such efforts; peasant cosmopolitans build their own futures.

Conclusion

The heterodoxy that seems to be such a feature of development in Southeast Asia arises not just because states have been pragmatic rather than ideological in their policies but also because those policies have connected with people and their everyday practices in surprising ways. Accordingly, heterodoxy-as-experienced arises from two divergent sources: first, there is heterodoxy-in-policy and, second, there is heterodoxy-in-practice. Here I have been interested in exploring the latter.

From the above discussion, the Asian developmental state may seem to have been highly effective – 'strong', as it is sometimes said. When we look at its operation at the societal level, we begin to discern greater contingency: policies do not operate in the ways that are intended and there is more scope than might be expected for alternative responses. The policies explored here in the context of Thailand and Vietnam indicate not so much a rejection of those policies or even a 'resistance' to them. Rather, what emerges in the interstitial spaces that almost always exist on the ground is something that is both less overt but also perhaps more important: it is a disjuncture between political economy and individual experience. 'There is', as Hobson and Seabrooke write, 'always a space, however small, for the expression of agency' (2007: 14). This space to express agency is wider than often thought, even in one-party states, and ordinary people more inventive than their characterization as 'ordinary' would lead one to think.

What does this mean, however, for the wider question of the relationships between vernacular modernities, everyday practices, state intentionalities and directional history (see Table 2.1)? Essentially, it means that we need to pay attention to the boundaries in Table 2.1: at the points of contact between everyday practices and state intentionalities, and between vernacular modernities and directional histories. If it is at the boundaries that we find explanatory purchase, then the binaries become blurred. In their introduction to this volume, Elias and Rethel argue that a focus on the everyday 'allows for the probing and ultimate rearticulation of a number of binary understandings: states versus markets as agents of economic development; the traditional and the modern as the opposite ends of the development process; and inclusion and exclusion as different modalities of progress and transformation'. The discussion here has tried to do just this, to show that up close and personal the binaries begin to dissolve: policies-as-practiced take on new forms with different implications; modernities are reworked in ways that rhyme with local customs; and histories are pursued in novel means.

This is not to underplay the sometimes seemingly instrumental ways that policies operate in everyday terms. Take the case of the thirteen million Chinese who do not just have the 'wrong' *hukou*, but no *hukou* at all, known colloquially as *heihu*, or 'black *hukou*'. Li Xue, a second child born in Beijing in violation of China's one-child policy, is one of these thirteen million. Her parents could not pay the fine incurred which amounted to six times her father's annual income and, in consequence, she has no *hukou*:

As a result she could not go to school. She now cannot get a job, nor get married, nor even buy a train or plane ticket.... It means she has barely any legal identity at all. She cannot, on her own, even enter the law courts where her battles for *hukou* are fought. She has to use her sister's library card to borrow the books she needs to help her. (*Economist* 2014: 29)

In this case there is no doubting the power of state policies. But Li Xue continues to struggle to be officially recognized and to bring her existence as a non-person to an end. She has a Weibo account[14] where she parades her case and she returns to court time and again. To be sure, Li Xue cannot change

[14] China's Twitter.

China's *hukou* system by herself, just as our migrants in Hanoi were unable individually to change the *ho khau* system they encountered. But even in China the system is incomplete and partial, unable to govern without giving some room for manoeuvre, some fissures of possibility for action and reaction, some contingency. In their call for an everyday international political economy (EIPE), Hobson and Seabrooke write that:

a central purpose of EIPE is neither to marginalize the importance of the dominant, nor to reify the agency of the weak. Rather, it is to analyse the interactive relationship between the two; one that in many ways constitutes a dialogical, negotiative relationship. (2007: 15)

When we look at the Vietnamese migrant frustrating the household registration system or the Thai villager both acknowledging but then ignoring the King of Thailand's sufficiency economy, we are viewing one in relation to the other. It is in the here-and-now of livelihoods that we can discern the relativity of living. Political economy and 'everyday' political economy are not two circuits of understanding, separated across political and economic space, but intersecting ways of understanding both national processes *and* local and personal experiences. The migration of rural Vietnamese to Hanoi is shaped by national policies; the nature of rural work (and its absence) in Thailand is similarly partially explained by the policies of *kaanpattana* (development) over the last half century. This can go some way in elucidating, at an aggregate level, the nature of rural and urban development. What it cannot do, however, is explain individual decisions and the textures of living. Goss and Lindquist (1995: 345) argue that migration is the 'outcome of a complex combination of individual actions and social structures [... in which] the capacity for such action is differentially distributed according to knowledge of rules and access to resources, which in turn may be partially determined by their position within other social institutions'.

While recognizing their individuality, the directional histories of our interviewees in both northern Vietnam and north-east Thailand were fairly clear. In livelihood terms, they wished to live more secure lives, with robust livelihoods, higher incomes, greater levels of material consumption and a better standard of living or quality of life. Our respondents in both countries also recognized that there were often trade-offs between higher incomes (in the city) and a better quality of life (in the countryside). It is in the gap between policies and the aggregate, and practices and the individual, that an everyday political economy and its utility takes root.

References

Bryant, J. (2002) 'Patrilines, patrilocality and fertility decline in Viet Nam', *Asia Pacific Population Journal* 17(2): 111–128.

Chan, A. and Wang, H.-Z. (2004) 'The impact of the state on workers' conditions: Comparing Taiwanese factories in China and Vietnam', *Pacific Affairs* 77(4): 629–646.

Dapice, D., Gomez-Ibanez, J. A. and Nguyen, X. T. (2010) *Ho Chi Minh City: The Challenges of Growth*. Harvard Kennedy School, Ash Center for Democratic Governance and Innovation, Policy Dialogue Paper number 2. Ho Chi Minh City: UNDP. Downloaded from: www.un.org.vn/index.php?option=com_docman&task=doc_details&gid=14 4&Itemid=211&lang=en

Dayley, R. (2011) 'Thailand's agrarian myth and its proponents', *Journal of Asian and African Studies* 46(4): 342–360.

Dove, M. R. and Kammen, D. M. (2001) 'Vernacular models of development: An analysis of Indonesia under the "New Order"', *World Development* 29(4): 619–639.

Economist, The (2014) 'Fighting for identity', *The Economist*, 17 May, p. 29.

Ekman, B., Liem, N. T., Duc, H. A. and Axelson, H. (2008) 'Health insurance reform in Vietnam: A review of recent developments and future challenges', *Health Policy and Planning* 23: 252–263.

Elinoff, E. (2014) 'Sufficient citizens: Moderation and the politics of sustainable development in Thailand', *PoLAR: Political and Legal Anthropology Review* 37(1): 89–108.

Ferguson, J. (2010) 'The uses of neoliberalism', *Antipode* 41: 166–184.

(2011) 'Toward a left art of government: From "Foucauldian critique" to Foucauldian politics', *History of the Human Sciences* 24(4): 61–68.

Friedman, J., Knodel, J., Bui, T. C. and Truong, S. A. (2003) 'Gender dimensions of support for elderly in Vietnam', *Research on Aging* 25(6): 587–630.

Fukuyama, F. (1995) 'Reflections on the end of history, five years later', *History and Theory* 34(2): 27–43.

Gainsborough, M. (2009) 'The (neglected) statist bias and the developmental state: the case of Singapore and Vietnam', *Third World Quarterly* 30(7): 1317–1328.

(2010) *Vietnam: Rethinking the State*. London: Zed Books.

Goss, J. and Lindquist, B. (1995) 'Conceptualizing labour migration: A structuration perspective', *International Migration Review* 29: 317–351.

GSO (2006a) *The 2004 Vietnam Migration Survey: Internal Migration and Related Life Course Events*. Hanoi: General Statistics Office and United Nations Population Fund.

(2006b) *The 2004 Vietnam Migration Survey: The Quality of Life of Migrants in Vietnam*. Hanoi: General Statistics Office and United Nations Population Fund.

Hardy, A. (2001) 'Rules and resources: negotiating the household registration system in Vietnam under reform', *Sojourn* 16(2): 187–212.

(2003) *Red hills: Migrants and the State in the Highlands of Vietnam*. Honolulu: University of Hawaii Press.

Hewison, K. (2008) 'Review of *Thailand Human Development Report: Sufficiency Economy and Human Development*', *Journal of Contemporary Asia* 38(1): 212–215.

Hewison, K. and Tularak, W. (2013) 'Thailand and precarious work: An assessment', *American Behavioral Scientist* 57(4): 444–467.

Hobson, J. M. and Seabrooke, L. (2007) 'Everyday IPE: Revealing everyday forms of change in the world economy', in Hobson, J. M. and Seabrooke, L. (eds.) *Everyday Politics of the World Economy*. Cambridge: Cambridge University Press: 1–23.

Kerkvliet, B. J. T. (2005) *The Power of Everyday Politics: How Vietnamese Peasants Transformed National Policy.* Singapore: Institute of Southeast Asian Studies.

(2009) 'Everyday politics in peasant societies (and ours)', *Journal of Peasant Studies* 36: 227–243.

Krishna, A. (2010). *One Illness Away: Why People Become Poor and How They Escape Poverty.* Oxford: Oxford University Press.

Le, B. D. (2009) 'Social protection for rural–urban migrants to large cities in Viet Nam', in *Regional Trends, Issues and Practices in Urban Poverty Reduction: Social Protection in Asian Cities.* Bangkok: UNESCAP: 18–34.

Le, B. D., Tran, G. L. and Nguyen, T. P. T. (2011) 'Social protection for rural–urban migrants in Vietnam: Current situation, challenges and opportunities', *Research Report 08.* Brighton: Centre for Social Protection, Institute of Development Studies.

Le Mare, A., Buapun, P. and Rigg, J. (2015) 'Returning home: The middle-income trap and gendered norms in Thailand', *Journal of International Development.* 27 (2): 285-306.

Leaf, M. (1999) 'Vietnam's urban edge: The administration of urban development in Vietnam', *Third World Planning Review* 21(2): 297–315.

Mansuri, G. and Rao, V. (2012) *Localizing Development: Does Participation Work?* Washington, DC: World Bank. Downloaded from: https://openknowledge .worldbank.org/bitstream/handle/10986/11859/9780821382561.pdf?sequence=1

NESDB (2011) *Eleventh National Economic and Social Development Plan, 2012–2016.* Bangkok: National Economic and Social Development Board, Office of the Prime Minister. Downloaded from: http://eng.nesdb.go.th/Portals/0/news/ plan/eng/THE%20ELEVENTH%20NATIONAL%20ECONOMIC%20AND%20 SOCIAL%20DEVELOPMENT%20PLAN%282012–2016%29.pdf

Nguyen, T. P., Tran, N. T. M. T., Nguyen, T. N. and Oostendorp, R. (2008) 'Determinants and impacts of migration in Vietnam', Working Paper Series No. 2008/01. Development and Policies Research Centre. Downloaded from: www.depocenwp.org/

Nguyen, T. A., Rigg, J., Luong, T. T. H. and Dinh, T. D. (2012) 'Becoming and being urban in Hanoi: Rural-urban migration and relations in Viet Nam', *Journal of Peasant Studies* 39(5): 1103–1131.

Niimi, Y., Thai Hung, P. and Reilly, B. (2009) 'Determinants of remittances: Recent evidence using data on internal migrants in Vietnam', *Asian Economic Journal* 23(1): 19–39.

NSO (2013) *The Informal Employment Survey 2012.* Bangkok: National Statistical Office.

Painter, M. (2003) 'The politics of economic restructuring in Vietnam: The case of state-owned enterprise "reform"', *Contemporary Southeast Asia* 25(1): 20–43.

(2005) 'The politics of state sector reforms in Vietnam: Contested agendas and uncertain trajectories', *Journal of Development Studies* 41(2): 261–283.

Reynolds, C. (2013) 'Chatthip Nartuspha, his critics, and more criticism', in Pasuk, P. and Baker, C. (eds.) *Essays on Thailand's Economy and Society for Professor Chatthip Nartuspha at 72*, Bangkok: Sangsan: 1–22.

Rigg, J., Buapun, P. and Le Mare, A. (2014a) 'Personalizing the middle-income trap: An inter-generational migrant view from rural Thailand', *World Development* 59(7): 184–198.

Rigg, J., Nguyen, T. A. and Huong, T. T. L. (2014b) 'The texture of livelihoods: Migration and making a living in Hanoi', *The Journal of Development Studies* 50(3): 368–382.

Rodrik, D. (2007) *One Economics, Many Recipes: Globalization, Institutions, and Economic Growth*. Princeton and Oxford: Princeton University Press.

Rydstrom, H. with Trinh Duy, L. and Burghoorn, W. (2008) 'Introduction to volume on rural families in transitional Vietnam', in Trinh Duy, L., Rydstrom, H. and Burghoorn, W. (eds.) *Rural Families in Transitional Vietnam*. Hanoi: Social Sciences Publishing House: 7–36.

Thai Chamber of Commerce (2010) *Sufficiency Economy: 100 Interviews with Business Professionals*. Bangkok: Amarin Publishing.

UNDP (2007) *Thailand Human Development Report 2007: Sufficiency Economy and Human Development*. Bangkok: United Nations Development Programme.

(2010) *Internal Migration and Socio-economic Development in Viet Nam: A Call to Action*. Hanoi: United Nations Development Programme.

Unger, D. (2009) 'Sufficiency economy and the bourgeois virtues', *Asian Affairs: An American Review* 36(3): 139–156.

Walker, A. (2012) *Thailand's Political Peasants: Power in the Modern Rural Economy*. Madison: University of Wisconsin Press.

World Bank (2003) *Red River Delta – Ha Tay and Hai Duong: Participatory Poverty Assessment*. Hanoi: Poverty Task Force.

(2008) *Vietnam Development Report 2008*. Joint Donor Report to the Vietnam Consultative Group Meeting, Hanoi, 6–7 December 2007.

(2010) *Vietnam Development Report 2010: Modern Institutions*. Joint Donor Report to the Vietnam Consultative Group Meeting, Hanoi, 3–4 December.

Zhang, H. X., Mick, P., Locke, C., Winkels, A. and Adger, W. N. (2006) 'Migration in a transitional economy: Beyond the planned and spontaneous dichotomy in Vietnam', *Geoforum* 37(6): 1066–1081.

3　　Neoliberalism, Resource Governance and the Everyday Politics of Protests in the Philippines

Jewellord T. Nem Singh and Alvin A. Camba

> I have challenged the mining industry to provide evidence of at least one case of a town that developed through large-scale mining. Up until now, they cannot provide a concrete example.
>
> Danny Arias[1]

The quote above vividly captures the recent conflicts on the role of mining and social development in the Philippines. Danny Arias, responsible for linking local communities to national campaigns against large-scale mining, contests the possibilities of transnational investments bringing long-term economic development to a country characterized by challenging geographies for mineral extraction, political violence and a history of socioenvironmental disasters. Importantly, his critique opens up an important intellectual space for academic research that places questions of rights, agency and political mobilization as key organizing concepts in understanding why the 'logic of globalization' is neither inevitable nor necessarily desirable. As the pace of neoliberal reforms intensifies in the region, ordinary people – especially those with limited material and political resources – make justice claims in very difficult circumstances, sometimes not always successfully, in order to alter the configuration of global and local power structures.

Danny Arias's position reflects two important countervailing ideas about neoliberalism and development in Southeast Asia, which we will develop in this chapter. First, Arias's critique reflects the contestation of a neoliberal model of mining management expressed specifically by local political actors sidelined in national political debates. Market reforms in the natural resources sector involved designing complex privatization and liberalization policies. The consolidation of a national anti-mining movement indicates the strength of resistance against foreign direct investment (FDI)-led, large-scale mining (as

[1] Interview with Danny Arias, Campaign and Advocacy Officer, ATM, Quezon City, 19 June 2014.

We thank Alyansa Tigil Mina (ATM) coalition and Philippine Association for Intercultural Development (PAFID) for providing the photographs for this chapter. We would like to acknowledge Raymond Baguilat for facilitating access to interviews with local organizations, community leaders and anti-mining activists.

opposed to *mining* per se). The movement links the diverse efforts of activists, community leaders and the Catholic Church to think about alternative policy paradigms in the mining industry. Civil society actors question the promise of mining-led development, particularly the government's strategy of attracting transnational investments as a way of spurring growth and raising the contribution of mining to the country's exports, revenues and potential for technological development. In addition to the national movement, local communities and regional elites have also challenged the normative commitment of the government towards private capital participation through a nuanced critique of large-scale mining. These actors have come to constitute a somewhat unified political voice against neoliberalism as a development paradigm.

Second, justice claims determining just payments for the host communities in mineral ventures and fair compensation for the negative externalities are complex and heterogeneous, and two competing visions of mining and development exist within the Philippine civil society. The first position, led by the ATM coalition, takes a more reformist stance and negotiates with the state. The second perspective articulated by the *Kalikasan* (Nature) coalition offers a more radical critique of mining-led development by refusing to work within the parameters of reform set by industry participants and state actors as well as stressing the legitimacy of small-scale mining as a livelihood strategy for poor communities. These positions demonstrate the conflicting views around the promise of mining for poorer communities. The division is also historically defined by the ideological rifts within the Left in the country (Quimpo 2007). Their differences are notably more difficult to reconcile, which are based on divergent organizational strategies and alliance-building politics. As a tactical decision to amplify opposition to mining, however, both coalitions have cooperated through ad hoc mobilization. Both rely on local community support in the mining regions for their campaigns. Crucially, their campaigns are constrained by their limited impacts in national politics in terms of pressuring the Philippine government to reverse its position encouraging the private sector to invest in the mining industry.

Our chapter tells a larger story about the changing political economy of the Philippines, one that is frequently characterized by regional specialists as a 'post-developmental state'.[2] By this, we refer to the emergent strategy of domestic elites to extend the reach of the markets across the economic, political and social spheres, thereby subjecting ordinary people to the imperatives

---

[2] With the aftermath of the 1997 Asian financial crisis and the accompanying financial reforms in the relationship of state and capital, some have started to use the 'post-developmental' state as an alternative framework. The post-developmental state denotes 'a new kind of relationship whereby the state, through a plurality of forms, seeks to produce the kind of subjects that are attractive to global capital, both as low-skilled and technical workers and as newly affluent consumers' (Ong, 1999: 57).

of capitalist accumulation in a globalized world economy (Nevins and Peluso 2008; Carroll 2012). While the initial discussion presented in this chapter focuses on the emergence of large-scale mining in the Philippines in terms of systemic factors and elite-centred narratives, later sections of the chapter explore responses of ordinary people and local communities as they become subject to the forces of globalization. Indeed, in the later sections of the chapter, the case of 'anti-mining' in the Philippines demonstrates the everyday forms of civil society activism that have emerged as a response to the dislocations brought about by the rise of large-scale mining – a discussion that will be placed within the wider literature on everyday politics of resistance (Scott 1985). By stressing the ordinary weapons of relatively powerless groups, we are able to understand how ordinary people devise their livelihood and resistance strategies as they become integrated in global circuits of production and consumption (Ong 2006; Nevins and Peluso 2008; Elias 2010; Gomez 2012). In the highly globalized mining industry, the advance of market reforms meant that national elites moulded the model of resource exploitation around the increasing legitimacy of transnational investments as the primary source of social development in the peripheral mining regions. As efforts to institutionalize neoliberalism intensify, local communities have resisted the expansion of large-scale mining. This, in turn, leaves the future of the mining industry uncertain and sensitive to domestic political challenges.

Field research was conducted in Metro Manila and Luzon from 2009 to 2014. We visited several mining sites in Camarines Norte and Nueva Vizcaya, as well as several municipalities in the provinces of Benguet, Ifugao and Mt Province. Semi-structured interviews were conducted with leaders or representatives of people's organizations, as well as national actors ranging from transnational companies, state officials and non-governmental organizations (NGOs). For this chapter, we focused on acquiring the perspectives of NGOs, people's organizations and indigenous group organizations, including national anti-mining movements, indigenous groups, leaders of Islamic and non-Islamic communities in Mindanao and the Christian communities in Luzon. Their perspectives reveal the ways in which they deal with, and resist, the neoliberal mineral regime. Interviews conducted with mining companies and government officials also serve to affirm, build or, at times, contradict civil society perspectives. In addition, the views and perspectives collected were triangulated with data from government reports and news sources.

Neoliberal Mineral Governance in the Philippines

Neoliberalism in the mining industry promotes specific norms, practices and discourses associated with private sector participation – specifically foreign capital – as a key element of growth (Nem Singh and Bourgouin 2013).

But it is also a *political project*, whereby national elites deploy a combination of co-optation and coercion in order to cement political support for market-based ideas of development. In this context, neoliberalism was adopted in sector-specific ways through institutionalized market-conforming policies in a globalized industry.

The mining industry bears particular characteristics that enable state elites to legitimately make a case for a governance arrangement aimed at attracting multinational companies. Large-scale mining requires huge sunk costs and long-term investments in technological development, both of which depend on the existence of political conditions deemed attractive to MNCs. Without private capital, the responsibility falls unto the state to make the investments in the sector. In the post-war years, the Philippine mining industry was nationalized and purchased by domestic businesses. Filipino-owned mining companies such as Benguet, Atlas, Marcopper, Lepanto and Philex were established and began to export minerals to Japan (Holden & Jacobson 2008; Orfenio 2009; Marzan et al. 2010). Under Ferdinand Marcos (1965–86), the state supported the capitalization of domestic firms and aggressively promoted mineral exploration of peripheral regions. From a passive, non-interventionist policy framework based on the colonial treaties with the United States, Marcos shifted the mining regime towards an active, state-led development model which favoured large, established business interests that could mobilize financial resources to explore, develop and exploit minerals, but at the same time sought to prevent the entry of foreign mining companies into the sector (Lopez 1992; Holden 2006; Orfenio 2009).

After 1986, the succeeding democratic governments drastically shifted the country's economic policy orientation towards open markets and deregulated industries. Corazon Aquino (1986–91) laid down the initial foundations of the neoliberal political economy model by stressing the role of foreign companies in national recovery, which was expressed in National Economic and Development Authority's Medium-Term Philippine Development Plan (1987–92). These reforms were further consolidated under the government of Fidel Ramos (1992–7) which via the *Philippine Mining Act 1995* (RA 7942) established a neoliberal mining framework for the sector (Orfenio 2009). But alongside the new mining framework, progressive reforms were also implemented, for example, the recognition of indigenous peoples' rights through the *Indigenous Peoples Rights Act of 1997* (IPRA).

Ramos's mining policy framework became – and remains – the cornerstone of natural resource management in the country. There exist three distinctive elements that shape the governance of natural resources. First, there is undoubtedly a state preference for foreign companies with their huge financial resources to become the engine of mineral exploration and extraction, to the extent that small-scale mining was publicly (and erroneously) perceived as unsafe and environmentally disastrous compared to large-scale mineral extraction. To complement new mining rights and generous tax exemptions to private capital, RA 7942 mandated land to be used for mineral exploration; otherwise, it would be confiscated by the state to be sold again for mineral-related activities.[3]

Second, the law attempted to promote a 'socioenvironmental model', whereby international financial institutions, most notably the World Bank group, sought to contain the social and ecological consequences of resource extraction without jeopardizing the main objective of enhancing the role of private investment in financing extractive industry expansion (Hatcher 2014). What is striking is that the ministry in charge of protecting the environment – the Department of Environment and Natural Resources – is also the regulatory state agency responsible for signing and approving contracts for exploration and exploitation through environmental licenses. In other words, the neoliberal policy framework brought together irreconcilable objectives within a weak state that created frictions within the bureaucracy.

Third, the mining regime attempted to contain social conflicts through hollow participatory, consultative mechanisms as enshrined in two distinctive laws approved around the same period. The Local Government Code (RA 7160) provides jurisdictional powers to sub-national governments to make decisions as regards revenue collection and allocation, including the capacity to challenge national ordinances under conditions in the name of local autonomy.[4] This means, in practice, that mining provinces can make important decisions regarding whether or not large-scale mining activities can operate in the locality. The IPRA passed at the same time as the Philippine Mining Act has been an effective instrument for civil society actors, local communities and indigenous peoples to frame their economic justice demands against mining operations.[5]

After Gloria Macapagal Arroyo (2001–10) became president, she attempted to revive the country's mining industry by issuing Executive Order 270 (EO 270) and the Mineral Action Plan. These policy manoeuvres signalled a renewed focus on a resource-based developmental strategy embedded within a neoliberal policy paradigm. Furthermore, the policy alterations took place when resource investments had been intensifying in the developing world, partly as a result of Chinese economic growth and its search for resource security but also in part due to the restructuring of the global extractive industry.

---

[3] Interview with mining consultant Geograce Resources Philippines, Quezon City, 31 December 2009.

[4] Interview with congressional staff, Committee on National Communities, Quezon City, Philippines, 19 October 2013.

[5] Alongside ILO Convention 169, which respects indigenous rights, IPRA has empowered affected communities of mining operations to challenge their license to operate on the basis of the rights to their ancestral lands, self-determination and cultural rights.

Table 3.1 *Economic impact of the Philippine mining industry (in US$ million)*

	2008	2009	2010	2011	2012[a]
Mining contribution to GDP[b]	$1.205	$1.381	$1.955	$2.237	$1.724
	0.70%	0.80%	1.00%	1.00%	0.70%
Total mining investment	$604.2	$719.5	$1,053.1	$1,149.7	$791.7
Export share (metal mining)	$2,498	$1,470	$1,929	$2,840	$2,265
	5.2%	3.9%	3.8%	6.0%	4.9%
Export share (non-metallic)	$211	$156	$162	$177	$145
	0.4%	0.4%	0.3%	0.4%	0.3%

[a] Preliminary figures.
[b] In US$ billion.
Source: Adapted from Mines and Geosciences Bureau (2013).

External circumstances pushed investments towards emerging resource producers, which had low taxes and pro-foreign investment regimes (Nem Singh
and Bourgouin 2013; *World Investment Report* 2007).[6] But as Table 3.1 details,
despite the steady growth in mining investments, the contribution of the sector
to GDP remains marginal. We detail the developmental impact of the neoliberal regime in the next section, which looks at the national campaign to halt the
expansion of large-scale mining.

The mining regime undoubtedly incorporates social development in the
policy framework. Given the need for enormous capital to explore potential
mineral areas, the law allows foreign investors to use their capital through several kinds of mineral applications. In return, mining companies are required to
invest 1 per cent of their profits into communities through their social development mineral plan (SDMP). The companies usually invest in local communities during the exploration phase of mineral development to acquire
community consent. These firms directly engage with communities through
the construction of schools, day-care centres, roads, basketball courts and the
provision of scholarships and community-building funds. Some notable examples include SMI-Xstrata's 100,000 scholarships for young people over twelve
years, numerous day-care centres and primary schools in Didipio, and even
wage payment for schoolteachers and nurses. These corporate social responsibility (CSR) initiatives reflect not only the growing legitimacy of private actors
in governance arrangements (Cutler et al. 1999), but they are equally indicative
of the lack of institutional capacity of Third World governments to provide
universal welfare for the poor. In extreme situations, notably in resource-rich
Mindanao, mining companies are caught up within the web of violence and

---

[6] While total metal mining operations increased from 23 in 2008 to 35 in 2012, the approved mining contracts soared from 545 in 2008 to 730 in 2012 (Mines and Geosciences Bureau 2013b).

conflict in mining zones. To achieve basic security, large mining firms pay for the wages of paramilitary officials to keep the towns and mining areas safe from rebel group attacks.[7]

The legitimacy of the neoliberal mining model rests, above all, on its development impacts through FDI. Given the geographical isolation of mining towns from more prosperous cities, these enclave economies are characterized by high levels of income poverty, absence of interconnected grids of electricity and water pipelines, and scarce infrastructures for education and health. For this reason, mining companies have argued that mining communities will be the direct beneficiaries of mining operations.[8] As in Africa's resource-rich regions today, mining activities in the Philippines paved the way for road constructions that have gradually connected peripheral regions into cities. Direct social investments also provided new opportunities for low-skilled mining workers to put their children in schools, and company employees have benefited from new hospitals in the mining regions. In addition, the SDMP requires mining companies to purchase their materials from the local communities and mining provinces, thereby encouraging low-skilled work in the *sitios* or villages through higher demand for food, clothing, laundry and other types of household work. It is apparent then that it is not technological transfer or the spillover effects of the mining industry to the broader regional and national economies that encourage mining in the periphery. Nor do we find that mining communities have benefited greatly from new employment opportunities in the sector. It is, in fact, the livelihoods and the small gains from the margins in the context of an overwhelming strategic absence of the state which make mining a tolerable employment opportunity for some of these mining provinces. Given the weak, if not virtually absent, political consensus around mining as a development strategy, it is not surprising that the push towards large-scale mining driven by FDI as a growth model received enormous resistance from civil society, indigenous peoples and local communities. We turn to the process of mobilization in the following section.

Constructing the 'Anti-Mining' Movement

The rise of the 'anti-mining' movement in national politics should be understood in the context of complex interactions between states, multinational firms and local communities. Specifically, the movement offers a general critique of the Philippine government's emphasis on FDI as the only way to revitalize the mining industry. This position is clearly in line with the neoliberal policy paradigm advocating for the strategic absence of the state. Crucially, the mining

---

[7] Interview with former local government unit official, Bayombong, Nueva Vizcaya, 26 June 2014.
[8] Interview with Kayzer Llada, commercial specialist, Philippine Associated Smelting and Refining Corporation, Makati City, 11 June 2014.

regime after the 1995 Mining Act makes important compromises with regard to the process of acquiring local community consent and guaranteeing mitigation measures against the social and ecological impacts of large-scale mineral exploitation. Below we outline the main criticisms that civil society actors have raised regarding the ways in which processes aimed at making the mining regime accountable and sensitive to the demands of local communities have been either ignored or hijacked by corporate interests. Raising these criticisms has clearly resonated with the general public granting the national anti-mining coalitions some credibility in public policy debates.

The 1995 Philippine Mining Act incorporates weak mechanisms for local communities (together with civil society organizations) to channel their grievances towards state institutions. The expansion of large-scale mining in particular has undermined safeguards for political consent and social acceptability. The primary instrument of local accountability in the mining industry – the principle of *free, prior and informed consent* (FPIC) facilitated by the National Commission of Indigenous Peoples (NCIP) – has been casually treated as a formality which companies must tick off from a vaguely defined checklist rather than opening a genuine dialogue between local communities and multinational firms.[9] More importantly, the FPIC is also susceptible to self-interested individuals in the mining communities, leading to numerous allegations that the consultation processes are largely hollow. Some problems identified by critics include the arbitrary selection of new leaders in the indigenous communities who are supportive of large-scale mining, the numerous consultations with the communities until they acquiesce to mining, minority support from few members of the community treated as 'majority' vote or consent, and the lack of specific procedures in the FPIC that subject the consent-building process to multiple and often competing interpretations. Because of the numerous, repetitive and arbitrary consultation procedures, multinational firms and local elites are given opportunity to exploit the FPIC process, pushing numerous communities to acquiesce to mineral industry demands. To provide an example from our fieldwork, in the province of Nueva Vizcaya, the regional branch of the Mines and Geosciences Bureau (MGB), the key regulatory agency, approved a mineral exploration permit whether or not the Titan Mining Corporation conducted a FPIC process with the Ikelahans, an indigenous group, in the province.[10] The Nueva Vizcaya office of the MGB gave the final permit even though it did not have the power to do so because of the size of the tenement. Instead of scrutinizing the application, the Manila office subsequently approved the permit in less than thirty days.[11]

[9] Interview with Robbie Halip, Officer Asia Indigenous People's Pact, Bangkok, 12 June 2014.
[10] Interview with Former local government unit Official, Bayombong, Nueva Vizcaya, 26 June 2014.
[11] Interview with Kail Zingapan, Mapping Officer, PAFID, Quezon City, 6 June 2014.

Second, the 1995 mining regime also fails to delineate government land, ancestral domains and protected areas, on the one hand, and appropriates land with mining potential for exploitation, on the other. With civil society organizations unable to participate in allocating and planning land use for mining,[12] the process of undertaking environmental impact assessments (EIAs) becomes ineffective in protecting local communities and indigenous domains. Mining companies, which are required to conduct EIAs to be verified by the Provincial Environmental Board of mining provinces, are able to acquire mineral tenements covering ancestral lands and protected areas through various means.[13] In one highly controversial case from Southern Cotabato in Mindanao, the mining firm, SMI-Xstrata, submitted an EIA that has missing information in its geographic simulation that would affect the health of the river basins in the surrounding provinces. Social movements and peoples' organizations believed that the mining firm and the national government deliberately presented an incomplete, biased report. This was exacerbated by the government's efforts to make the controversial EIA difficult to obtain for civil society organizations.[14] The larger issue, of course, is the limited institutional capacity of the national and regional governments to monitor, tax and regulate the mining industry. There appears to be very weak technical capacity on the side of the regulatory agency, the MGB, which makes the state dependent on multinational companies from undertaking the EIAs (Nem Singh et al. 2014).

Finally, civil society organizations have argued that CSR initiatives underpinned by the FDI-driven growth model have largely ignored the negative externalities of large-scale mining, especially deprivation, income poverty and health hazards that result from mining activities. Often this is a result of the fact that SDMPs themselves have come to reflect the rent-seeking practices of the mining industry, for example, the ways gifts and sponsored events are used to acquire favours from government officials and community leaders. As such, the emergence and practices of the anti-mining mobilization go beyond the class relations, or the social identities inferred directly from the mode of production. Anti-mining mobilization, instead, goes back to the concrete experiences of engaging both multinational and domestic mining companies, as well as the ways in which state frameworks direct the struggles of communities towards particular issues.

What we see then is that the neoliberal mineral regime has in many ways acted to limit the spaces for local communities to participate meaningfully in

---

[12] Interview with Maramie Diego, Mangyan Taga-Bukid, Atsmata Indigenous Group, Quezon City, 6 June 2014.
[13] Interview with Farah Sevilla, Policy and Research Officer, ATM, Quezon City, 19 June 2014.
[14] Interview with Dave de Vera, Executive Director, PAFID, Quezon City, 6 June 2014.

Figure 3.1 Mobilization of *Akbayan* party-list group against the 1995 Act.
Source: Alyansa Tigil Mina

political debates. The purported benefits and safeguards of the 1995 Philippine Mining Act fail to strike a balance between its socioenvironmental safeguards and pro-investment position. Given the lack of developmental impacts on the communities, the government's attempts to revitalize large-scale mining as a growth strategy have generated political resistance. The next section details the complex and heterogeneous national anti-mining movement, supporting local communities in contesting the current policy in favour of resource exploitation.

Everyday Politics of Resistance

We blockaded the roads for days, months, and years. They were only able to penetrate when military forces arrived and started a series of intimidation, destruction, and assassination.

Timuay Fernando Daing[15]

Our allies from the barangay [local municipalities] near the border of Pangasinan will send text messages to the people in Casigbu [which is near the mining areas]. We usually have approximately an hour or two to gather whatever we have and get what we need to create a barricade. We take what we have and see what happens.

Maria Eva Budong[16]

These quotes reflect upon the oftentimes spontaneous and/or banal aspects of social mobilization. Nonetheless, such mobilizations are grounded in the

[15] Interview with Timuay Fernando Daing, *Simbuan* tribal leader, Quezon City, 18 June 2014.
[16] Interview with Eva Barong, Mapping Officer, PAFID, Quezon City, 6 June 2014.

concrete experience of marginalization by local communities and indigenous peoples that serve as the starting point for organized political resistance against large-scale mining. While the Philippines enjoys a long history of civil society activism dating as far back as the anti-dictatorship movement (Thompson 1996; Quimpo 2007), what is particularly striking is the ways in which local movements and regional elites have mobilized and generated the push for a national anti-mining coalition to be formed. In the previous section, we focused on the criticisms that have been used by civil society activists in order to form a national movement against large-scale mining. In this section, we turn to focus less on the critiques and more on the politics of mobilization that play out in terms of three specific sets of practices: the strategies of activists; the politics of building alliances with other actors; and the emerging conflicts concerning the role of small-scale mining as an alternative strategy to large-scale mining. These three highly contentious processes are pivotal to evaluating the strengths and limits of civil society activism in the Philippines.

The 'anti-mining' movement is far from uniform and homogenous. There exist two huge nationally organized coalitions which represent contending approaches to mining and social development. There are some clear differences between their coalition-building strategies, methods of mobilization and prognosis of the mining industry. Crucially, these distinctive approaches to mining and social development reflect the historical fragmentation of the Left in the Philippines, and therefore, compromises over key positions have been difficult. Nevertheless, there is ad hoc cooperation among social groups to prevent large-scale mining in the country. We summarize these different positions in Table 3.2.

The first group involves approximately 250 civil society and people's organizations, which consolidated their strength in a single, informal anti-mining coalition, the ATM. The coalition's members range from multi-sectoral organizations to indigenous and mining-affected communities to human rights groups. However, one prominent actor within the coalition is the Catholic Church alongside other faith-based organizations that support the ban against mining. The members sought three interrelated but distinctive goals: (a) scrapping the 1995 Philippine Mining Act and replacing it with a new mining law; (b) revoking Arroyo's executive order revitalizing mineral activities; and (c) passing a national moratorium on mining.[17] Their key contention is the incapacity of the existing mining framework to address effective revenue collection and in accordance with political spaces for affected communities to decide whether mining should operate in their provinces.

---

[17] Phone interview with Jaybee Garganera, Secretary General, ATM, 4 July 2012.

Table 3.2 *Contending visions on mining and social development*

Coalition	Goals	Nature of coalition	Methods and approaches	Political alliances	Position over small-scale mining
ATM	Stop large-scale mining as a least common denominator Open up a dialogue among actors for alternatives	ATM comes from Philippine Network for Human Rights in the rural areas and was previously housed in PNHRA Its funding comes from international NGOs	Opposition to the 1995 Philippine Mining Act through legalistic, institutional and non-violent methods There is a need for state action to change the laws and conduct studies about impacts of mining ATM methods come from a more advocacy-based NGO strategy of international NGOs such as Harribon Foundation; they emphasize non-violent, peaceful means (fact finding, scientific missions and working with officials) to promote their advocacies ATM strategies have evolved because of its 'success' to penetrate national and local governance bodies (Cielo Magno in the Mining Working Group, MWG) for mineral-related decisions	ATM is part of an alliance of 16 NGOs, which includes Bantay Kita, Action for Economic Reform, and others ATM is directly affiliated with political parties but the coalition has members from these organizations ATM works very closely with key legislators Strong political relationship with church-based organizations at national and sub-national levels The ATM has developed ties with businesses and other actors in mobilizing against mining, especially in Tampakan, Santa Fe and Romblon	The ATM is unclear when it comes to small-scale mining given its position is to reject the 1995 Philippine Mining Act Because the ATM has some support from small-scale mining communities, it advocates for an alternative small-scale mining bill

Kalikasan	Stop transnational, large-scale mining as a least common denominator	Kalikasan chairs *Defend Patrimony*, a broad coalition of people's organizations, NGOs and civic institutions that opposes liberalization and advocates resource nationalism	Opposition to the 1995 Philippine Mining Act through legalistic methods but strong emphasis on community mobilization	Strong alliance with radical left political parties, evidently shown in Bayan Muna and Makabayan bloc's sponsorship of the People's Mining Bill	ATM advocated for case-by-case discussions of specific approaches emerging from the communities as a way of deciding whether mining operations should take place or not	Kalikasan supports and pushes for small-scale mining as part of a national development strategy
	Promote state-led, large-scale mining based on a strong domestic market and self-sufficiency	Some of its funding comes from international sources	More radical view as regards the negative role of transnational capital in local communities	Few links with domestic businesses		Emphasis on local communities and the domestic market as opposed to large-scale, FDI-led mining
			Emphasis on empowering local communities as a way of opposing large-scale mining	Strong belief in the legitimacy of confrontational methods which constrain possible alliances with church-based organizations		Kalikasan recognizes small-scale mining as a *livelihood* strategy but not as a means of developing mining for exports and revenues
			Kalikasan puts forward a national development strategy across all sectors, with mining seen as a key industry to spur state-led industrialization	Kalikasan does not profess to support violence but argues that the structural problems of the Philippine economy mean that armed resistance has become prevalent in these poor, resource-rich regions		

Source: Authors' compilation based on reports, interviews, and newspaper archives. Alyansa Tigil Mina, 2011a, 2011b.

Figure 3.2 Tao Muna Hindi Mina (People First Before Minerals) campaign of ATM in Roxas Boulevard, Metro Manila. *Source*: Alyansa Tigil Mina.

The second coalition is *Kalikasan* with approximately 200–300 civil society and indigenous organizations. Unlike the ATM, Kalikasan takes a radical stance as regards the neoliberal mineral regime by pointing towards the structural dependency of the Philippines on the 'imperialist, Western influence'.[18] Using a national industrialization framework, Kalikasan members oppose large-scale mining because of the inherently 'exploitative relations of mineral extraction'. This argument reflects more orthodox, Marxist perspectives on resource production as a way to instil new forms of imperialism in the global economy. Their campaign is geared towards national self-sufficiency as expressed in state-led visions of industrialization, which signifies a more nuanced position regarding the possibility of utilizing minerals for growth and development. Given that raw materials are increasingly vital for industrialization, the coalition argues for structural change in governance frameworks as well as state reforms that reflect a nationalist policy orientation.

Needless to say, the construction of a strong, unified opposition movement to large-scale mining is fraught with tensions, contradictions and, in many

[18] Interview with Leon Dulce, Campaign Officer, Kalikasan-PNE, Quezon City, 13 June 2014.

cases, irreconcilable differences. The divergent visions on mining and development between and within the two political coalitions pose some challenges in sustaining a national movement. Indeed, the diverse members in each political coalition mean that their actions are based on a politics of pragmatism rather than ideological cohesion. While both coalitions conceive of 'anti-mining' as resisting the current mining policy framework promoting FDI and large-scale mining in the country, they carry quite nuanced policy positions, especially the question of small-scale mining. For these reasons, ATM and Kalikasan are, at best, networks of loose social groups and political movements bearing within themselves competing objectives, strategies and organizational interests.

The position of ATM over small-scale mining has been perceived as tenuous, if not unclear. With over 250 member organizations, 'there is a 60-40 divide with people who are fine with mining and those who are absolutely against it'.[19] The ATM faces challenges in maintaining a unified coalition, so their approach is to take the *least common denominator* to express their policy perspective. The ATM furthers pluralism and a case-by-case approach to small-scale mining with the view to strengthening the fiscal capacity of the Philippine government to capture resource rents. By contrast, the Kalikasan coalition argues for structural changes and policy reorientation in the fiscal, macroeconomic and environmental dimensions to advance a more statist version of mineral extraction. Kalikasan imagines mining as a pivotal sector due to the potential enormous rents which can then spur the creation of new chains of national industries in the Philippines. Similar to arguments of resource nationalism in Latin America and Africa during 2000s (Nem Singh and Bourgouin 2013), the coalition conceives natural resources as *national* commodities to be used for investments in other sectors. This, in turn, can build the foundations for long-term growth and structural transformations of the economy.

Other important differences are noticeable. The coalitions have expressed dissatisfaction with each other in terms of their mobilization strategies as well as the timing of their initiatives. For Kalikasan, the ATM has the tendency to be satisfied with legal and institutional methods owing to their reformist, compromising position with the state. For ATM, Kalikasan lacks sincerity in coordinating mobilization, petitions and strikes, resulting in covert initiatives during ad hoc partnerships. To put it simply, the tensions and political conflicts with big coalition movements remain, and their members are aware of the difficulty in maintaining a focus on their shared goals and reconciling their organizational differences. Owing to the history of the movements, their campaigns are separated by their presence in different provinces, towns and municipalities. At the local level, peoples' organizations and indigenous communities call upon

---

[19] Interview with Danny Arias, Campaign and Advocacy Officer, ATM, Quezon City, 19 June 2014.

both coalitions in organizing anti-mining campaigns, culminating in ad hoc coordination and parallel programs.

Nevertheless, the role of these national movements is to help local communities to organize, analyze and decide whether they would like large-scale mining to operate in their provinces. Beyond understanding the strategies and politics of resistance claimed by these national movements, we argue that there is also a need to explore everyday practices of activism at the local level. Broadly, we categorize two distinctive approaches here. On the one hand, some local organizations employ militant methods such as organizing human barricades, economic sabotage, protests and rallies. Human barricades, by the virtue of their visibility and public display, provide protection to the communities and keep the state away from using violence readily. People from municipalities and the smaller villages gather at specific locations to form human barricades, temporarily halting their activities in the formal and informal economies. While men provide the physical and manual labour to keep the barricade strong, the social status of elderly, women and children on the barricades hinder the state from pursuing violent action. Through human barricades, communities are able to shift the struggle from economic and political rights to human rights, ultimately making the state wary to act. Additionally, barricades garner the attention of the local media, as well as support from other sympathetic communities, creating an environment to openly highlight and speak about the local mining issues, as well as the broader national-level mining policy. Human barricades, therefore, transform communities into agencies of resistance, putting the lives of the people on the line, as well as reopening national and institutional policy debates at the local, community level.

On the other hand, some local groups resort to legalistic and institutionalized methods to engage with states and mining companies, notably through national petitions, fact-finding investigations, environmental scientific studies, and campaigns for moratoriums through alliances with sub-national elites. Mapping (the creation of counter-cartographies using local indigenous knowledge) is an interesting resistance strategy because it engages the mining applicants in their own terrain. Multinational firms and states often have a monopoly of claiming scientific legitimacy through the methods and tools for estimating mineral reserves and simulating environmental change. As we discussed in the previous section, SMI-Xstrata and the MGB presented an incomplete, erroneous EIA, which had some initial persuasive power because of its claim to methodological rigor and scientific accuracy. In response, civil society and people's organizations conducted their own geographic simulations and constructed their own 3D models, revealing the erroneous and incomplete projections of the mining firm and the state. The new studies delegitimized the mineral application and swayed the population to vote against the application in a public referendum.

It is worth noting that these approaches blur on the ground; local groups tend to switch their strategies when the effectiveness of their methods are exhausted; others change their tactics based on the political environment.[20] This is particularly the case when affected mining communities are subject to political violence and the growing militarization of mining regions. The national movements help provide material and political resources to the local communities depending on their mobilizing capacity, the urgency of the situation, as well as the specific demands of the local anti-mining campaign.[21] The use of telecommunications technology such as cellular phones has also assisted in coordinating spatially dispersed municipalities. In one of the quotations that opened this section, Maria Eva Budong of PAFID recounted her experience of political mobilization when she was part of an anti-mining community in the province of Nueva Vizcaya during her younger years, emphasizing the importance of closely coordinating activities among the residents of other *barangay* (small towns) who live near the mines.[22] Given the short amount of time to mobilize - for instance, forming barricades takes about one or two hours – spontaneous actions become more useful to generate immediate responses. However, the national organizations contribute food, supplies, and other forms of material support to sustain the human barricade.[23] These everyday and localized practices of resistance form some synergy with national mobilizations, creating some opportunities for national coalitions to align these specific local claims with the broader national framing of 'anti-mining' discussed earlier in this chapter.

Human barricades are effective because sustained blockades can derail mineral projects for years. However, they also exacerbate levels of political violence especially in highly militarized mining regions. In interview, Timuay Fernando Daing, one of the leaders of the *Simbuan* tribes in Zamboanga province in Mindanao, recalled their lengthy blockade as taking place over 'days, months, and years' – but these tactics also made communities vulnerable to military forces using intimidation, destruction and assassinations as methods of pacification in the region.[24] Indeed, as a result of the growing tensions in mineral-related areas, there have been extrajudicial killings – for example, the family of Daguil Campeon, a representative of the B'laan indigenous group in Mindanao and a former employee of Social Development Management Institute who turned member of the ATM. Another example is Dr Gerry

---

[20] Interview with Eva Barong, Mapping Officer, PAFID, Quezon City, 6 June 2014.

[21] Interview with Santos Mero, Deputy Secretary General, Cordillera People's Alliance, Baguio City, 28 June 2014; and with Maramie Diego, 6 June 2014.

[22] Interview with Maria Eva Budong, Mapping Officer, PAFID, Quezon City, 6 June 2014.

[23] Interview with Tony Bagay, labour leader, Kilusan Mayo Uno-Cordillera Chapter, Baguio City, 28 June 2014.

[24] Interiew with Timuay Fernando Daing, Simbuan tribal leader, Quezon City, 18 June 2014.

Ortega, a well-known anti-mining advocate in the Palawan mining region, as well as attempted kidnappings of civil society activists like Ka-Bandong from the ATM coalition (Rovillos et al. 2003). While in theory the state should protect and respect the primacy of rights of marginalized communities and groups, the FPIC process has been deemed weak in its implementation, and in some cases, social consent has deliberately been ignored by military and paramilitary security forces. This, in turn, leads to the escalation of mining-related social conflicts.

In response, one important strategy of national NGOs is to sponsor week-long exposure trips to other national and international supporters. In some instances, visitors are able to live with the communities and participate in the barricades, thus providing 'the community with the feeling of solidarity to their justice claims'.[25] In involving national and international participants, communities become part of a wider network of political activism that can tame mining-related violence and abuses from all sides. With the active participation of human rights NGOs in the national campaign, local communities are better able to openly discuss human rights abuses which are now internationally recognized as taking place systematically, sometimes with state parties involved in crimes. As Goodland and Wicks (2009) suggest, the impacts of mining on social development have been negative and the indigenous communities and local populations have been vulnerable to political violence related to large-scale mining. In addition, between 2010 and 2013 there have been thirty cases of mining-related violence against indigenous persons filed in the House Committee of Indigenous People. Moreover, most of the FPICs awarded to mining companies have been acquired as a result of weak state capacity to monitor abuses by multinational capital and domestic firms (NCIP 2012). Hamm et al. (2013) claim that civil and political rights are routinely infringed upon or violated on a larger scale, as backed up by UN reports, in which these conflicts over land and natural resources can be traced back to state parties. Overall, there are growing concerns that mining activities are generating violent political conflicts that lead to systematic human rights abuses and violations of indigenous peoples' rights.

Local communities and national campaigners have established patterns of ad hoc cooperation that allow complementarities between everyday practices of resistance based on their concrete experiences of class relations, violence and livelihood strategies, on the one hand, and more organized politics of collective action at the national level, on the other. For example, one important outcome of this synergy between local and national mobilizations has been the merging of two separate mining bills in Congress into one alternative mining bill,

---

[25] Interview with Piya Macling Malayao, Spokesperson, Kalipunan ng mga Katutubong Mamayan ng Pilipinas, Quezon City, 15 June 2014.

which was forged through the help of the Legal Rights and Natural Resources Center and Friends of Earth Philippines.[26]. Alliances do, therefore, appear to be challenging the neoliberal mining framework in meaningful and significant ways. Nonetheless, the state's response to both civil society and the industry has been variegated. The final section analyzes the state's response to these emerging policy debates.

State Responses to Social Mobilization

The anti-mining campaign both increased public awareness regarding the socioecological consequences of large-scale mining and opened up new debates around taxation, human rights and long-term development policy. The response of President Benigno Aquino (2010 to present) has been mixed. In an attempt to clarify the position of the government, Aquino issued EO 79 in July 2012, wherein the government recognized 'the need for extractive industries to pay more revenues given the nature of the tax regime'.[27] Aquino's executive order began with the discourse on 'sustainable mining' as a development strategy. In contrast to the Arroyo government, '[President] Aquino has been more responsive to the indigenous peoples' demands and notable reforms in the mineral sector have been implemented'.[28] In May 2013, Aquino enacted a moratorium on mineral exploration that halted the expansion of mineral extraction to new areas. At the same time, he created the Mining Industry Coordinating Council (MICC), which brings together various government agencies to review existing mining operations in line with the goal of enhancing compliance and adherence to the environmental and regulatory standards covering EO 270.[29]

Working with the MWG, the MICC was tasked to address complex institutional reforms on mining governance, which include, inter alia, renegotiating new mining contracts, changing the terms of licensing, seeking a balance on revenue sharing between national and regional governments, increased transparency and introducing some degree of local community participation before mining is allowed. As of June 2013, the MICC drafted a new mining bill aimed at replacing the 2 per cent excise tax, corporate duties and fees on capital imports with a fixed share of 7–10 per cent from the gross income and windfall revenues of mining firms.

---

[26] Interviews with Danny Arias, Campaign and Advocacy Officer, ATM, Quezon City, 19 June 2014; Farah Sevilla, ATM, 19 June 2014; and Leon Ducle, Campaign Officer, Kalikasan-PNE, 13 June 2014 (see also Recidoro, 2013)

[27] Skype interview with a senior official, National Anti-Poverty Commission, 16 October 2013.

[28] Interviews with congressional staff, 19 October 2013; and Jaybee Garganera, December 2011.

[29] The members of the MICC include the DENR, MGB, NCIP, Department of Interior and Local Government, Department of Trade and Industry and the Department of Finance.

While coordination among the state, industry and civil society has been taking place, and a moratorium was put in place by the Aquino government, managing potential resource wealth remains to be the key priority of the state. Aquino is challenging the low-tax regime imposed by Ramos and Arroyo. Civil society organizations, notably *Bantay Kita*, are supportive of the proposed increase in effective tax rates in the industry. However, in the Philippines and elsewhere, economic growth does not lead to social development. The expansion of mining, therefore, does not necessarily or naturally lead to better developmental outcomes. If there is anything the experiences of local communities tell us, it is the opposite. As the debate to pass a new mining law continues, the concerns of civil society organizations and local communities cannot be ignored in the policy-making process.

Overall, the emergence of civil society mobilizations particularly at local levels has begun to demystify the neoliberal veil of the mining regime in the country. Given the patchy history of large-scale mining and the weakness of the national state, the socioenvironmental consequences borne by local communities have generated vital political opportunities for national and local civil society actors to coalesce around socioeconomic justice claims. Although an emerging discourse today focuses on expanding mining activities alongside an unambiguous progressive agenda on welfare spending and taxation (see Nem Singh et al. 2014), the neoliberal orientation of the Philippine state has prevented any meaningful social dialogue taking place between states, multinational and big businesses, and civil society actors.

Conclusion

This chapter demonstrates that Philippine mining governance has been repoliticized by civil society actors, affected regional communities and local power holders in ways that challenge the national discourse of large-scale mining and its unambiguous role in social development. The pressure for repoliticization stems from the historical inequalities in distributing economic gains to the mining provinces; but it also hinges on the concrete experiences of being vulnerable to the socioecological impacts of large-scale mining. This vulnerability is further complicated by the growing militarization of some mining regions, especially in Mindanao, where communities are caught up in the armed struggle between different rebel groups and the military, with mining companies increasingly resorting to private security as a way of sustaining their mining operations.

It is worth noting that the scale of collective mobilization and degree of public opposition against mining is enormous. Thus, when the approval for mining in Simbuan, Tampakan, and Santa Fe was granted by the Philippine government, these approvals were eventually revoked in the face of sustained local protests and human barricades. Through these resistance practices, every-day actors are able to frame place-specific and concrete local demands in terms of broader questions of economic justice that are used in national political debates. Through civil society mobilization, the link between mineral rents and inclusive development is challenged. Overall, there appears to be a lack of political consensus over the place of large-scale mining in the country's development strategy.

Debates on state autonomy and institutional capacity have informed schol-arly understandings of the nature of the state and of state-citizenry bargains in Southeast Asian political economies (see Slater 2010; Kuhonta 2011). Our chapter analyzes how development strategies imposed by national elites can be challenged through both coordinated and everyday forms of activism. By pointing to the resistance strategies used by less powerful groups, we are able to locate the place of everyday political economy in understanding changes under market developmentalism. The anti-mining movement articulates a critique of not just the limits of economic growth as conceived by national elites, but they also challenge the everyday practices in the political economy that naturalize inequality, poverty and a narrow conception of development based on foreign investment and material income. In analyzing the com-plexity of mobilization, we showed that ordinary citizens and less powerful groups can deploy a variety of tactics and spontaneous actions to invoke a sense of collective injustice and resist hegemonic ideas around economic development.

References

Alyansa Tigil Mina (2011a) 'Palawan Case Study: Mining and Biodiversity Draft', accessed from Alyansa Tigil Mina: www.alyansatigilmina.net
   (2011b) 'Indigenous Peoples (IP) Rights in Resource Conflict Areas Zambales Experience', accessed from Alyansa Tigil Mina: www.alyansatigilmina.net
Carroll, T. (2012) 'Working On, Through and Around the State: The Deep Marketisation of Development in Asia-Pacific', *Journal of Contemporary Asia* 42(3): 378–404.
Cutler, C., Hauffler, V. and Porter T. (eds.) (1999) *Private Authority and International Affairs*. Albany: State University of New York Press.
Elias, J. (2010) 'Locating the "Everyday" in International Political Economy', *International Studies Review* 12(4): 603–609.
Gomez, E. T. (2012) 'State-Business Linkages in East Asia: The Developmental State, Neoliberalism and Enterprise Development', in A. Walter and X. Zhang (eds.) *East Asian Capitalism: Diversity, Continuity and Change*. Oxford: Oxford University Press.
Goodland, R. and Wicks, C. (2009) *Philippines: Mining or Food*. London: Working Group on Mining in the Philippines.
Grugel, J. and Riggirozzi, P. (eds.) (2009) *Governance After Neoliberalism in Latin America*. Basingstoke: Palgrave Macmillan.

Hamm, B., Schax, A. and Sheper, C. (2013) *Human Rights Impact Assessment of the Tampakan Copper-Gold Project*. Aachen, Germany: Institute for Peace and Development (INEF), MISEREOR, Fastenopfer, and Bread for All.

Hatcher, P. (2014) *Regimes of Risk: The World Bank & New Mining Regimes in Asia*. London: Palgrave Macmillan.

Holden, W. N. and Jacobson, R. D. (2008) Civil Society Opposition to Nonferrous Metals Mining in Guatemala', *Voluntas: International Journal of Voluntary and Nonprofit Organizations* 19(4): 325–350.

Kuhonta, E. (2011) *The Institutional Imperative: The Politics of Equitable Development in Southeast Asia*. Stanford: Stanford University Press.

Lopez, S. (1992) *Isle of Gold: A History of Mining in the Philippines*. Oxford: Oxford University Press.

Marzan, A., Garganera, J., Arayata, R. and Rodne, G. (2010) 'CSO Assessment of the MTPDP (2006–2010)', accessed from Alyansa Tigil Mina: www.alyansatigilmina.net

Mines and Geosciences Bureau (2013a) *Complete List of Mineral Sharing Production Agreement*. Quezon City, Philippines: Mining Tenements Management Division, Department of Environment and Natural Resources.

(2013b) *Mining Industry Statistics*. Quezon City, Philippines: Department of Environment and Natural Resources.

National Commission on Indigenous People (2012) *The Revised Guidelines on Free and Prior Informed Consent*, NCIP Administrative Order, No. 3. Quezon City, Philippines: Office of the President.

Nem Singh, J. T. and Bourgouin, F. (eds.) (2013) *Resource Governance and Developmental States in the Global South: Critical International Political Economy Perspectives*. Basingstoke: Palgrave Macmillan.

Nem Singh, J. T., Grugel, J. and Hatcher, P. (2014) *The Philippines: The Political Economy of Financing Children's Rights through Extractive Industries*. Geneva: UNRISD and UNICEF.

Nevins, J. and Peluso, N. (eds.) (2008) *Taking Southeast Asia to Market: Commodities, Nature, and People in the Neoliberal Age*. Ithaca and London: Cornell University Press.

Ong, A. (2006) *Neoliberalism as Exception: Mutations in Citizenship and Sovereignty*. London and Durham: Duke University Press.

(1999) 'Clash of Civilizations or Asian Liberalism? An Anthropology of the State and Citizenship', in H. L. Moore (ed.) *Anthropological Theory Today*. Malden, MA: Polity Press, pp. 48–73.

Orfenio, R. (2009) 'Failure to Launch: Industrialization in Metal-rich Philippines', *Journal of the Asia Pacific Economy* 14(2): 194–209.

Quimpo, N. (2007) *Contested Democracy and the Left in the Philippines after Marcos*. New Haven: Yale University of Southeast Asian Studies.

Recidoro, R. (2013) 'THE "ALTERNATIVE" MINING BILL – A Bill Designed to Kill Responsible Mining in the Philippines'. Pasig City, Philippines. Chamber of Mines of the Philippines.

Rovillos, R. D., Ramo, S. B. and Corpuz, Jr., C. (2003) 'When the Isles of Gold Turns into the Isle of Dissent: A Case Study on the Philippine Mining Act of 1995'. Paper presented at the meeting on Indigenous Peoples, Extractive Industries and the World Bank. Oxford, England: Tebtebba Foundation, 1–32.

Scott, J. (1985) *Weapons of the Weak: Everyday Form of Peasant Resistance*. New Haven: Yale University Press.

Slater, D. (2010) *Ordering Power: Contentious Politics and Authoritarian Leviathans in Southeast Asia*. Cambridge and New York: Cambridge University Press.

Thompson, M. (1996) *The Anti-Marcos Struggle: Personalistic Rule and Democratic Transition in the Philippines*. New Haven: Yale University Press.

World Investment Report (2007) *World Investment Report 2007: Transnational Corporations, Extractive Industries, and Development*. Geneva: United Nations Conference on Trade and Development.

4   Everyday Agents of Change: Trade Unions in Myanmar

Nicholas Henry

Introduction

On 1 May 2013, members of trade unions in Yangon openly celebrated International Workers' Day for the first time in decades. In previous years, members of the Federation of Trade Unions of Burma (FTUB) had crossed the border from Thailand into Myanmar, accompanied by troops from the armed wing of the Karen National Union, to hold clandestine Mayday celebrations in Karen villages. Union organizers would give speeches and lead discussions about the core labour rights guaranteed by the International Labour Organization (ILO). In the villages they passed through, they would gather reports of forced labour and other abuses by military units commanded by the ruling State Peace and Development Council (SPDC). When five union activists attempted to hold a Mayday meeting in Yangon in 2007, they were arrested and sentenced to lengthy jail terms.

In 2013 it was different. Union activists, together with other political prisoners, had been released from prison. The union federation, renamed the Federation of Trade Unions of Myanmar (FTUM), held their annual celebration on a public stage in Myanmar's largest city, attended by hundreds of members of newly legalized trade unions along with the deputy labour minister and an official from the ILO liaison office in Yangon. The day before, at a Labour Organisations Conference sponsored by the ILO, union members elected delegates to the ILO conference in Geneva. Those delegates subsequently participated in the ILO's decision to lift sanctions previously imposed on Myanmar for non-compliance with international labour standards. Union activists had been instrumental in persuading ILO member-states to impose sanctions on Myanmar's military regime in 2000 and in working with the ILO to establish processes to monitor and combat forced labour. In 2013, unions were moving from the margins to the centre of Myanmar's national politics and preparing to take up the challenge of organizing a movement capable of transforming the conditions faced by ordinary workers.

In the following discussion of Myanmar's reforms and the evolving industrial relations regime, I highlight the agency of workers and union organizers as everyday actors in shaping the conditions of economic governance and the role of trade union organizations as emerging structures that are beginning to act as bridging mechanisms between everyday and elite politics. Everyday actors, including workers, basic union leaders and union activists, are shown to be making strategic and deliberate use of the promotion of tripartite processes by the ILO to advance their interests, even in conditions where they lack trust in either government or employers' groups.

The new government, with the aid of lobbying and assistance from the ILO, has established legal rights to freedom of association and collective bargaining. These legal rights are a necessary but not sufficient condition for the transformation of Myanmar's industrial relations regime towards the form of tripartite corporatism promoted by the ILO, in which government labour institutions, trade unions and employers' organizations are oriented towards partnership and compromise centred on formal processes of collective bargaining (Hughes 2002). The work programme of the ILO in Myanmar has consistently focused on the establishment of basic labour rights, initially focused on the elimination of forced labour and the worst forms of child labour, and expanded since 2012 to include promotion of the rights to freedom of association and collective bargaining guaranteed by ILO Conventions 87 and 98, respectively.[1] This work programme is described by the ILO liaison officer in Myanmar as making both an immediate and a long-term impact in building conditions for tripartite cooperation in industrial relations between workers, employers and government.[2] While Myanmar's new labour laws allow for the basic conditions in which such a system could develop, the legal regime itself is insufficient to create corporatist social relations of industrial partnership. I argue in this chapter that the everyday agency of workers through processes of trade union organizing will determine the pattern of substantive economic change to emerge out of the current reforms to Myanmar's industrial relations regime.

International norms such as the core labour standards overseen by the ILO provide the basis for some kind of policy convergence between states but do not dictate the processes by which states and local actors achieve compliance or the institutional form that compliance takes. As Acharya (2004: 242) argues, most paths to the recognition of international standards and/or norms in local contexts ('norm acceptance') lie partway between complete congruence with international norms and outright rejection. This formulation bears a striking similarity to Scott's description of everyday politics as inhabiting the political terrain 'between quiescence and revolt' and suggests a role for everyday politics in explaining what might best be termed 'norm localization'. Acharya's

[1] Telephone interview with Ross Wilson, chief technical advisor to the ILO Freedom of Association Project in Yangon, Myanmar, June 2012–June 2013, July 2013
[2] Interview with Steve Marshall, ILO liaison officer in Myanmar, Yangon, January 2014.

(2004: 248) account of this process emphasizes local initiative and agency in 'borrowing' ideas and practices from outside in ways that amplify particular aspects of existing social relations and processes of normative change. For instance, as Gurowitz's (1999) study of migrant workers' activism in Japan shows, international norms are localized by subordinate groups in support of their political claims and campaigns. In other words, political activism situated in local contexts involves the negotiation of international and everyday norms.

Foregrounding the role of everyday actors in norm localization provides an alternative view to structuralist approaches that elide everyday agency. While top-down approaches are endemic to much International Relations and International Political Economy (IR/IPE) scholarship, this is more a matter of habit than a necessary limitation. Turning our theoretical perspective to consider the view of governance regimes from the ground of everyday politics can give a refreshing shake-up to existing theories of IR/IPE. In fact, as Herod (2007) argues, taking everyday agency seriously as a force in international politics involves challenging the spatial categories of IR/IPE thinking, in which the local is subordinated to the national and the global within a fixed hierarchy of nested spaces. This is because the experience of everyday politics involves inseparable connections to relations of power that operate across local, national and global scales in a manner more similar to a capillary network than to a series of distinct levels.

The involvement of non-state actors in processes of governance has been studied as part of the efforts of states and international organizations to render social life legible (Broome and Seabrooke 2012). For instance, Sending and Neumann (2006) examined the activities of international development NGOs in terms of a process of governmentality in which populations are constructed as governable and subject to policy interventions. Where these authors use the Foucauldian concept of governmentality, neo-Marxists such as Cox (1977) used Gramsci's theory of hegemony to respond to a similar puzzle of explaining the involvement of relatively autonomous non-state actors in supporting the work of international organizations. In his analysis of the ILO as a hegemonic institution, Cox was scathing in his analysis of international trade union activity, particularly by US-based unions, as a cross-class alliance with imperialism. For Cox, the reactionary international role of trade unions during the Cold War was an extension of the domestic role of unions in managing capitalism through their integration into corporatist social planning. However, less attention has been paid to the other side of hegemony or governmentality as a site of social struggle and compromise through which everyday actors define the terms of their compliance with the authority of states and international organizations. This perspective can help to explain the participation of everyday actors in producing the forms of legibility and cooperation that enable economic governance.

When Cox (1977) described the ILO model of tripartism as an expression of global hegemony, he was writing at the height of Cold War antagonism. The United States had given notice of withdrawal from the ILO, frustrated at what was seen as increasing Soviet influence on the leadership. Yet, Cox argued, the ILO remained committed to the corporatist integration of organized labour into state-managed capitalist social relations that had been championed by the United States throughout its membership of the organization. In the particular conjuncture of politics in the 1970s, corporatism could accurately be described as the consensus on industrial relations policy among developed capitalist states. As such, the practice of corporatism became loaded with the many contradictions and dubious compromises inherent in attempts to create social peace within capitalist economies. When Cox described corporatism as hegemonic, he could therefore legitimately combine two related meanings of the word. First, that the ideas of corporatism had attained a status of acceptance to the point that they could be assumed as common sense rather than seen as ideology. Second, that the practices of corporatism served an integrative function in promoting a cross-class alliance of the type described in Gramsci's (1971) theory of hegemony.

The situation today is somewhat more complicated. The ILO's model of tripartite industrial relations has survived the end of the Cold War and the associated process by which neoliberal economic theories overtook corporatist models of integration in the ideological orthodoxy of international financial institutions. In its annual *World of Work* reports, the ILO has made strong criticism of rigid applications of neoliberal economics in austerity responses to economic crisis. ILO economists have promoted policies that prioritize sustainable job creation and targeted social assistance as alternative forms of economic stimulus (ILO 2012, 2013). This has often left the ILO in the somewhat incongruous position of adopting a moderately counterhegemonic ideological position in defence of policies that promote hegemony in the sense of social integration.

Outside of the ILO, the tripartite model of partnership in industrial relations is more often championed by trade unions than by governments or employers' organizations. This raises a puzzle to explain why organizations of workers would promote the conditions of their subordination to the authority of governments and relations of exploitation with employers. The explanations offered by Cox's view of hegemony and by theorists of governmentality seem to deny active agency to workers in this process. For Cox, workers are denied agency by unaccountable union hierarchies captured by elite interests, whereas theorists of governmentality attribute causal power to more diffuse discursive structures but still end up denying the agency of everyday actors to resist or negotiate the terms of their cooperation with elites. Without contradicting the significance of structural and discursive power relations of the kinds highlighted by theories of hegemony and governmentality, this chapter addresses the relative absence of accounts of everyday agency in the literature on international institutions.

Myanmar's Reforms

If a regime is defined by the convergence of actor expectations around a coherent set of principles, norms, rules and procedures (Krasner 1982), then Myanmar since November 2010 has been in a state of profound regime uncertainty. In the context of such uncertainty, everyday political actors have greater opportunities to organize in ways that can reconfigure unsettled power relations and influence the form of the new regimes of governance that emerge (see also Rosser's chapter in this volume on everyday actors in post-New Order Indonesia). As Krasner argues, change is possible within a regime when different rules and procedures are introduced within the context of consistent principles and norms that remain unchanged. One possible outcome of such change within a regime is that the new rules and procedures are implemented in such a way as to contribute to a more profound shift in the norms of governance, leading to a more substantial change of regime than was initially expected.

As other scholars and commentators on Myanmar have noted, one of the unexpected effects of government reforms since 2010 has been the extent to which change which initially appeared to be superficial window-dressing has in fact been implemented in substantive ways (Turnell 2012). Prior to the 2010 elections, the odds seemed firmly stacked against any genuine democratic change. The national houses of parliament, for instance, were elected according to a constitution which reserves 25 per cent of seats for the military and which bars anyone with a foreign citizen as their spouse or child from serving as president, a clause specifically designed to exclude Aung San Suu Kyi from this role. Likewise, restrictions on party registration and campaigning for the elections would have required Suu Kyi, who remained under house arrest and as a prisoner was barred from running for office, to give up leadership of the National League for Democracy (NLD) that she founded in 1990 in order to register the party. Instead, the NLD boycotted the election, and the Union Solidarity and Development Party (USDP) dominated the resulting parliament. As well as being led by top generals of the former military regime, the USDP had inherited the apparatus and membership of the Union Solidarity and Development Association that had been established as the civilian proxy of the SPDC regime. This included an extensive patronage network based on effectively compulsory membership for civil servants and anyone seeking government support or contracts, plus an associated militia – the *Swan Arr Shin* – that was mobilized to intimidate political opponents and attack protests. The USDP leader and new president, Thein Sein, was prime minister under the previous

SPDC regime and, like most government ministers, is a former general in the *Tatmadaw* (Armed Forces of Myanmar).

Despite their deep connections to the military and the former regime, Thein Sein's USDP government has embarked on a series of reforms that have relaxed the more draconian aspects of government control utilized by the SPDC while maintaining the dominance of current and former military leaders. The reforms have been greeted as a dramatic departure from the isolationist and repressive political trajectory of the previous regime (Holliday 2013) but are more akin to the lifting of martial law than full-scale democratization. The changes have also been uneven, as government repression has intensified in some areas, especially in Kachin state and for the Rohingya population of Rakhine state. The reforms can usefully be understood as an effort by military elites in Myanmar to safeguard their influence and core interests while accommodating demands for change (Huang 2013). However, even if the reforms overall cement the central political role of the Tatmadaw, this does not diminish the significance of the changes in creating space for other political actors (Pedersen 2011). Political reforms allowing ordinary people to form associations and express their grievances through protest and representations to government are important changes, even as government and military activities, including land confiscation, contribute to those grievances (Ware 2012; Karen Human Rights Group 2013). The new ability of trade unions to legally organize is part of the contradictory process of economic reform, in which workers face new threats from marketization as well as new opportunities to organize collectively.

Evolution of Trade Union Agency in Myanmar

Trade unions have played a significant role in Myanmar's history, despite being outlawed for most of the last five decades under military rule. The country's first trade union federation, the All Burma Trade Union Congress, was formed in 1939 after a series of protest strikes against the British colonial government. In the immediate post-independence period, trade union activity was organized by factions of the ruling Anti-Fascist People's Freedom League. Rival union federations, along with national youth organizations and peasants' organizations, were mobilized as the personal power bases of high-level politicians in the League (Badgely 1958). Although the existence of multiple union federations was primarily explained by competition among political elites, it offered opportunities for everyday actors such as union committees at the workplace level to pursue their interests by switching allegiance between the rival organizations (Boudreau 2004: 46–7). Overt trade union activity went into abeyance during the 1962–88 period of military rule. However, trade union networks continued to organize as part of the underground opposition, with widespread anti-government strikes occurring in 1974 and 1988 without centralized leadership (Lintner 1990: 28). In 1988, as part of a widespread uprising against the military government, workplace and township strike committees formed to coordinate protests including general strikes and to demand the right to organize trade unions free from political interference.[3] Activists from the workers' movements met to re-form the national trade union movement, first in Rangoon in September 1988 and later on the Thai–Burma border in 1991. At this stage, the FTUB was formed to bring together affiliated unions, organize an underground labour movement and oppose the military regime.[4]

During military rule from 1962 to 2011, the international networks developed by union activists provided an 'abeyance structure' (Taylor 1989) for Myanmar's union movement. Unions established prior to military rule had been active in the International Confederation of Free Trade Unions (ICFTU) and other international groupings such as the Socialist International, as well as submitting complaints to the ILO of repression of trade union rights from 1962 onwards. Union activists in exile and in underground networks maintained these contacts and, in the case of the Seafarers Union, were able to continue operating with assistance from the International Transport Federation. Union activists coordinated by the FTUB collected reports and documentation of forced labour from inside Myanmar, often at great personal risk, and, through connections with the ICFTU and its successor, the International Trade Union Confederation, were able to present these reports to the ILO despite the objections of the Myanmar government. ILO sanctions, imposed under unprecedented use of Article 33 powers, persuaded the SPDC regime to agree to the establishment of an ILO liaison office in Yangon in 2002 and, under a supplementary agreement signed in 2007, to wide-ranging powers for ILO officials to travel to restricted areas and collect reports of forced labour (Poole 2013: 21). Although complainants were harassed and even prosecuted and regime forces continued to practice forced labour, activists reported a reduction compared to previous years, particularly on large projects under central government control. Trade unionists attributed this significant victory of ordinary people in Myanmar to pressure exerted through the ILO, with the support of the international union movement.[5]

In the period of direct military rule from 1988 to 2011, trade union activity in Myanmar was organized through clandestine networks. Trade union

---

[3] Interviews with union members and organizers from FTUB, Federation of Trade Unions of Kawthoolei, Karen Education Workers' Union and Joint Action Committee, Mae Sot, Thailand, October 2006.

[4] Interview with Maung Maung, general secretary of the FTUB, now general secretary of the FTUM, Bangkok, Thailand, November 2006.

[5] Interview with Maung Maung, November 2006.

activists were trained by the FTUB on the Thai–Myanmar border and returned to organize underground political activity and collect information. In particular, activists trained by the FTUB were essential in gathering evidence of systematic forced labour that formed the basis of complaints to the ILO. The reputation of the FTUB as a powerful opposition force was aided by clumsy state propaganda accusing the organization of terrorism. Thurein Aung, one of the union activists who was arrested for organizing the 2007 May Day meeting in Yangon, travelled to the border to make contact with the FTUB after reading accusations in state-run media that the organization was training trade unionists to attack the regime. International radio stations such as the BBC Burmese Service and Radio Free Asia were also important sources of information, carrying news reports about the ILO censure of Myanmar and programmes about trade union rights.[6]

Myanmar's Industrial Relations Regime

The new industrial relations regime in Myanmar is primarily codified in two recent pieces of legislation: the Labour Organization Law passed in October 2011 (Pyidaungsu Hluttaw 2011) and the Settlement of Labour Dispute Law of March 2012 (Pyidaungsu Hluttaw 2012). The former establishes the right of workers to form trade unions, while the latter governs negotiation of conditions of employment and provides for the formation of arbitration and conciliation councils at township levels. A further law governing minimum wages has been passed but not yet implemented. The law sets a process for minimum wages to be decided by a committee appointed by the president (Bu and Naing 2013).

The reforms have allowed for the creation of new collective actors and institutions at local levels, although the extent and pace of change has been highly uneven and dependent on local circumstances. Trade unions formed at the workplace level are the basic units of the industrial relations system, with a minimum of thirty members or 10 per cent of workers employed by the enterprise, whichever is greater. Over 600 trade unions representing approximately 150,000 workers were registered by July 2013.[7] A significant feature of the regulations is that small farmers are also eligible to form unions, with no requirement for an employer to be identified. This extends the potential scope of the industrial relations system to allow for farmers' organizations ranging from township associations up to national federations. Around half of the unions registered by 2013 were of self-employed small farmers.

---

[6] Interview with Thurein Aung, January 2014.
[7] Telephone interview with Ross Wilson, chief technical advisor to the ILO Freedom of Association Project in Yangon, Myanmar, June 2012–June 2013, July 2013.

Forming Unions

In the current context in Myanmar, trade unions can best be understood as community-based collective actors, organizing within the informal networks of everyday politics alongside other community-based organizations (CBOs). CBOs are particularly involved in everyday political economy, since they are based in particular non-elite communities and are actively involved in the informal political life and economic activity of those communities. At the same time as they are involved in the everyday politics of their communities as activists and organizers, members of CBOs are able to mobilize their collective agency to engage with elite politics. This dual function is discussed by Appadurai (2001) in his study of an alliance of CBOs formed by communities of the urban poor in Mumbai. He describes the operation of the alliance as an example of 'deep democracy' because of the commitment of activists to 'build on what the poor themselves know and understand' (Appadurai 2001: 29). By situating themselves within the everyday politics of their base communities while focusing on building collective strength and by maintaining a strategic approach to engaging with elites without being co-opted by any particular apparatus of elite politics, CBOs are able to constitute a non-elite democratic force. However, translating between everyday and elite forms of politics is fraught with difficulties for CBOs. As Appadurai (2001: 28–9) makes clear, the process of building democratic engagement at the level of everyday politics requires a 'politics of patience' to negotiate the contradictions of non-elite social relations as well as the impacts of elite forms of coercion and co-optation.

For ordinary people in Myanmar, the trade unions able to be formed under the new laws are their first opportunity to legally join an independent CBO that can organize collective action and advocacy. In urban industries, workers face low wages, long hours and poor health and safety conditions. At a Yangon meeting of union members and basic union leaders organized by the FTUM in January 2014, workers from a range of industrial factories reported a similar range of problems.[8] Workers faced dangerous conditions with a lack of personal protective equipment. For example, workers from a local bottling plant contracted by international soft-drink brands, including Coca-Cola, reported working without protective equipment, receiving chemical burns and breathing fumes from ammonia gas used in cooling and caustic soda used to clean bottles. Workers also reported difficulties with management and supervisors. One union delegate from a Yangon shoe factory reported that supervisors worked on every line of the factory, acting 'like the personal workers of the boss, telling us when our work is wrong to do it again and always telling us to go faster'. This

---

[8] Conference titled *Industrial Relations, Productivity and Labour Management Cooperation*, Kanaung Hall, Hlaingtharyar, 17 January 2014. Quotes from author's notes of contemporaneous translation.

kind of pressure was often worse for union members, with widespread reports of harassment and discrimination. A garment factory union delegate warned others to be prepared that 'when a union is formed at a factory there is often immediate retaliation'. The broader message of her warning was that workers should not attempt to form small unions in isolation but should join together for strength. As well as working her full-time factory job, she regularly travelled to other factories to talk to workers about forming unions:

where the unions have been formed the conditions are gradually improving, but there are so many factories that don't have a union and when we approach them to try to organize they have never heard of unions.

In rural areas, farmers face insecure land tenure, as well as difficulty accessing credit, modern equipment and technical assistance, and access to markets for their products. In Khayan township outside of Yangon, farmers reported confiscation of land without compensation for roads that were yet to be built.[9] One farmer complained, 'if they take away our land to make a road, they should at least make a good road.' In addition to transport difficulties, the farmers wanted to improve farming methods and yields but lacked access to modern farming equipment: 'The big crony companies are using large equipment, but we don't have this.' By forming unions, these farmers hoped to be able to prevent further land confiscation, gain access to international assistance for improved farming methods and form a welfare fund for families in hardship. Union activists organize around these issues as well as promote the role of trade unions as legal associations that can advocate on behalf of their members and promote democracy. In the absence of telephone or postal systems in rural Myanmar, all communication with union members had to be done in person, which made well-developed networks of delegates especially important. To call a union meeting, organizers would send invitations by post to the nearest union office, which would then be relayed by messengers on motorbikes to outlying villages. Through these networks, union organizers based in Yangon were in regular contact with the rural unions, but the majority of organizing work in signing up new members and establishing branches was being done by the members themselves by sending delegates to other villages. When the elected leaders of the village-level unions were able to gather with U Than Swe, an educated lawyer who leads the AFFM of the FTUM, the meeting was part motivational speech, part training session and part update on the union's progress in organizing development assistance and a farmers' insurance scheme. In January 2014, the AFFM had township unions of this kind in 35 townships, comprising 210 legally registered village-level unions, with 190 more having submitted requests for registration.

---

[9] Meeting of the Agriculture and Farmers Federation of Myanmar (AFFM), Khayan Township, 4 January 2014. Quotes from author's notes of contemporaneous translation.

Organizers from unions such as the FTUM maintain contact with a national network of village- and township-level union activists, coordinating access to training provided by the union and the ILO, distributing educational material on workers' rights and organizing for village-level union delegates to travel to Yangon for meetings and training. A group of union delegates visiting Yangon from the Naga area of North Myanmar had organized unions to have a 'voice for the Naga people' and to resist confiscation of land by mining and forestry companies with political connections. The idea to organize unions had come from refugees who returned to the Naga area having formed connections with trade union activists in the Karen community on the Thai–Myanmar border that shared membership in the Baptist Church.[10]

A similar combination of existing social networks and concerns over land and development motivated the formation of township-level unions of farmers in Central Myanmar. FTUM organizers attended meetings to vote on the formation of township unions in Pakokku and Kyauk in January 2014. The concerns in these regions were similar to those of other rural areas, except that there was less immediate concern about land confiscation and more focus on access to development assistance, markets for produce and addressing the consequences of government neglect, such as the lack of schools and hospitals. One village in Pakokku township had built the foundations and frame for a school building, having been promised building materials and a teacher's salary by the Ministry of Education, but neither had eventuated. Villagers speaking at the union meeting expressed hope that forming a legal union would help them to advocate on these issues of local development. They also discussed plans with the visiting union organizers to arrange a barter system to exchange produce such as beans and vegetables for rice from the paddy farmers in the south of the country. At the meetings in both Pakokku and Kyauk, there was considerable enthusiasm from the village-level union delegates for the process of electing the officials for the township union. The process was taken very seriously by everyone present and involved speeches by the candidates followed by a secret ballot and a public tallying of the votes watched vigilantly by the whole crowd. For many of those present, especially younger people, the meeting would have been their first experience of a democratic election process.

To organize in an environment of uncertainty about the extent of legal rights and the possibility of retaliation by employers, union activists make use of skills and tactics developed during periods working in underground movements in Myanmar and among migrant workers in neighbouring countries. Organizers work through informal networks to make contact with workers through other community organizations or in public settings nearby workplaces. A union organizer in Yangon described how FTUM organizers make initial contact with

---

[10] Interview with Naga Labour Union organizers, January 2014.

workers at large factories by waiting at local teashops to start conversations with workers after work. Once contact is made with interested workers, further meetings are arranged where those attending are engaged in discussion about the role and function of unions and asked to bring more of their co-workers to the next meeting, until numbers grow enough to form a legal union. Union organizers also visited churches and monasteries to make contact with workers at nearby factories.[11]

To organize workers in more dispersed occupations such as domestic work, contact with community organizations is especially important. For instance, union organizers in Yangon identified ethnic Karen women as a particularly vulnerable group of domestic workers who are often locked in the houses where they work, only allowed one day off in two months and are subject to physical abuse with impunity. To begin the process of organizing a union, organizers made contact with a Karen Christian organization that provides vocational training to these workers and had the right, negotiated with employers, to call the workers for a meeting once in three months. By first persuading the religious organization of the potential benefits to the Karen workers of organizing a union, activists were able to attend a meeting of the workers to discuss unionizing. In this way, union organizers were able to make use of the existing relationships of trust the religious organization has with the workers without arousing suspicion from employers who exercise a large degree of control over the movements of the women they employ as servants.[12]

Strike Action

In the initial period of the new labour laws in early 2012, there was a wave of strikes by industrial workers in urban areas of Myanmar. These strikes were partly motivated by specific demands to address low pay, long hours and poor working conditions, but they were also expressive of a more generalized frustration and resentment. These early strike actions can be considered as acts of political protest signalling an ongoing crisis in industrial relations. The grievances underlying the crisis are long-standing, built up over decades of underdevelopment, corruption and economic mismanagement, combined with authoritarian suppression of dissent. The strike wave in 2012 was a result of new freedoms to express old grievances rather than any fundamental change in the conditions of work. Workers responded to changes in legislation as a signal that authorities would refrain from acting harshly against strike action, even if such actions were technically outside the law.

---

[11] Interview with FTUM organizer, July 2013.
[12] Interview with FTUM organizer, July 2013.

Most of the strikes in early 2012 were unsuccessful in achieving their demands as workers lacked strong organizations to maintain solidarity and present a united front in negotiations with employers. In some cases, only a minority of workers went on strike and were easily isolated while factories continued production. In other cases, employers were able to intimidate or bribe leaders and divide striking workers by spreading rumours. In this early period, strike actions were treated as political crises and provoked a high-level response, with factories on strike surrounded by riot police and government ministers involving themselves in negotiations. If workers could maintain unity, they were, therefore, able to capitalize on this sense of crisis, with heavy pressure put on employers to settle disputes. The degree of government involvement in these disputes and the fact that they were at times settled in the workers' favour is especially interesting given that this early wave of strikes occurred without legal notice by a registered union and were therefore outside the law. A further wave of strike action in April 2013 was more successful, as industrial workers demanded pay increases commensurate with those granted to civil servants. When most employers still refused to negotiate after three days of strike action, union representatives took cases to the township negotiation committees (a level of mediated negotiation below the formal arbitration and conciliation councils) where they were successful in gaining pay increases at many of the factories. In June of 2013, FTUM organizers in Yangon responded to twelve industrial disputes and were able to assist with negotiating wage increases of at least US$ 50 per month for workers earning an average of US$ 120 per month. At one large factory in Yangon, more than 1,000 workers demonstrated outside the factory and some went on hunger strike. In another factory, workers were concerned that exposure to industrial chemicals was contributing to high rates of lung disease and miscarriages among the workers and have, rather than seeking a wage increase, sought assistance from the FTUM with negotiating better health and safety protection.[13]

Relationships with Government

A lack of trust on all sides characterizes the present state of industrial relations in Myanmar. As a union organizer for the FTUM put it, 'In some townships, some officials are our friends, but as a department we don't trust them and they don't trust us.'[14] The implementation of processes for union registration is uneven across the country. Township registrars are generally appointed from among Ministry of Labour staff, but not all townships have effectively established processes for registering unions, and the reasons that may be given

[13] Interview with FTUM organizer, July 2013.
[14] Interview with FTUM organizer, July 2013.

for refusing or delaying registration vary from region to region. With farmers' unions generally not having employers to deal with, the accessibility and willingness of township registrars to assist with union registration was the main factor affecting the uneven process of unionization. Organizers affiliated with the FTUM reported difficulties registering unions of farmers in some areas where officials perceived the union-organizing process to be overly political, for instance, where union organizers were also members of political parties such as the NLD: 'they said that our unions are fake and that some politicians are involved with the union issues'.[15] While the involvement of political party members in unions is, of course, permitted under the law, where officials are suspicious of the motivations of union organizers, they may tend to delay or refuse to process applications.

Difficulties with implementation of the new law are not always a result of government reluctance to recognize unions. Workers are also unfamiliar with the requirements for registration or struggle to complete documentation. The ILO liaison office had spoken to local registrars who had received forms that were incomplete or in a dirty and tattered state and were unsure whether to process them. Low levels of literacy also make filling in forms a challenge for some groups of workers and, with township registrars lacking resources and often unwilling to actively assist workers to form unions, the task of coordinating and documenting registration falls to union activists who coordinate between workers and government representatives. Another frequent problem was the requirement to register an office for the union. One union of mine workers who lacked a permanent residence registered their office as the local teashop, which the township registrar was unsure whether to accept, but was advised to do so by the ILO.[16]

Outside of major cities, the contradictory effects of the reforms in creating new opportunities and new threats for workers have been concentrated in areas where state-led development projects are being implemented. New threats to the land and livelihood of small farmers have come with the acceleration of large-scale infrastructure, power generation, resource extraction and industrial zone projects. In some areas, especially East Myanmar, large-scale development projects are now possible as a result of ceasefires between the government and insurgent groups (Karen Human Rights Group 2013). In other areas, such as the Kyaukse Industrial Zone near Mandalay or the Dawei deep-water port development area, expansion and acceleration of existing projects is anticipated with increased access to foreign investment and markets. At the same time as villagers in areas affected by the projects are threatened with displacement and loss of their land, they have been able to make use of new rights to organize

---

[15] Interview with FTUM organizer, July 2013.
[16] Interview with Ross Wilson, July 2013.

and protest to appeal to local and national authorities to consider their needs and to make contact with political allies. In some cases, where local protest has been able to connect with a wider national constituency, the government has responded. The Myitsone mega-dam project in Kachin state, a joint venture between the government and a Chinese construction firm, was suspended in response to public pressure after the effect of the project on Myanmar's iconic Irrawaddy river raised nationwide concern, but thousands of villagers remain displaced (Mungchying Rawt Jat 2013). In another high-profile case, the Letpadaung copper mine project came to national attention after protests against land confiscation by villagers, led by Buddhist monks, were violently attacked by police. In response, the government appointed a commission led by Aung San Suu Kyi, which has not halted the project but has promised to consult with villagers and monitor the social and environmental effects of the mine.

Such conflicts are played out on a minor scale throughout the country, as villagers' claims under the new and unevenly implemented system of land rights for small farmers are pitted against state and commercial development projects based on land confiscation. In this context, trade unions formed among farmers in rural areas are focused on establishing and defending land rights, both by assisting farmers to fulfil the requirements for documentation of legal title and by organizing collective action to oppose encroachment. Unions are also in the process of organizing workers employed on large development projects and in the industrial zones. Workers in urban industrial estates such as Yangon's Hlaingthaya industrial zone were among the first to take strike action in 2012 and now form a core membership of new industrial unions. More isolated industrial zones such as Kyaukse are more tightly controlled by authorities hostile to union organizing, but unions have begun to make contact with workers and to collect information on working conditions in the garment and cement factories in the zone. A union organizer involved in these efforts referred to the Kyaukse zone as a site of conflict with the government's development agenda. This organizer was sympathetic to the policies of the ILO to promote tripartite cooperation for development. He argued for pay rises, for instance, in terms of the wider benefits for economic growth: 'if the workers are paid more, they will buy from other factories, and this will be the real development.' The organizer cited the 'Nissan model' to argue that cooperation between unions and employers could have mutually beneficial effects on productivity as well as working conditions. But when asked about the current potential for mutually beneficial cooperation with government agencies, the organizer responded: 'we have to go step by step and then maybe we can communicate or work together but not now.' He saw the government's reform efforts as 'half-hearted' and as characterized by a continuing competition between reformers, hardliners and 'the majority who sit on the fence'. While hoping for gradual changes over the next three or four years, depending on the outcome of elections in 2015, that would make cooperation with government more possible, unions will continue the cautious approach of taking advantage of new rights to organize while remaining wary of placing too much trust in government process or dialogue with employers.[17]

Union Training – ILO Involvement

The first step in the ILO Freedom of Association project was to design training programmes to educate workers and employers about the new industrial relations regime established by legal reforms. The ILO had run similar programmes in other countries, such as the activities of the ILO-ACTRAV workers' branch in post-Suharto Indonesia, but there were no materials or models immediately available to implement in Myanmar. As Ross Wilson, chief technical advisor to the ILO project, put it: 'I had an office and a desk and I had to get started.' The first event of the ILO project in June 2012 was run as an open forum in Yangon with more than 300 people attending: 'It was the first time that they'd had an opportunity, certainly in any kind of public forum like this, to talk about the issues and the rights that we were referring to of freedom of association, freedom of assembly, and freedom of speech.'[18]

Those attending, mostly factory workers from Yangon, took the opportunity to express their anger and frustration at the working conditions and hours that were imposed on them and the lack of opportunity to affect change. In addition to this frustration, workers expressed cynicism about 'whether the new regime was going to make any difference' and whether the government could be trusted to implement the law as it was written. In the context of this political uncertainty and lack of established channels for political debate and dialogue, the newly established right to form unions takes on a broader political significance. While other legal reforms have allowed political demonstrations and meetings that would previously have been illegal and dangerous under military rule, these still require permits and are heavily restricted. The legal ability of unions to organize meetings of members and to hold demonstrations during industrial disputes are, therefore, of wider significance in creating the kinds of democratic political spaces that are still unusual and unfamiliar in Myanmar.[19]

---

[17] Interview with FTUM organizer, July 2013.
[18] Interview with Ross Wilson, July 2013.
[19] A legal ambiguity exists in interpreting the right to freedom of association and the right to strike in combination with the more restrictive conditions of the Decree on the Right to Peaceful Assembly and Peaceful Procession 2012 (for text and commentary, see Article 19, 2012). ILO officials had raised this issue with government and received assurances that industrial relations law would take precedence in handling industrial disputes. There have been cases, however, of workers involved in industrial action being arrested and charged with participation in an unauthorized protest (interview with Ross Wilson, July 2013).

With many workers initially cynical about the legal changes and employers suspicious or hostile, the training programme initiated by the ILO Freedom of Association Project aimed to build the basic skills and knowledge necessary to facilitate dialogue and collective bargaining between the newly elected union leaders and their employers. Workers were eager to participate in the training, with many travelling large distances to attend the training sessions in Yangon, arriving up to two hours early to wait for morning sessions to begin. Despite the sessions being held only in Yangon, by June 2013 almost all of the 600 registered unions had sent at least two elected leaders to attend the ILO training. In the initial open forums, workers had reported feeling uncomfortable talking openly with employers present. Accordingly, the format of the subsequent workshops was designed specifically to redress the balance, with two union leaders from each enterprise invited along with one employer representative, and the programme split across two days with workers attending the first day on their own and joined by employers on the second day. In the initial sessions, workers were able to overcome their caution and gain confidence with discussion of leadership and organizing skills and strategic planning. The latter was seen as particularly important by ILO staff, who had 'identified the need for them to think very carefully about their strategies, particularly rushing into strike action'.[20] This discouragement of spontaneous strike action reflects both a concern for the interests of workers who could face retaliatory action from employers if they took industrial action from a position of weakness, and a more general preference on the part of ILO for a more managed process of collective bargaining as part of tripartite cooperation.[21]

The inclusion of employers in the training sessions was seen as important to meet the ILO's goals of promoting economic partnership. Training sessions modelled negotiation processes for collective bargaining around working conditions and occupational health and safety and ended with discussion of tasks to complete in the workplace. Among employers who attended the sessions, ILO staff observed a shift from suspicion to acceptance of negotiating relationships with unions, with workplace follow-up visits confirming that changes were being implemented. However, the ILO is cautious about interpreting these results as generally representative of the broader state of industrial relations, emphasizing that the employers attending the ILO sessions are those who are willing to at least tolerate unions and consider cooperative approaches, whereas some other employers are more hostile.[22]

Whereas the ILO is focused on the basic rights codified in conventions and other instruments and agreed to through the tripartite international structure of

---

[20] Interview with Ross Wilson, July 2013
[21] Interview with Ross Wilson, July 2013. Interview with Steve Marshall, January 2014.
[22] Interview with Ross Wilson, July 2013

the organization, trade unions at the local level are free to take a more partisan approach in their organizing and training activities. FTUM organizers have initiated training programmes for elected delegates and union activists with support from international partners, including the AFL-CIO's American Center for International Labor Solidarity, with funding from the National Endowment for Democracy and smaller agencies such as New Zealand's UnionAid programme (National Endowment for Democracy 2013; UnionAid 2013). Training programmes run by the FTUM draw heavily on the material produced by the ILO, but frame the discussion with a more explicit class analysis. The need to develop strong independent unions is described as part of a global struggle in which workers who have come before have 'given their blood, and now we have to fight for our rights'.[23] This analysis of workers' rights as won through collective struggle also provides a context for the presentation of the role and function of the ILO in FTUM training sessions. The ILO has a high profile in Myanmar and is seen as an important protector of workers' rights. A union organizer with the FTUM described how when ILO project officers visited union events, 'everywhere they go, people are ready to clap'. Union trainers seek to build on workers' existing knowledge of the ILO as an organization concerned with protecting workers' rights by emphasizing the significant role of trade unions within the tripartite structure of the organization: 'The ILO is not only for the governments. Also there is a huge influence of the workers. This is workers' power for the world. We would like to be part of the world to improve things.'[24]

This is an important reframing, as it allows workers to perceive themselves as agents of change and as participants in global politics, rather than as passive recipients of rights bestowed from above by powerful international organizations. It is a transformational perspective on rights that successfully appropriates the institutionalist perspective of ILO training materials while reframing legal rights as the product of a transnational movement driven by the everyday agency of workers. Where the ILO 'goes straight for the middle' in seeking to establish tripartite compromise between workers, employers and government, union trainers emphasize the need to build workers' power through unions to counterbalance the existing power of employers and government. By framing the conversation in this way, trainers are able to make use of the frustration and resentment that ordinary workers feel towards employers and government, to discuss issues of social justice and government corruption in terms of how to build unions as a counterbalancing power. Training sessions can then turn this sense of political purpose and motivation towards practical issues of union building, such as establishing

---

[23] Interview with FTUM organizer, July 2013.
[24] Interview with FTUM organizer, July 2013.

systems for collecting dues, recruiting new members and developing democratic decision-making processes.[25]

Conclusion

Myanmar's industrial relations regime is in the midst of a transformation made possible by legal changes but driven by the everyday agency of workers through the process of union organizing. The involvement of union activists who have been able to openly return to the country for the first time since 1988 has allowed Myanmar's nascent union movement to draw on support from a network of international trade union contacts. These activists have used the skills they gained as participants in underground union networks and in organizing migrant workers on the Thai–Myanmar border to contribute to training and organizing a new generation of union delegates and organizers. The importance of training programmes in organizing new trade unions in Myanmar is similar to the experience of other CBOs in Myanmar and among migrant populations on the Thai–Myanmar border (Henry 2011, 2013). To some extent this reflects Chatterjee's (2001) argument that the organization of civil society organizations such as trade unions in post-colonial societies is a 'pedagogical project'. While Chatterjee focuses on the elite politics of mobilization in nationalist movements, CBOs like trade unions can also be seen as processes of translation between everyday and elite politics. Training of union delegates and organizers can then be seen as an important component of building the power of workers and basic labour organizations as everyday actors to counterbalance the existing politico-economic power of employers and the state. Ordinary workers and union activists remain sceptical of any immediate possibility of tripartite cooperation in the style promoted by the ILO. However, the active involvement of the ILO in Myanmar through training programmes, advocacy of legal reform and monitoring of workers' rights has provided opportunities to workers and unions as everyday actors to build collective power in their workplaces and communities. On the basis of these organizing efforts, workers will be in a stronger position to defend their interests in future conflicts with employers and government and to influence the terms of any tripartite cooperation as Myanmar's industrial relations regime continues to evolve.

References

Acharya, A. (2004) 'How ideas spread: whose norms matter? Norm localization and institutional change in Asian regionalism', *International Organization* 58(2): 239–275.

---

[25] Interview with FTUM organizer, July 2013.

Appadurai, A. (2001) 'Deep democracy: urban governmentality and the horizon of politics', *Environment and Urbanization* 13(2): 23–43.

Article 19 (2012) *Myanmar: The Decree on the Right to Peaceful Assembly and Peaceful Procession.* London: Article 19 Law Programme. http://www.article19.org/data/files/medialibrary/3440/12-09-19-LA-Myanmar.pdf.

Badgley, J. (1958) 'Burma's political crisis', *Pacific Affairs* 31(4): 336–351.

Boudreau, V. (2004) *Resisting Dictatorship: Repression and Protest in Southeast Asia.* Cambridge: Cambridge University Press.

Broome, A. and Seabrooke, L. (2012) 'Seeing like an international organisation', *New Political Economy* 17(1): 1–16.

Bu, M. and Naing, K. (2013) *Highlights of Myanmar's New Law on Minimum Wages.* Yangon: VDB Loi. www.vdb-loi.com/vdb/wp-content/uploads/2013/04/Myanmar's-New-Law-on-Minimum-Wages_(VDB%20Loi%20Analysis)_30Apr13.pdf

Chatterjee, P. (2001) 'On civil and political society in postcolonial democracies', in S. Kaviraj and S. Khilnani (eds.) *Civil Society: History and Possibilities.* Cambridge: Cambridge University Press, pp. 165–178.

Cox, R. (1977) 'Labor and hegemony', *International Organization* 31(3): 385–424.

Gramsci, A. (1971) *Selections from the Prison Notebooks.* New York: International Publishers.

Gurowitz, A. (1999) 'Mobilizing international norms: domestic actors, immigrants, and the Japanese State'. *World Politics* 51(3): 413–445.

Henry, N. (2011) *People Power: The Everyday Politics of Democratic Resistance in Burma and the Philippines.* PhD Thesis, Victoria University of Wellington, New Zealand. http://researcharchive.vuw.ac.nz/handle/10063/1750.

(2013) 'A place on the platform: the participation of women in Karen community organizations', in J. Smith (ed.) *Journeys from Exclusion to Inclusion: Marginalized Women's Successes in Overcoming Political Exclusion.* Stockholm: International Institute for Democracy and Electoral Assistance, pp. 235–266.

Herod, A. (2007) 'The agency of labour in global change: reimagining the spaces and scales of trade union praxis within a global economy', in J. M. Hobson and L. Seabrooke (eds.) *Everyday Politics of the World Economy.* Cambridge: Cambridge University Press, pp. 27–44.

Holliday, I. (2013) 'Myanmar in 2012: toward a normal state'. *Asian Survey* 53(1): 93–100.

Huang, R. L. (2013) 'Re-thinking Myanmar's political regime: military rule in Myanmar and implications for current reforms', *Contemporary Politics* 19(3): 247–261.

Hughes, S. (2002) 'Coming in from the Cold: Labour, the ILO, and the international labour standards regime', in R. Wilkinson and S. Hughes (eds.) *Global Governance: Critical Perspectives.* London: Routledge, pp. 155–171.

International Labour Organisation (2012) *World of Work Report 2012: Better Jobs for a Better Economy.* Geneva: Department of Communication and Public Information of the ILO. www.ilo.org/global/publications/books/WCMS_179453/lang--en/index.htm.

(2013) *World of Work Report 2013: Repairing the Economic and Social Fabric.* Geneva: Department of Communication and Public Information of the ILO. www.ilo.org/global/research/global-reports/world-of-work/2013/WCMS_214476/lang--en/index.htm.

Krasner, S. D. (1982) 'Structural causes and regime consequences: regimes as intervening variables', *International Organization* 36(2): 185–205.

Karen Human Rights Group (2013) *Losing Ground: Land conflicts and collective action in Eastern Myanmar*. http://khrg.org/2013/03/losing-ground-land-conflicts-and-collective-action-eastern-myanmar.

Lintner, B. (1990) *Outrage: Burma's Struggle for Democracy*. London: White Lotus.

Mungchying Rawt Jat [Kachin Rights Organisation] (2013) *Model Villages Are Not a Model*. www.burmacampaign.org.uk/images/uploads/model_villagers_are_not_a_model.pdf.

National Endowment for Democracy (2013) *Burma*. www.ned.org/where-we-work/asia/burma.

Pedersen, M. (2011) 'The politics of Burma's "democratic" transition: prospects for change and options for democrats', *Critical Asian Studies* 43(1): 49–68.

Poole, M. (2013) 'Myanmar Turns a Corner', *World of Work: Magazine of the ILO*. Geneva: Department of Communication and Public Information of the International Labour Organization, pp. 19–31. www.ilo.org/global/publications/magazines-and-journals/world-of-work-magazine/issues/WCMS_216068/lang--en/index.htm.

Pyidaungsu Hluttaw (2011) 'The Labour Organization Law', *Pyidaungsu Hluttaw Law*, 11 October: 7. www.mol.gov.mm/en/wp-content/uploads/downloads/2012/05/Labour-Org-Law-ENG.pdf.

  (2012) 'The Settlement of Labour Dispute Law', *Pyidaungsu Hluttaw Law*, 28 March: 5. www.mol.gov.mm/en/wp-content/uploads/downloads/2012/06/Settlement-dispute-lawEng.pdf.

Sending, O. J. and Neumann, I. B. (2006) 'Governance to governmentality: analyzing NGOs, states, and power', *International Studies Quarterly* 50(3): 651–672.

Taylor, V. (1989) 'Social movement continuity: the women's movement in abeyance', *American Sociological Review* 54(5): 761–775.

Turnell, S. (2012) 'Myanmar in 2011: confounding expectations', *Asian Survey* 52(1): 157–164.

UnionAid (2013) *Railway Workers' Project on Track*. www.unionaid.org.nz/2013/05/railway-workers-project-on-track/.

Ware, A. (2012) *Context-Sensitive Development: How International NGOs Operate in Myanmar*. West Hartford, CT: Kumarian Press.

Part III

Widening and Deepening Markets

5   The Political Economy of Muslim
      Markets in Singapore

Johan Fischer

Introduction

On 26 March 2010, I was in the audience for the *Fourth International Halal Food Conference* held at the Sheraton Hotel in Brussels, Belgium. From around the world, Islamic organizations, halal certifiers and companies had come to attend this conference held by the Islamic Food Council of Europe, one of the world's major halal certification bodies. A Malaysian woman in the Q&A session wants to know why and how it could happen that halal pork turned up in the Supermarket NTUC FairPrice Co-operative in Singapore when everybody knows that pork cannot possibly be halal. Fierce competition exists between Malaysia and Singapore, not least in the struggle for world leadership in global halal production, trade and regulation. The representative from the Majlis Ugama Islam Singapura (MUIS) – the Islamic Religious Council of Singapore – that acts as Singapore's state halal certification body agrees that pork can never be halal and that it would compromise Shariah principles (Islamic law) if it were labelled as such. She explains that the incident arose because of a rumour in an email that halal pork was on sale in Singapore.

MUIS inspectors did not find any halal pork when investigating, and the MUIS representative calls this a 'sabotage' incident. The subsequent police investigation could not place the responsibility. This incident was big in the media, and the picture of 'halal pork' allegedly sold by the supermarket showed a packet of FairPrice's Pasar brand pork bearing a green 'halal' sticker. A FairPrice spokesman said that the incident was regarded as 'a deliberate and wilful act of mischief' (*Straits Times*, 25 November 2007). MUIS carried out its own checks at eight FairPrice outlets and found that none of the specified items bore the MUIS logo. A MUIS spokesman said, 'We treat the case of the MUIS halal certification mark on the packaging containing pork very seriously as the halal mark has been abused.' He added that under the Administration of Muslim Law Act (AMLA) that governs Islam and halal in Singapore, an

This chapter forms part of a larger research project with the title *Islam, Standards and Technoscience: In Global Halal Zones* (Fischer 2016).

abuser of the MUIS halal certification mark is liable to a fine not exceeding S\$ 10,000 or to a jail term not exceeding twelve months, or both. This means the perpetrator is culpable even if the mark is a sticker, a fake or was digitally added (*Straits Times*, 25 November 2007).

In Arabic, halal literally means 'permissible' or 'lawful' and traditionally it signifies 'pure food' with regard to meat achieved through proper Islamic practice such as ritual slaughter and pork avoidance. In the modern and globalized industry for not only food but also biotechnology as well as care products, a number of Muslim requirements have been met, such as an injunction to avoid any substances that may be contaminated with porcine residues or alcohol, gelatine, glycerine, emulsifiers, enzymes, flavours and flavourings. These requirements are setting new standards for production, preparation, handling, storage and certification. In the modern world, halal is part of a huge and expanding globalized market that by some accounts is estimated to be worth more than US\$ 2.3 trillion, with the value of the halal food sector thought to have reached US\$ 700 billion annually (World Halal Forum 2013).

The Koran and the Sunna (the life, actions and teachings of the Prophet Muhammad) exhort Muslims to eat the good and lawful food God has provided for them. However, a number of conditions and prohibitions have to be observed. Muslims are expressly prohibited from consuming carrion, spurting blood, pork and foods that have been consecrated to any being other than God himself. These substances are *haram* ('unlawful' or 'forbidden'). The lawfulness of meat depends on how it is obtained. Ritual slaughtering (*dhabh*) entails that the animal is killed in God's name by making a fatal incision across the throat. In this process, the blood should be drained out as fully as possible. Because the sea is seen to be pure in essence, all marine animals, even if they have died spontaneously, are halal. Land creatures such as predators, dogs and, in the eyes of some jurists, donkeys are haram, despite the fact that unlike pork they are not mentioned in the Koran. What is more, crocodiles, weasels, pelicans, otters, foxes, elephants, ravens and insects have been condemned by the *ulama* (literally those who know the law or religious scholars). Another significant Islamic prohibition relates to wine and any other alcoholic drink or substance, all of which are haram, whatever the quantity or substance (Denny 2006: 279). Indeed, alcohol has become a highly controversial question in divergent halal zones. To determine whether a foodstuff is halal or haram 'depends on its nature, how it is processed, and how it is obtained' (Riaz and Chaudry 2004: 14). In the end, however, the underlying principle behind the prohibitions remains 'divine order' (Riaz and Chaudry 2004: 12).

In a Southeast Asian context, taboos distinguish between groups and individuals in everyday life. Moreover, taboos operate in terms of the production, preparation and distribution of food (Manderson 1986: 10). In modern Singapore, many Malays are fastidious about halal, but they practice this fastidiousness pragmatically in the context of the ethnic Chinese majority (Nasir *et al.* 2009). During fieldwork in Singapore, I found a large number of food as well as non-food products certified by the state in convenience stores, grocery stores, supermarkets and hypermarkets. What is more, in Singapore virtually all of the multinational fast food chains such as McDonald's and Burger King are fully halal-certified by MUIS, and this is also the case with many smaller restaurants, even those owned and run by ethnic Chinese. In Singapore and the modern world at large, halal commodities and services are no longer expressions of esoteric forms of production, trade and consumption but part of a huge and expanding globalized market.

In the global market for halal products, Singapore holds a special position in that it is state bodies that certify halal products and spaces (shops, factories and restaurants) as well as work processes. In shops around the world, consumers can find state halal-certified products from Singapore that carry distinctive halal logos. Globally, companies are affected by the proliferation of halal that to a large extent is evoked by Southeast Asian nations such as Singapore, Malaysia, Indonesia and Thailand. I situate my analysis of halal in a framework of new governing practices by different Southeast Asian countries such as Singapore (Ong 2006). Sovereign rule invokes the exception to create new economic possibilities, spaces and techniques – for instance, an increased legal focus on halal in Singapore (Ong 2006: 7). Current studies on the entanglements of capitalism, Islam and the state in Southeast Asia explore, for example, how moderate Islamic 'spiritual reform' movements in Indonesia combine business management principles and techniques from popular life-coaching seminars with Muslim practice. This form of 'market Islam' and 'spiritual economies' merge entrepreneurship as a way to produce new Muslim subjects, Islamic practice, capitalist ethics and effective self-management (Rudnyckyj 2008, 2009, 2010).

The everyday political economy of halal commodities and services such as certification by MUIS raises some broader questions about how the state and Islamic authorities in Singapore attempt to create and regulate new markets around halal products in a local context. I explore the rise of a halal commodity regime and how and why processes are changing and their implications for everyday life in Singapore (Nevins and Peluso 2008: 1). More specifically, in analyzing how this emerging commodity regime relates to the production of people and places in Singapore, this chapter traces how cultural, economic and political processes shape, consolidate and expand the market for halal products. An important question in this chapter is how supermarkets/hypermarkets such as FairPrice live up to increasing halal requirements in terms of keeping halal/haram products separate, but also the way in which more and more supermarkets are designed according to halal requirements. Another issue is how the state, Islamic bureaucrats and halal inspectors subject the everyday workings of supermarkets to expanding 'Islamic' requirements and forms of regulation and how FairPrice responds to, and is affected by, these processes. Singapore is small in size and there are not many manufacturing industries in the country. Moreover, the number of Muslims in Singapore is limited, and most of these are relatively relaxed about everyday halal consumption. Consequently, the Singaporean market for halal products and services is not so much driven by local demand; the main impetus for the widening and deepening of halal markets in Singapore is the country's vision to become the world leader in global halal markets. This is not unlike similar ambitions in Malaysia with regard to promoting the country as an international centre for Islamic finance, as will be discussed by Lena Rethel in the next chapter. Thus, the marketing and regulation of halal in Singapore is to a large extent framed and formatted by a number of transformations in the global market for halal that took place from the 1990s onwards.

The connection between Singapore and Muslim Southeast Asia more generally and the global proliferation of halal is no accident. As this chapter will show, halal has a particular and unique historical, political and cultural trajectory in Singapore. This chapter is based on participant observation and interviews carried out among halal producers, traders, Islamic organizations, companies, Islamic authorities, restaurant owners and supermarkets in particular. It is complemented by extensive archival research on halal in Singapore, mainly drawing on the *Straits Times* (established in 1845). This is a censored newspaper that expresses state ideologies in Singapore.

Everyday Political Economy, Standards and Audit Culture

Over the past three decades, the state in Singapore has effectively certified, standardized and bureaucratized halal production, trade and consumption, and this has had a profound effect on the everyday experiences of consumers, companies and regulatory institutions in the country. I am inspired by a take on political economy that explores how anthropological subjects in everyday life are situated at the 'intersections of local and global histories' (Roseberry 1988: 173), that is, ways in which the lives of informants, in this case FairPrice representatives, can be studied in particular conjunctions or tensions between capitalism and the cultural freedom of subjects that define anthropological political economy (174). Studies in this tradition typically examine their subjects in the context of the world economy, the development of capitalism and structures of power that shape and constrain activity (Roseberry 1988: 179) – for example, how markets and MUIS as a regulatory institution interact and diverge in Singapore. A classic study in this tradition is Aihwa Ong's (1987) ethnographic analysis of spirit possession among young Malay women working in electronic assembly plants in Malaysia. Ong explores how spirit possessions can be seen as a response to the introduction of capitalist relations – not unlike the way in which halal in Singapore is commoditized. Comparable to Ong's placement of the young women within a complex set of contradictory experiences, I explore halal commodities and services at the intersections of commoditization, regulation and microsocial responses to this by supermarkets and their staff.

As halal proliferated in the 1980s in Singapore, it contributed to new forms of space making, thus lifting halal out of its base in halal butcher shops and wet markets into standardized space such as abattoirs and super/hypermarkets. Economic growth, the emergence of large middle-class groups and globalization of the food market have pluralized shopping choices – that is, in urban Singaporean shops and restaurants there is availability of a very wide range of local and imported foods. My research shows that before super/hypermarkets became dominant, halal was mainly about trusting the authority of the local halal butcher shop. Consumers now rely on the authority involved in proper Islamic branding through marking commodities with logos or accompanying certificates (Fischer 2008, 2011). Standards and standardization can be seen to be instruments of control and forms of regulation attempting to generate elements of global order (Brunsson and Jacobsson 2000: 1). The Singaporean state can impose sanctions on companies that do not live up to halal standards. What is more, standards can also refer to persons with certain qualifications, knowledge or skills (Brunsson and Jacobsson 2000: 5). An example of this is the mandatory requirement that supermarkets such as FairPrice must set up a Halal Team to ensure not only the halalness of products but also as a means of mitigating the risk of non-halal contamination, that is, as a form of standardized Muslim risk management.

These transitions can be conceptualized as a move from a 'bazaar economy' to a 'standardized' economy (Fanselow 1990) characterized by standardized and substitutable commodities in terms of quality/quantity. In standardized shopping spaces such as super/hypermarkets, a vast amount of information on product logos and labels is transmitted (Fanselow 1990: 258). Hence, this form of standardized and impersonal shopping warrants detailed information on labels and in the form of logos signifying certification by a recognizable certifier. What is more, super/hypermarkets are themselves standardized spaces in terms of design that allow for the proper handling of halal, on the one hand, and readiness for audits/inspections, on the other. Below I will show how this shift from a bazaar economy (wet markets) to a standardized one (abattoirs and super/hypermarkets) took place in Singapore.

An important theme is the emergence, consolidation and expansion of an audit culture around halal commodities and practice. This affects everyday life in FairPrice as well as the shopping practices of ordinary consumers. Halal certifiers such as MUIS regulate halal by performing 'on-site' audits and inspections in factories, restaurants and shops. There is a large body of literature on the rise of an 'audit society', but there is need for further scholarship on the ways in which audits and inspections are understood and practiced in locally specific contexts and their implications for everyday life. The pervasiveness of an audit culture within and around halal practices is not well understood, but, as I will show, it links everyday economic subjects such as supermarket staff and consumers, halal and markets in novel ways. Audit and inspection systems are a feature of modern societies. They exist to generate comfort and reassurance in a wide range of policy contexts (Power 1999: xvii). To a large extent, auditing is about cultural and economic authority granted to auditors (Power 1999: xvii), based on the assumption that those auditors are competent and their practices effective. A central aspect of audit culture that is also highly relevant to the market for halal is the pushing of control and self-control further into organizations to satisfy the need to connect internal organizational arrangements to public ideals (Power 1999: 10). Staff policies as well as establishing sections in shops that specialize in halal are examples of the increasingly prominent role of internal control systems that can be audited.

Audit culture cuts across notional state–market divides. New Public Management (NPM) is a change in style of public administration borrowed from private sector administrative practices towards quality assurance among other things (Power 1999: 42). The *Fourth International Halal Food Conference* was entitled *Establishing a Halal Quality Assurance System* – quality assurance has been transformed from an engineering/science to a management/cultural/ control concept that can be sold and certified. Quality assurance initiatives demonstrate how the control system is becoming the principal focus of audit practice and that quality must be measurable (Power 1999: 60). Audit culture has been explored from an anthropological perspective focusing on consensus endorsing government through economic efficiency and good practice. In this form of modern accountability, the financial and the moral converge to form a culture of what are deemed acceptable forms (Strathern 2000: 1). Audits and audit practices are discussed as descriptors 'applicable to all kinds of reckonings, evaluations and measurements' and as 'distinct cultural artefacts' in the market that work as a platform for both individual interest and national politics (Strathern 2000: 2).

To sum up, standards and standardization can refer to the design and qualities of products as well as proper conduct of shops – for example, with regard to the production, preparation, handling and storage of halal. Halal standardization represents a particular take on political economy that explores how everyday life in Singapore is situated at the intersections of a range of oppositions: between local economies of consumption and a globalizing halal industry; between religious principles and NPM-style administrative practices; between the country's economic ambitions and the everyday experiences of supermarket staff and ordinary consumers. A key question I explore is to what extent audit culture is compatible with the point that the underlying principle behind halal and its commoditization is 'divine order'.

Halal in Singapore

The Singaporean vision is to become a world leader in halal. To achieve this, halal commodities and handling are subjected to increased forms of everyday regulation. This section offers a broader context for understanding halal in Singapore. Singapore is a Chinese majority country where Muslims – of whom most are ethnic Malays (Singapore is the top destination country for outmigration from Malaysia; see also Tyson, this volume) – constitute the largest minority, and this has a significant bearing on halal production, trade, consumption and regulation. Out of 3.77 million Singaporean residents in 2010, the Chinese formed about 74 per cent, Malays 13 per cent and Indians 9 per cent, while 'Others' accounted for the remaining part.[1] Singapore exists in a 'double minority' setting: Chinese are a majority in Singapore but a minority in the region, whereas the Malays are a minority in Singapore but a strong majority in the immediate region (Mauzy and Milne 2002: 99–100). This complex relationship is essential to understanding halal in Singapore.

Singapore's colonial history dates back to 1819 when the British East India Company chose it as a settlement because it was centrally located for trade. In 1959, the People's Action Party (PAP) formed a government led by Lee Kuan Yew, who was the first prime minister of the Republic of Singapore. Lee governed for three decades until 1990 and he has been considered the architect behind Singapore's impressive performance and continuous economic growth. The reasons for this growth are many, but his strategies to make use of technology with multinational corporations have helped the country achieve first-world status. To this day, PAP governs Singapore driven by the pursuit of economic growth, which it delivers – and this is PAP's 'performance' principle and single legitimacy to rule. The party will go to all lengths, including curtailing conventional democratic rights and practices, to 'deliver the goods' to the people (Chua 2003: 3). Certain laws and controls on political participation and civil rights such as freedom of the press can be said to determine that Singapore is not a liberal democracy, but rather some form of authoritarian state. More broadly, authoritarianism is intimately linked to the political history of Singapore and PAP's quest for political dominance (Chua 1995: 204). What is more, the 'moral performance' of the PAP state defines the political rule and shapes the quality of social and political life (Yao 2007: 180). Singapore's judicial system has received high international acclaim, and this

---

[1] The data can be accessed at www.singstat.gov.sg/pubn/popn/c2010acr/key_demographic_trends.pdf

is also relevant to the way in which religion – and in connection with halal, in particular Islam – is regulated and managed legally.

All unions are under an umbrella organization called National Trades Union Congress (NTUC) of the government that supervises its activities. NTUC owns Singapore's largest supermarket chain, as I will discuss in detail later (Hefner 2001: 41). From the early 1980s, the Singaporean nation-building project moved towards a more 'ethnic-cum-racial form', with conceptions of 'Chinese' ethnicity and a peculiar Singaporean notion of 'Chinese values' playing increasingly important roles (Barr and Skrbis 2008: 5). What is more, this ethnicization includes the upholding of Singapore's two main national myths, that is, multiracialism and meritocracy that facilitate and legitimize rule by a self-appointed Chinese elite (Barr and Skrbis 2008: 5). Interestingly, halal aspirations that emerged in the 1980s occurred in parallel to the stress on Confucian ethics and, more broadly, a form of Chinese ethnicization of society. Confucian ethics includes obedience to benevolent and paternalistic hierarchical authority and emphasizes societal duties and obligations. Ironically, it is this transformation that plays a key role in the proliferation of halal in Singapore and beyond.

The state promotion of halal in Singapore presents a paradox: halal as an ancient Muslim food taboo is promoted as a national and neutral brand that benefits the economy, while the moral implications are downplayed – especially in a Chinese majority cultural context where Chinese social, religious and economic rituals are unavoidably intertwined. Gambling, eating pork and drinking alcohol are important ways of establishing identity and group membership, and rituals involving these things permeate all aspects of Singaporean life (Stimpfl 2006: 74). It is in this context that Malay Muslims are called upon to handle halal properly. In other words, no matter how forcefully halal is promoted as a highly lucrative global market in which countries such as Singapore want to find their rightful place, halal is essentially an Islamic moral injunction and not socially neutral in nature. Before halal became part of a global and growing market, the state in Singapore considered it an expression of excessive religiosity and minority rights that separate Muslims and non-Muslims in a 'multiracial context'.

MUIS and Halal Regulation

Islam is heavily state-regulated in Singapore. MUIS is the state Islamic institution, and its main decision-making body is the council headed by a president. It also comprises the Mufti of Singapore and members nominated by Muslim organizations. The state in Singapore promotes religiosity even though Singapore is officially a secular state, that is, the 'religious economy' is heavily regulated and governed by a very pragmatic state (Pereira 2005: 172). When the AMLA was enacted in 1965, it allowed for the establishment of MUIS in 1968 and the consequent culmination of the fusion of Malay and Muslim identities in Singapore (Kadir 2004: 360). The management of Islam in Singapore is done through the institutionalization of AMLA and the formation of MUIS. Issues addressed in AMLA are the Shariah Court, Muslim financial provisions, mosques and religious schools, halal and *haj* (pilgrimage), marriage and divorce, property, conversions, religious offences and miscellaneous others. MUIS's functions, duties, responsibilities and powers are clearly defined in AMLA. It states that MUIS was established and functions to administer matters relating to the Muslim religion and Muslims in Singapore, including any matter relating to halal certification.[2] MUIS started to provide halal services in 1972, and the first halal certificate was issued in 1978. MUIS is solely responsible and performs a regulatory function in halal under the state. MUIS also facilitates halal food trade through certifying local exporters to export their products to a global halal market, certifying local establishments and participating in forums on standardization of halal certification (Riaz and Chaudry 2004: 53).

An amendment of AMLA was passed in 1999 giving MUIS new powers in allowing it to regulate, promote and enhance the halal business. This bill endows MUIS with the sole authority to regulate the halal certification of any product, service or activity in Singapore. On 1 December 2009, a further amendment of AMLA with specific reference to halal certificates took effect so that it was now a serious offence to display false halal logos, that is, false MUIS logos. On MUIS's website, its halal services are described as follows:

MUIS is vested with the powers to act as the sole authority to administer and regulate halal certification in Singapore. This is clearly stipulated in AMLA:

Section 88A(1): The Majlis may issue Halal certificates in relation to any product, service or activity and regulate the holders of such certificates to ensure that the requirements of the Muslim law are complied with in the production, processing, marketing or display of that product, the provision of that service or the carrying out of that activity.

Section 88A(5): Any person who, without the approval of the Majlis a) issues a Halal certificate in relation to any product, service or activity; or b) uses any specified Halal certification mark or any colourable imitation thereof, shall be guilty of an offence and shall be liable on conviction to a fine not exceeding $10,000 ... or to imprisonment for a term not exceeding 12 months or both.[3]

A number of requirements are related to audits and inspections specifically. Upon submission of application and in the course of being halal-certified, random audits and surprise inspections are performed on the applicant's premises

---

[2] http://statutes.agc.gov.sg/
[3] www.muis.gov.sg/cms/services/hal.aspx?id=1714

to ensure compliance with the halal requirements. These audits check one or more of the following concerns: assess the seriousness of intention to go halal; verify the authenticity of information and supporting evidence submitted; assess the overall halal compliance and internal control systems; assess the effectiveness and consistency of implementation; assess the role and efficacy of the Muslim staff in guiding and ensuring compliance in the production process; educate and reinforce understanding of halal requirements and compliance by employees; assess risk of non-compliance; and report on areas for improvement (Riaz and Chaudry 2004: 224). In a MUIS (2007: 11) publication, the definition of the mandatory Halal Team is outlined as follows:

A group of appointed personnel responsible for implementing, monitoring and maintaining the Halal system, as well as ensuring that all requirements have been met in accordance with this document. The team shall be led by an appointed management representative and shall comprise at least one Muslim staff and members from the multi-disciplinary background, who possess relevant knowledge and expertise. The company shall ensure that the Muslim staff and at least one other member of the Halal team are sent for Halal training recognized by MUIS.

Obviously, this can be a controversial aspect of halal production, trade and regulation.

Halal in the Singaporean context evolved from being a sensitive Malay minority question to becoming a major national focus of state and market. Singapore's 'double minority' setting has been a driving force in the promotion of halal – Malay Muslims are simultaneously seen as a 'problem' as well as instrumental to the production, promotion, regulation and consumption of halal. The stress on Chinese ethnicity, ethics and values also embodies a powerful narrative about the hard-working and economically successful Chinese that must 'tap' the global and expanding market for halal. All this takes place in the framework of Singapore's unique form of government that can be characterized as some kind of authoritarianism that allows for close networking between key organizations and institutions, but also a standardized audit culture around the commoditization of halal. MUIS as a statutory body plays a pivotal role in regulating the halal market in Singapore.

Halal Visions, Laws and Logos

From the early 1990s onwards, Singapore was presented as a 'logical choice' as a processing and trading centre for halal food based on strong trading and cultural links with the Muslim world. This involved modern, efficient and cost-effective infrastructure; a technologically advanced food products industry; availability of halal certification by competent authorities; and an export-oriented food industry (*Straits Times*, 16 August 1990). In 1997, it was estimated that over the previous six years the number of halal certificates issued by MUIS had jumped from 19 to 271 and that this expansion included new products such as mooncakes (*Straits Times*, 5 September 1997). As the global market for halal expanded in the 1990s, MUIS envisioned a new service certifying make-up products, for example, 'to ease the doubts of Muslims' (*Straits Times*, 18 May 1999).

At around the same time, PAP launched a new series of dialogue sessions to gather feedback on issues affecting the Malay Muslim community, and a key issue was the use of false halal certificates by some restaurants and hawkers (*Straits Times*, 30 May 1991). This point relates to the way in which the halal discourse intensified in the early 1990s, and a central theme is the prolifera-tion and regulation of halal into more and more areas, for example, the begin-ning of MUIS certification of abattoir poultry (*Straits Times*, 23 May 1992). When these abattoirs apply for halal certification, they must comply with MUIS requirements and ensure that they have enough Muslim workers to comply with these guidelines. It is only Muslim staff that can attach the halal labels (*Straits Times*, 12 July 1992). This is an important point because it testifies to the trend that Muslims must be involved in proper handling and not only the actual ritual slaughter in light of rising halal requirements. Another important issue here is techniques and technologies of certification and logos. When the move from wet market to abattoir slaughter was completed, logos in the form of 'paper tags' tore when wet and had to be replaced by stallholders. Poultry hawkers in some wet markets resorted to 'do-it-yourself' tagging. Hawkers called for waterproof plastic or aluminium tags to be used instead of the paper tags. In these markets, stallholders must sell only poultry labelled by the abattoirs. The penalty for not doing so is a fine of up to S\$ 1,000 for the first offense and S\$ 2,000 for the second and subsequent offenses (*Straits Times*, 16 July 1992).

From the mid-1990s onwards, the halal discourse focused on calls to tap the growing global market for halal production, trade and consumption through MUIS certification – that is, from around that time, the state and companies in Singapore realized that halal had grown into a truly global assemblage with immense business potential. In 1994, Singapore's exports of halal food amounted to S\$ 1.2 billion, making up 24 per cent of the country's total food and beverage exports of S\$ 5 billion (*Straits Times*, 17 August 1995). In 1995, MUIS introduced its first logo that was to standardize existing logos labelled on halal food products. Previously, food manufacturers with halal certificates merely used the Arabic halal symbol, which was not a 'standardized' logo. Food manufacturers now had three months to change their halal logo to the new one issued by MUIS (*Straits Times*, 21 August 1995). Thus, centralized regulation transformed diverse classifications of logos into one national stan-dard. With the amendments to the AMLA, MUIS's role as the highest Islamic authority in Singapore was 'expanded' and 'strengthened', and MUIS could form part of companies as well as joint ventures. Moreover, MUIS was given the authority to issue halal certificates and punish those who violated the rules (*Straits Times*, 30 April 1998, 28 June 1998).

In the late 1990s, the halal discourse focused on the successes of halal-certified companies. MUIS reported a steady increase in issued halal certificates. The certificate was said to 'draw business' because Muslims were assured that their food was halal, especially in Malay areas. Supermarkets, including NTUC FairPrice, set up halal sections and reported increased sales. This success reinforced MUIS requirements that companies have to pass stringent checks before they are given the certificates. Food must be prepared properly for Muslim consumers, and companies must use equipment free from contact with non-halal food. A coordinator from a certified catering firm explained that this process was not easy – the firm spent about S$ 4,000 to restructure the kitchen and had to look for new halal suppliers, but profited in the end (*Straits Times*, 25 September 1999).

As a recent article in the *Straits Times* reports, in the context of the 'booming' global halal market, Singapore's halal industry is 'on a roll' with the number of halal-certified premises rising five-fold within the last ten years to 2,650 in 2011, with a further increase up to 5,000 expected by 2015 (*Straits Times*, 8 October 2011). These trends have prompted MUIS to seek to move beyond certification. Together with organizations such as International Enterprise Singapore and SPRING Singapore (the Standards, Productivity and Innovation Board), MUIS seeks to build up the country's halal brand through product development, trade and consultancy. At stake is a multibillion-dollar global halal market. MUIS's president explained that 'going halal' can increase takings by 20–25 per cent for businesses (*Straits Times*, 8 October 2011). In the same article, the minister-in-charge of Muslim affairs (who is also minister for information, communications and the arts) was reported to expect that the quintupling of halal-certified premises over the last ten years was also a boost for tourism, especially with regard to Muslim tourists from Malaysia, Indonesia and the Middle East staying in halal hotels.[4] At the same time, it was suggested that multinational fast food chains such as Delifrance (halal-certified since 2001) had achieved a 20 per cent boost in revenues. Similar stories are told about local companies, extolling the similar experience of the Chinese owner of a pizzeria – once the challenge of buying only halal-certified raw materials was overcome, business prospered (*Straits Times*, 8 October 2011; see also, e.g., SPRING 2011).

Such government narratives and media commentaries point to important transformations driven by the expanding halal industry, including

---

[4] The minister launched a MUIS Singapore Halal Eating Guide iPhone app (a digital version of the hard copy available at bookstores and some mosques), which can be downloaded for free – a sure sign that halal has reached the Digital Age.

the increasingly global flow of products, ideas and people. Considering Singapore's size and history, halal visions and halal altogether take up much space in the Singaporean media. In Singapore, actions speak louder than words, especially in a political context where halal is relatively uncontested and comfortably situated within a form of bureaucratized authoritarianism. Halal is constantly evoked as a global and growing market, and this fact legitimizes state involvement and regulation. At the same time, halal has become a global market in which legality plays an increasingly important role. The ongoing expansion of both the domestic and global halal markets was underpinned by significant changes in how halal is regulated and promoted in Singapore. This in turn has influenced how halal is experienced and acted upon in everyday life.

The Everyday Political Economy of Halal in FairPrice

FairPrice stores were set up in the 1970s by the NTUC Welcome Consumers' Cooperative Ltd with the objective 'to sell daily necessity goods such as rice and other utilities to consumers at a low price or at cost' (Lee and Jao 1982: 312). FairPrice has since then evolved into Singapore's biggest grocery retailer. I will now discuss a case that attracted attention in the Singaporean media during my fieldwork. In a news release in 2009, FairPrice announced Singapore's first supermarket audited by a local halal consultancy organization at Joo Chiat Complex in eastern Singapore (NTUC FairPrice 2009). This supermarket was 'aimed at addressing the needs of Muslim customers' by introducing a wider range of halal-certified 'offerings' within its store, catering to the 'significant Muslim population residing in the vicinity of this new store'. FairPrice at Joo Chiat Complex was the first supermarket to appoint a local halal consultancy organization, the chairman of NTUC FairPrice announced. Moreover, FairPrice had plans to extend this to other bigger stores.

The news release further detailed that in order to attain the audit approval by the halal consultancy organization, FairPrice stores undergoing the audit program set up by this consultant 'must go through a series of at least four stringent audits. The programme covers the processes of handling Halal products, training of key staff on Halal requirements and recommendations on areas for improvement' (NTUC FairPrice 2009). This audit program, the chairman stressed, supplements 'ongoing efforts to build a closer relationship with the Muslim community'. In addition to the variety of products offered at other FairPrice stores, in the newly launched outlet '[a] third of its in-store products are Halal-certified. Of these, about 400 are new Halal products, including a wide range of baking needs and spices, meat products such as chicken salami and beef pepperoni and even toiletries' (NTUC FairPrice 2009).

The halal consultancy's objective was to ensure that 'all facilities, practices and processes' in FairPrice outlets comply with requirements recommended by MUIS. This work is done through a series of steps by the halal consultant that include spending a month minimum with the outlet to develop halal process flows and food-handling procedures to ensure compliance with MUIS requirements; training of key staff to understand more about halal and the processes that will ensure halal status of products; auditing the branches (minimum four times) that have been trained; reporting and recommendations to FairPrice; and regular meetings with FairPrice to exchange ideas (NTUC FairPrice 2009). Consequently, increased halal regulation transformed the everyday relationship between auditors and FairPrice staff. In the media, this move was described as FairPrice 'stepping up its standards in the stocking of halal foodstuffs' in its new store in Joo Chiat Complex that was audited by the halal consultant, meeting 'strict requirements' as recommended by MUIS (*Straits Times*, 21 August 2009). The article continued:

This extends from halal food being imported into Singapore to the way it is stored with other products. For example, food from purportedly halal sources overseas will have to be checked and verified by the supermarket staff. Halal and non-halal food will also be kept distinctly separate, not just on displays, but in backroom operations as well. Also, a team will be specially designated to handle halal food only.

However, that same day, another article appeared whose heading read 'Only MUIS can certify' (*Straits Times*, 21 August 2009). This article stated that MUIS had 'taken issue' with FairPrice's new halal auditing program and noted that MUIS's president 'stressed that the council is the sole authority that can certify establishments and products as halal'. FairPrice had, the article said, 'announced it is helping its Muslim customers with a halal auditing programme – done by another Muslim body'. MUIS stressed that it had not yet certified the Joo Chiat outlet. The day after, this point was repeated in an article headed 'MUIS sole authority on halal certification' (*Straits Times*, 22 August 2009). In the article, FairPrice's managing director explained that the halal consultant's audit would give Muslim customers a greater level of assurance. But MUIS 'threw a question mark over the claim', stating that it had not yet certified the outlet and that FairPrice had merely approached the council for advice in December of the previous year on choosing a consultant. In response to this request, MUIS had earlier referred FairPrice to the halal consultant. A spokesman for the halal consultant confirmed this and argued that MUIS should speak to both the consultant and FairPrice about the issue so that people would know what MUIS's 'jurisdiction' and 'scope' were. It was established that the consultant's role was only to consult and audit and not provide any form of certification for halal. The main outcome of this case was to firmly establish that MUIS is the sole authority on halal certification in Singapore. FairPrice stated that it fully recognized this authority.

All this should be seen in relation to some wider transformations outlined in the same article: halal certification in Singapore and overseas had boomed and '[w]ith the Singapore halal mark becoming a recognized one, the number of certified establishments has nearly quintupled from 500 in 2000, to 2,300 last year'. This only shows how the commoditization of halal interacts with the standardization of a localized audit culture. A day later, it seemed to be back to 'business as usual' when the FairPrice supermarket in Joo Chiat Complex offered 'new halal products for keen cooks' (*Straits Times*, 23 August 2009).

During fieldwork, I met a FairPrice director of food safety and quality. FairPrice received its first International Standards Organization (ISO) certificate in 1993 and Hazard Analysis and Critical Control Points (HACCP) certification around the same time. According to the director, these types of certification work as 'everyday platforms and procedures for standardization and standardized practices in all Fairprice outlets'. Around 2006, FairPrice started to receive more and more requests about halal from Muslim customers, and as a cooperative, it was necessary to address all needs from organic to halal, but the question was how to do it: 'A specific halal counter is not enough. There has to be a mindset in terms of a system.' Halal has become increasingly important for FairPrice, and the organization has tried to focus on 'mass requirements' and 'streamline basic platforms' to address issues such as everyday standard operating procedures for doing things.

However, during my fieldwork in 2009, halal was mainly to do with counters in individual outlets, and this posed challenges to a company like FairPrice. This was the case in the FairPrice outlet in Joo Chiat Complex that I frequently visited during fieldwork. According to the director, it was challenging to comply with the individual store approach when MUIS had introduced the Halal Quality Management System (HalMQ) in 2008 – a new certification scheme that was to ensure new levels of halal standardization and audit culture in Singapore. FairPrice suggested that HalMQ had to be a 'quality system' similar to ISO, which was 'company-wide and not store specific'. However, after discussions between FairPrice and MUIS, implementing halal became more standardized. According to the director, establishing the Halal Corner or 'partition', that is, a designated halal-certified service corner, is very different from Muslim countries such as Malaysia in which local and multinational super/hypermarkets keep non-halal products in a separate room because strict Muslims would not accept a partition only. Previously, halal was more of an ad hoc question of 'where to put the freezer' in this or that outlet, but now everyday procedures have been standardized and centralized in the Halal Team comprising representatives from various departments of FairPrice from corporate communication to purchasing administration. As the director explains, the Halal Team is a constructive forum for discussing and standardizing halal.

When the director and I discuss the advantages and disadvantages of halal becoming big business not only in Singapore but also globally, she comments that it is important for Singapore to take part in this market as the country is strategically located between Malaysia and Indonesia which are major halal markets. Even if the number of Muslims is limited in Singapore, shops must cater for all 'races', and the Chinese do not mind the proliferation of halal as long as this does not replace products such as pork. For instance, the FairPrice Joo Chiat Complex is located in an area with many Malays, and naturally this outlet must 'adapt to the surrounding community. We're a cooperative doing what's best for the community', the director stresses. Thus, this supermarket, like many other super/hypermarkets around the world, adapts to the specific everyday requirements of local consumers and this is why there was special attention to halal in the Joo Chiat Complex outlet that caters to the Malay community. In this outlet, some customers ask for Muslim staff that can advise them on halal. In general, halal and non-halal products are both available in FairPrice outlets and other supermarkets in Singapore except for the Halal Corners in which only halal products can be found.

FairPrice designs all packaging for their own brands and they also take into account how the MUIS halal logo fits in with the general design of their house brand products. The director explains that packaging is designed so that it is 'suitable' for all Singaporeans. Many products carry the nutritional informa- tion required under the Sale of Food Act on top. Below that is the Healthier Choice Symbol issued by the Health Promotion Board under the Singaporean government. Under this logo is the MUIS halal logo. The FairPrice design department is to a large extent responsible for these designs, and MUIS and other parties are flexible about it. However, MUIS does not accept red logos, for instance, and prefers green or black ones. The process behind the halal logo on specific packaging is as follows: the supplier applies for the halal certificate and normally it takes between nine and twelve months for the final approval to go through. When the supplier receives the logo from MUIS, this is sent to FairPrice, which fits it into the overall design of the packaging.

Having the MUIS halal logo on products helps FairPrice when consumers enquire about the halal status of products. At the same time, industry players in Singapore and MUIS are aware of the growing demand for halal-certified products together with increased competition from Malaysia and elsewhere. FairPrice finds itself in the interfaces between the industry, consumers and MUIS, and this is the reason it takes halal so seriously. During my fieldwork in Singapore, I found a wealth of different halal logos in FairPrice outlets: a MUIS logo on a bag of honey almonds together with a number of additional logos; a halal logo of the Majelis Ulama Indonesia (Indonesian Ulemas Council) on coffee; a Halal Authority Australia logo on muesli bars (this prod- uct was also halal-certified and labelled as kosher according to Jewish dietary requirements); International Food and Nutrition Council of America logos; and many other halal logos. In FairPrice, as in other super/hypermarkets in Singapore, most (food) products are halal-certified. In other words, it is not only halal meat and other products in the designated Halal Corner that are halal-certified.

Unsurprisingly, halal inspections are important for everyday management in FairPrice. As more and more outlets were halal-certified in Singapore, MUIS subcontracted inspection duties to Warees Halal Division, a subsidiary of MUIS, which helps firms attain MUIS halal certification through the process of consultation. The organization is also responsible for mandatory halal training of staff. Once companies are certified, Warees Halal undertakes the task of ensuring that firms comply with the requirements of halal certification, that is, conducting site audits, engaging local Muslim organizations abroad to conduct regular periodic audits and sending halal-certified products for laboratory tests on an annual basis. Typically, inspections take place in the wake of 'customer feedback', that is, customers inform MUIS about issues they would like to have checked, and MUIS then asks Warees Halal to perform an inspection. When certification expires, FairPrice contacts MUIS and inspections take place as part of the process of renewing certification. Lastly, because of HalMQ, more inspections take place. Inspections are both announced and unannounced, and the director does not feel that there is any real difference between the two. After an inspection in an outlet, this outlet then emails a report back to the FairPrice headquarters. Halal consultants carry out halal 'integrity audits' so that certified stores follow halal standards at all times.

After the FairPrice HalMQ was established in 2010, the organization fully complied with MUIS's halal standard requirements. The management system of the Food Safety and Quality Department in FairPrice also involves audits at suppliers and food safety partners all along the supply chain. More specifically, the 'building blocks' for HalMQ include 'commitment' as the management has endorsed a Halal Quality Policy; standards based on MUIS halal standards; ISO 9001 (deals with the requirements that organizations wishing to meet the standard have to fulfil) and HACCP; and audit programs in relation to suppliers, warehouses, headquarters and all supermarket outlets. The Operational Halal Integrity Program of FairPrice ensures that the halal control points are properly monitored at the stores with three key focuses – specifically that each store is designed in order to properly review the store layout to ensure minimal cross-contamination; to ensure product control which streamlines the list of halal-certified products versus non-halal products with regard to store layout and population needs; and to ensure facility/equipment control. FairPrice set up the mandatory Halal Team that attends halal training. Before this became a mandatory requirement, it was just, in the words of the director, a 'working team'. Every FairPrice outlet with a halal certificate must send one staff for training. This training was constructive for FairPrice in that it laid out the basic MUIS 'halal principles, standards': 'If we know that these are the mandatory standards then it's easier to talk to the officers and inspectors and to form our own system', the director explains. In addition to the above, employees at FairPrice must participate in an on-the-job training program to ensure that staff are aware of receiving, handling and displaying halal-certified products. Finally, the organization has a communication program including various platforms with suppliers, staff and customers to ensure all parties are aware of the proper handling of halal-certified products.

Around 2009 when my fieldwork in Singapore took place, proper halal handling was still characterized by multiplicity in staff's everyday work. For example, I met a Malay Muslim man from FairPrice at the mandatory halal training arranged by MUIS. He wondered why he as a Muslim had to take the halal course: he was supposed to be an indigenous Muslim expert on halal, but even so the MUIS course on halal understanding was mandatory for him. Even if most of the discussions in this chapter focuses on supermarket representatives, the stress on halal markets and their regulation has effects on Muslim as well as non-Muslim staff in supermarkets more generally. It is the staff's responsibility to translate somewhat abstract halal regulation into everyday work practices and these practices are increasingly subjected to new forms of religious standardization and audit culture. My findings show that this type of disciplining permeates work practices at many different levels in supermarkets as well as restaurants – from executive decisions to everyday discussions about storage and transportation.

In conclusion, the FairPrice case shows how an organization can comply with rising halal requirements. This process can be challenging at times, but by now this whole process has been 'standardized', meaning that with regard to supermarkets the roles of and relationship between MUIS as a regulatory institution and FairPrice have been settled.

Conclusion

In this chapter, I have tracked the ways in which halal in shops – and the audit culture that surrounds it – has been standardized in Singapore. Halal logos and certificates play major roles in shops selling standardized halal products. Standardization makes halal impersonal, and, in turn, this stresses the need for third-party visual assurance that also has legal implications. These points also stress the fact that as these halal spaces or landscapes are standardized they are subjected to new forms of halal audit culture in everyday life. What is more, the FairPrice case shows that in Singapore, halal certification is fully centralized in MUIS. Standardization of halal in shops smoothens compliance for companies, but ironically compliance is also driving up halal requirements to cover more and more products and processes, that is, audit culture pushes control and self-control further into shops.

In Singapore, halal was described as an ever-expanding global market that the country must 'tap' with the help of a unique form of state certification. Simultaneously, the state in Singapore promotes halal as a neutral, self-evident and lucrative business. This exploration situates modern and global halal in a framework of new governing practices by different Southeast Asian countries such as Singapore. With regard to staff policies, innovation and certification, these companies work hard to comply with halal. Another important issue was halal inspections in companies that can be said to be a new form of religious audit culture. Interestingly, the concern over halal is more pronounced in some Southeast Asian countries such as Malaysia, Indonesia, Brunei and Singapore than in much of the Middle East and South Asia. The reasons for this are many, but the proliferation of halal in Southeast Asia cannot be divorced from the fact that over the past three decades these countries have witnessed steady economic growth, the emergence of large groups of Muslim middle-class consumers and bureaucrats, as well as centralized state incentives to strengthen halal production, trade and consumption – as well as finance, which is the main focus of the next chapter.

References

Barr, M. D. and Skrbis, Z. (2008) *Constructing Singapore: Elitism, Ethnicity and the Nation-Building Project*. Copenhagen: NIAS Press.

Brunsson, N. and Jakobsson, B. (2000) *A World of Standards*. Oxford and New York: Oxford University Press.

Chua, B.-H. (1995) *Communitarian Ideology and Democracy in Singapore*. New York: Routledge.

   (2003) *Life is Not Complete without Shopping: Consumption Culture in Singapore*. Singapore: Singapore University Press.

Denny, F. M. (2006) *An Introduction to Islam*. Upper Saddle River: Pearson Prentice Hall.

Fanselow, F. S. (1990) 'The bazaar economy or how bizarre is the bazaar really?', *MAN New Series* 25(2): 250–265.

Fischer, J. (2008) *Proper Islamic Consumption: Shopping among the Malays in Modern Malaysia*. Copenhagen: NIAS Press.

   (2011) *The Halal Frontier: Muslim Consumers in a Globalized Market*. New York: Palgrave Macmillan.

   (2016). *Islam, Standards and Technoscience: In Global Halal Zones*. New York: Routledge.

Hefner, R. W. (2001) 'Introduction: multiculturalism and citizenship in Malaysia, Singapore, and Indonesia', in R. W. Hefner (ed.) *The Politics of Multiculturalism: Pluralism and Citizenship in Malaysia, Singapore and Indonesia*. Honolulu: University of Hawai'i Press, pp. 1–58.

Kadir, S. (2004) 'Islam, state and society in Singapore', *Inter-Asia Cultural Studies* 5(3): 357–371.

Lee, S. Y. and Jao, Y. C. (1982) *Financial Structures and Monetary Policies in Southeast Asia*. London and Basingstoke: The Macmillan Press.

Manderson, L. (1986) 'Introduction: the anthropology of food in Oceania and Southeast Asia', in L. Manderson (ed.) *Shared Wealth and Symbols: Food, Culture and Society in Oceania and Southeast Asia*. Cambridge and Melbourne: Cambridge University Press, pp. 1–25.

Mauzy, D. K. and Milne, R. S. (2002) *Singapore Politics under the People's Action Party*. London and New York: Routledge.

Majlis Ugama Islam Singapura (2007) *MUIS-HC-S002: General Guidelines for the Development and Implementation of a Halal Quality Management System: Principle 1 – Establish the Halal Team*. Singapore: Majlis Ugama Islam Singapura.

Nasir, K. M., Pereira, A. A. and Turner, B. S. (2009) *Muslims in Singapore: Piety, Politics and Policies*. Oxon: Routledge.

Nevins, J. and Peluso, N. L. (2008) 'Introduction: commoditization in Southeast Asia', in J. Nevins and N. L. Peluso (eds.) *Taking Southeast Asia to Market: Commodities, Nature, and People in the Neoliberal Age*. Ithaca: Cornell University Press, pp. 1–24.

NTUC FairPrice (2009) *News Release*. Singapore: FairPrice.

Ong, A. (1987) *Spirits of Resistance and Capitalist Discipline: Factory Women in Malaysia*. New York: State University of New York Press.

—— (2006) *Neoliberalism as Exception: Mutations in Citizenship and Sovereignty*. Durham and London: Duke University Press.

Pereira, A. (2005) 'Religiosity and economic development in Singapore', *Journal of Contemporary Religion* 20(2): 161–177.

Power, M. (1999) *The Audit Society: Rituals of Verification*. Oxford: Oxford University Press.

Riaz, M. N. and Chaudry, M. M. (2004) *Halal Food Production*. Boca Raton: CRC Press.

Roseberry, W. (1988) 'Political economy', *Annual Review of Anthropology* 17: 161–185.

Rudnyckyj, D. (2008) 'Worshipping work: producing commodity producers in contemporary Indonesia', in J. Nevins and N. L. Peluso (eds.) *Taking Southeast Asia to Market: Commodities, Nature, and People in the Neoliberal Age*. Ithaca: Cornell University Press, pp. 73–87.

—— (2009) 'Market Islam in Indonesia', *Journal of the Royal Anthropological Institute* 15: S183–S201.

—— (2010) *Spiritual Economies: Islam, Globalization and the Afterlife of Development*. Ithaca: Cornell University Press.

SPRING (2011) *Global Halal Food Industry: Guide to Tapping the Fast Growing Halal Food Market*. Singapore: SPRING Singapore.

Stimpfl, J. (2006) 'Growing up Malay in Singapore', in L. Kwen Fee (ed.) *Race, Ethnicity, and the State in Malaysia and Singapore*. Leiden and Boston: Brill, pp. 61–93.

Strathern, M. (2000) 'Introduction: new accountabilities', in M. Strathern (ed.) *Audit Cultures: Anthropological Studies in Accountability, Ethics, and the Academy*. London and New York: Routledge, pp. 1–18.

World Halal Forum (2013) 'Introduction', available at: www.worldhalalforum.org/whf_intro.html.

Yao, S. (2007) *Singapore: The State and the Culture of Excess*. Oxon: Routledge.

6   Islamic Finance in Malaysia: Global Ambitions, Local Realities

Lena Rethel

Introduction

In 2009, the 15Malaysia project brought together fifteen Malaysian filmmakers to reflect on sociopolitical issues in Malaysia.[1] The result is a series of fifteen short films that provide a snapshot of living in Malaysia during a period of rapid social and economic change. Some of these films are funny, some are serious; some are action-packed, some are more contemplative. They all share a commitment to shedding light on how ordinary citizens engage with Malaysia's ongoing transformation. A couple of these films are specifically targeted at drawing out some of the cultural misunderstandings that can occur in Malaysia's multiethnic society. One of them is on Islamic finance. In the short film *Potong Saga*, the Chinese boy Namewee tries to open an Islamic bank account.[2] A group of friends tell him that he has to undergo circumcision to be eligible. He follows their advice. Yet, when he goes to open his account, the bank manager tells him that this procedure would not have been necessary. This is when he wakes up and realizes that it was all a dream.

The film provides a satirical commentary on interethnic relations in Malaysia and on what it is to become part of Malaysia's aspiring consumer society and increasingly financialized political economy. According to Namewee's friends, 'Islamic banking is very stable', 'they are different from other banks', 'their interest [sic] rate is better also', 'Islamic bank is people power', 'your money is safe', 'globalization' and 'in order to have a better future sometimes you have to make sacrifices'. On the one hand, these statements closely echo elite discourses on Islamic finance. They could thus be seen as illustrative of the success of the development of Islamic finance as an elite project and its acceptance by ordinary Malaysian citizens. On the other hand, this humorous engagement with Islamic finance constitutes a cultural space for critical reflection about Islamic finance as positioned at the intersections of age, gender, race and class in Malaysia. As such, the film can serve as an entry point for thinking about the

---

[1] The films can be accessed at http://15malaysia.com/films/
[2] This film can be accessed at http://15malaysia.com/films/potong-saga/

116

dynamics of Islamic finance in Malaysia more broadly. This chapter will focus on the tensions within Islamic finance as an elite project first aimed at modernizing the Malaysian economy and now also increasingly part of Malaysia's international competitiveness agenda and on how Islamic finance is engaged with, sustained and challenged by ordinary Malaysian citizens.

The last three decades have seen a rapid expansion of Islamic finance in Malaysia. With a Muslim share of slightly over 60 per cent of the overall population according to Malaysia's most recent census, a dual financial system has evolved where Islamic banks operate alongside conventional financial intermediaries. Currently, Malaysia has the most advanced Islamic financial system in the world.[3] The share of Islamic finance in the Malaysian banking system is approaching 25 per cent (BNM 2013a: P2). Its market for sukuk, Islamic bond-like instruments, issued by both domestic and international corporations, multilateral agencies and the government, is both deep and mature. Indeed, corporate sukuk now have a share of around half of the domestic bond market (BNM 2013a: 69), while sukuk issued in Malaysia account for more than 70 per cent of the global sukuk market (BNM 2013a: 78). At the time of writing, Malaysia has just enacted a comprehensive legal, regulatory and supervisory framework for Islamic finance – the *Islamic Financial Services Act 2013* – while simultaneously maintaining a dual (conventional and Islamic) financial system. In addition to these domestic developments, Malaysian financial policymakers have played crucial roles in international initiatives to promote and regulate Islamic finance.

Early on, Malaysian financial elites identified Islamic finance as part of their economic modernization agenda. However, in so doing, they pursued multiple – at times conflicting – goals. On the one hand, Islamic finance was identified as a pathway to promoting greater financial inclusion.[4] It was seen as a means to improve the economic position of the economically marginalized Muslim Malays and to bring them into the formal financial system. In so doing, its objectives were closely aligned with the New Economic Policy (NEP), also discussed by Franck and Tyson in this volume. On the other hand, Islamic finance has become an integral part of the government's ambitious project of financial modernization and international competitiveness with the ultimate objective of achieving developed country status by 2020. Mapped onto these agendas are the patronage politics that have come to increasingly characterize Malaysia's political economy, especially so since the former Prime Minister Mahathir came into office in 1981 (Gomez and Jomo 1997).

---

[3] Not by volume of assets under management but, when it comes to financial innovation, including number and range of approved structures, and also in terms of the sophistication of its legal and regulatory framework for Islamic finance.

[4] Interview with a former Islamic banker, Kuala Lumpur, March 2013.

This takes us to one of the central conundrums of Malaysian elite politics, especially so when it comes to the financial sector. On the one hand, financial policy elites are well educated, and overall financial regulation is seen as effective with a 'relative high' degree of 'internal discipline', in particular when it comes to the central bank, Bank Negara Malaysia (BNM) (Hamilton-Hart 2002: 127). On the other hand, financial policy making cannot be disassociated from the patronage politics of Malaysia's ruling coalition, giving rise to multiple nodes of entanglement (discussed in more detail later). At the same time, ordinary Malaysians have become increasingly directly exposed to financial volatility, with the country having one of the highest household debt levels in the world (Rethel 2010, 2012).

Recent critical work on Islamic finance in Malaysia has looked into attempts by state elites to position Kuala Lumpur as Islamic financial capital and conceptualizes these efforts as a services sector–oriented continuation of Malaysian industrial policy (Rudnyckyj 2013; Lai 2015). Against this backdrop, considering the development of Islamic finance in Malaysia from an everyday political economy perspective can draw out a number of issues that these accounts tend to disregard but that are nevertheless important for understanding the increasing salience of Islamic finance in Malaysia. The recognition of the significance of non-Western contexts allows for interrogating the extent to which Islamic finance presents an alternative to conventional financial practice, which is potentially better suited to Malaysia's multiethnic and developmental context. It draws attention to the extent to which tensions within elites and between elites and ordinary citizens have had an effect on the development of Islamic finance in Malaysia and its distinctive character. And it highlights the changing dynamics of inclusion and exclusion that have shaped Malaysia's economic transformation with significant implications for people's daily lives (cf. Martin 2002).

To address these issues, the next section will discuss some of the core principles of Islamic finance and the ways in which it departs from conventional financial practice. The section thereafter will look at how Islamic finance in Malaysia was turned into an elite project, intimately bound up with an increasingly Islamic economic modernization strategy. This is despite a number of openings where Islamic finance could have been reconstituted as a more grassroots project, engaging ordinary Malaysians on a more equal footing and not primarily through the politics of patronage. This section will be followed by a discussion of Islamic financial practices in Malaysia at the intersection of the global ambitions of Malaysian financial policy and commercial elites and ordinary citizens' everyday practices and aspirations with a focus on Islamic consumer finance. The last section will review the core arguments and offer some concluding comments. In so doing, this chapter draws on documentary analysis; interviews with financial policymakers, Shariah scholars, market practitioners and activists; and participant observation of Islamic finance industry conferences and training and financial education seminars for Islamic financial consumers. The fieldwork was conducted between 2007 and 2013.

Everyday Political Economy and the Multiple Worlds of Finance

Islamic finance is distinct from mainstream finance in that it draws on religiously informed injunctions that set out the types of financial structures that are permissible and those which are not. Islamic financial products and services have to comply with the principles of the Shariah, the Islamic jurisprudential body of knowledge. The distinction between *halal* (permissible) and *haram* (forbidden), discussed by Fischer in the preceding chapter, also applies to Islamic financial instruments. Thus, products and activities related to pork, alcohol and prostitution, among others, are deemed as Islamically not acceptable, which also makes them not investible. Moreover, Islamic finance prohibits *riba* (interpreted as the paying and receiving of interest), *maisir* (gambling) and *gharar* (profiting from uncertainty). More specifically, the prohibition of interest is seen as reinforcing the productive orientation of Islamic finance. In Islam, 'making money from money' is deemed not acceptable as money is seen as a medium of exchange, where money only becomes capital when it is invested in business and through human effort (Venardos 2006: 57). Similarly, gambling is prohibited because of its zero-sum character where one party benefits from the other's misfortune. Stipulations against profiting from uncertainty are intended to avoid one party exploiting another party's ignorance and to ensure contractual clarity. In so doing, Islamic financial principles curtail speculative financial practices such as short selling.

Islamic finance promotes distinctive ideas about debt, creditworthiness and asset-specificity. Debt – no matter if sovereign, corporate or household – is not a legitimately profitable activity. Creditworthiness is based on the 'worthiness' (in terms of economic profitability but in some interpretations also social desirability) of an investment project, and not primarily the repayment capacity of the borrower. Asset-specificity in this instance means that there has to be a direct link to the 'real' economy, which rules out many of the synthetic financial products that were intimately tied up in the recent global financial crisis. In so doing, Islamic finance is thought to embrace the mutually constitutive roles of the financial and the productive dimensions of the economy. According to its advocates, this makes it a particularly suitable instrument not just for the development of the financial sector but for the economy as a whole (e.g., Zeti 2007a, 2007b). In particular, two pathways stand out in this regard – the potential of Islamic finance to foster financial inclusion, specifically the mobilization of savings of the poor; and the contribution that Islamic finance can make to infrastructure development.

On a number of points, Islamic finance clearly departs from financial practice developed in and promulgated by largely Western-based elite financial actors (Maurer 2012). For example, Bill Maurer (2008) argues that while contemporary Islamic financial products often mirror conventional financial products, they differ in their underlying reasoning, giving Islamic finance a greater inherent reflexivity. Gillian Rice (1999) sees Islamic financial products as endowed with a 'moral filter' of what is deemed socially desirable and thus not just subject to the market mechanism. At the same time, recent efforts to develop Islamic finance cannot be separated from global circuits of capital. This is in part because the two are highly interconnected – take, for example, the growing importance of big conventional banks such as HSBC (through its Amanah subsidiary) or Citibank in developing Islamic finance. It is also because while, in its current guise, Islamic finance is constructed by its advocates as a response to increasingly fickle and footloose global flows of money, it struggles to move beyond the conventional financial system as its reference point. Islamic finance thus sits at the intersection of everyday political economy and cultural political economy, with a particularly non-Western dimension. In so doing, the development of Islamic finance in Malaysia speaks to those literatures that explore the role of everyday practices, cultures and relationships in understanding the 'social sources of finance' (cf. Seabrooke 2006) and their importance for the constitution of the global political economy (Hobson and Seabrooke 2007; Best and Paterson 2010).

Economic (Financial) Modernization and Islamic Visions of Development

The origins of Islamic finance in Malaysia date back to the early 1960s when the Malayan Muslim Pilgrims Savings Corporations (now Lembaga Tabung Haji – Pilgrims Fund Board) was established (Cizakca 2011: 207–26). It was set up in 1963 on the initiative of Ungku Abdul Aziz, Professor of Economics at the University of Malaya (and incidentally the father of the current central bank governor), to enable mainly rural Muslims to save for the pilgrimage to Mecca, one of the five pillars of Islam. It was a deliberate attempt to promote the financial inclusion of the Muslim Malays. More specifically, Tabung Haji was targeted at fostering a savings habit and mobilizing the funds of the rural poor. However, it is important to stress that in Malaysia's early post-independence history, Islam, although the religion of the majority ethnic Malay population, played little public and/or political role (Khoo and Hadiz 2011: 477). Even its visibility was limited, as, for example, urban women went unveiled, in striking difference to today. More important for the development of Islamic finance in Malaysia than this first Islamic savings vehicle were the creation of an Islamic banking sector in the 1980s and the subsequent development of Islamic capital markets. This section will look at these developments and discuss how they relate to Islamic finance in Malaysia as foremost an elite project.

Economic Modernization and the Creation of Islamic Banking

The resurgence of political Islam in Malaysia in the 1970s is a complex phenomenon. Khoo (1995: 159–62) points out three major reasons for this development. One of them is the implementation of the NEP, an affirmative action programme to strengthen the economic position of the economically under-represented Malay political majority that was implemented following race riots in 1969 (see also Crouch 1996). He argues that its efforts at modernization had dislocating effects on Malays, while, at the same time, it generated class-based disaffection with these changes, which made Islamic notions of fairness and economic and social justice appealing. Second, missionary movements and the Angkata Belia Islam Malaysia (ABIM) – the Muslim Youth Movement of Malaysia – spread Islamic ideas and ideologies. ABIM, in particular, promoted an 'activist, reformist Islam' (Khoo 1995: 160). Third, Khoo points to the resurgence of Islam as political force. After the May 1969 riots, the Parti Islam SeMalaysia (PAS) – the Pan Malaysian Islamic Party – had joined the Barisan Nasional coalition in 1973. However, in 1977, having fallen out with the United Malays National Organization (UMNO), it was expelled from the coalition and became the source of a growing Islamic political opposition (Crouch 1996).

The UMNO-led government reacted with feeble attempts to reestablish its Islamic credentials, derided by its Islamic opponents. However, when Prime Minister Mahathir came into office in 1981, it took over the initiative in the Islamization process (Camroux 1996; Crouch 1996). Within a relatively short span of time, a series of Islamic institutions was set up. The establishment of the International Islamic University Malaysia (IIUM) and of Bank Islam Malaysia Berhad (BIMB), both in 1983, were significant events and a clear manifestation of Mahathir's liberal vision of Islam. For him, Islam and Islamic values could be understood as key elements of Malaysia's modernization drive. He saw them as strong foundations of a capitalist work ethic (Khoo 1995; see also Tripp 2006: 117). Similarly, Camroux (1996: 858) argues that it gave the necessary 'Islamic legitimization' to Mahathir's development strategy to be effective among the Malay population. In 1984, a year after the establishment of the first Islamic bank, the first Malaysian takaful (insurance) operator was established.

Thus, the creation of Islamic banking in Malaysia was very much a political project driven by the country's political elites (Thirkell-White 2006). On the one hand, the Islamization of the economy was shaped by increasing electoral competition between UMNO and PAS. On the other hand, especially taking into account the focus on commerce and finance, one could say that it was closely aligned with Mahathir's overall economic policy strategy of promoting an indigenous commercial and industrial class. In part, it served to empower ethnic Malays with regard to Chinese financial dominance (Venardos 2006: 146). However, early on it was identified as a potential area of economic growth and of unlocking Muslim Malay savings. Hence, the introduction of Islamic finance in Malaysia and subsequent developmental efforts are a clear reflection of Mahathir's growth-oriented interpretation of the NEP and economic strategy more broadly.

This is not to say that there were no bottom-up pressures for, and initiatives aimed at, creating Shariah-compliant financial services during this period. Perhaps the best example of this was Project Ikhtiar (PI), a microfinance scheme established in the mid-1980s with heavy involvement of Universiti Sains Malaysia (USM) (Lucock 1990). Following research into the plight of the rural poor and inspired by the example of the Grameen Bank in Bangladesh, PI was set up as an experiment with the provision of microfinance loans. It was institutionalized in 1987 as Amanah Ikhtiar Malaysia (AIM), a private trust (Al-Mamun et al. 2010). Organized according to the *quard hasan* (benevolent loan) principle, AIM does not charge interest but a service charge (Lucock 1990: 5; Norma 2012). This is a significant difference from the business model pursued by the Grameen Bank. Since its inception, AIM has developed into Malaysia's most important microfinance organization and extended finance to more than 320,000 borrowers (*The Star Online*, 23 June 2012).

However, AIM was quickly absorbed within Malaysia's elite politics of patronage and profit. Hamayotsu (2004: 240–2) discusses the politicization of AIM in the mid-1990s and suggests it was a means for then Finance Minister Anwar Ibrahim 'to extend his personal patronage networks to the poorest Malay communities'. Post-Anwar, the Malaysian government remains AIM's most important funding source; note, for example, the not uncontroversial allocation of RM 2.1 billion to AIM in the 2012 budget (*The Malaysian Insider*, 10 October 2011). Thus, despite its grassroots origins, AIM does not challenge the idea that the development of Islamic finance in Malaysia is very much an elite project and has instead become part of Malaysia's racialized politics of patronage. At the same time, the organization has significantly professionalized its operating structures (Chan 2010: 67–73).

Visions of Development and the Emergence of Islamic Capital Markets

In 1990, the market-oriented shift in the NEP under Mahathir was consolidated when he launched Vision 2020, setting the achievement of advanced industrialized country status by the year 2020 as Malaysia's new developmental target. In the financial sector, efforts were increasingly focused on developing capital markets. This included the development of Islamic capital markets, a move in stark contrast to the market-driven and bank-oriented development of Islamic finance elsewhere and another instance of Malaysian 'top-down' policy making. Following the creation of BIMB, the Malaysian government began to issue Islamic government securities, thus helping it to meet its reserve requirements in a Shariah-compliant way and to manage surplus funds (BNM 1994: 327). During the 'surplus years' of the early 1990s, an increase in domestic net borrowing was primarily intended to satisfy the increasing demand for Islamic paper (*Business Times*, 30 March 1995). In 1990, Shell Malaysia issued an RM 125 million bond based on the Islamic principle of *bai bithaman ajil* (deferred sale) to finance a middle distillate synthesis project in Bintulu, Sarawak, giving birth to the creation of an Islamic corporate bond market. In the same year, Islamic corporate bonds became eligible for secondary trading (*The Business Times Singapore*, 15 June 1990). The year 1994 saw the introduction of Islamic mortgage bonds, when Cagamas, Malaysia's National Mortgage Corporation, bought and sold on the housing loans from BIMB (*Business Times*, 2 March 1994; on Cagamas, see Rethel 2010).

Further progress was also made on the banking front. In 1993, BNM, the central bank, introduced an 'interest-free banking scheme', allowing existing conventional banks to offer Islamic financial products and services and taking the country one step closer to a fully operable dual financial system. A year later, the Islamic money market was established, making Malaysia, in the eyes of the regulating authorities, 'the first country with a fully fledged Islamic banking system which functions on a parallel basis with the conventional system' (BNM 1994: ix). Again, as with most other developments in the Malaysian financial system, Islamic banking did not emerge spontaneously, but was the product of the 'conscious planning' by the Malaysian financial authorities. In May 1997 the National Syariah Advisory Council (now Shariah Advisory Council) was established at Bank Negara to harmonize financial with religious practice at a national level. At the eve of the Asian financial crisis, Malaysia had fifty-two financial institutions (twenty-five commercial banks, twenty-two finance companies and five investment banks) offering Islamic financial products and services (Warde 2000: 127). However, the share of Islamic finance of the overall financial system was still relatively small.

This changed considerably in the period following the crisis. Not only did Islamic banks further increase their share of the banking system, but Malaysia also played a leading role in the development of both its domestic and the international sukuk market. Sukuk are financial instruments similar to conventional bonds, but instead of fixed interest payments (which are not Shariah-compliant), they typically generate a return through income streams based on lease or rent payments. Through a number of landmark issues and the creation of a supportive regulatory environment, Malaysia has become the global centre for sukuk issuance by both domestic and foreign entities, including, for example, the International Finance Corporation, the private sector arm of the World Bank. In promoting sukuk, two reasons, in particular, stand out for policymakers given the country's past experiences: its (perceived) stability and potential contribution to economic development.

More specifically, it is a widely held belief that the asset-specificity of sukuk and its resulting connection to real economic activity make sukuk more stable than conventional financial instruments and thus less crisis-prone (Zeti 2007b). At a major industry conference in Kuala Lumpur in 2007, I observed how government officials, in order to promote Islamic finance, use anecdotes and moral tales of corporate business leaders and fund managers who burnt their fingers in the 1997–8 crisis, decisively turning to this apparently safer route of funding and investment. Similarly, the wider public is increasingly encouraged to invest in sukuk, and a number of bond market funds have emerged in recent years that invest in these assets. Thus, in the aftermath of the Asian financial crisis and even more so with the global financial crisis, the view that Islamic finance provides a safer alternative has gained meaning and is successfully harnessed by the state and financial elites in an effort to promote Islamic finance (as Namewee's friends bear testimony). The second reason pertains to Malaysia's role as a successful (Muslim) developing country. It is the potential seen in using sukuk for project finance and infrastructure funding, to finance the further development of Malaysia, but also its potential in other parts of the world, in particular in Asia and the Middle East, given the relatively early stage of economic development of many countries with sizable Muslim populations (Zeti 2007a).

As this brief overview has shown, despite certain impulses from academia and the grassroots level, the development of Islamic finance has been very much an elite project. Warde (2000: 126) describes Islamic finance in Malaysia as a 'principal tool in the country's developmental policy, ... designed to form the vanguard of financial modernization'. On the one hand, Islamic finance, at least in the early days, is a clear example of how, under the auspices of the NEP and on state initiative, the stratification of Malaysian society along ethnical groups was reproduced in the financial sector. On the other hand, and increasingly so following the announcement of Vision 2020 and then the shock of the Asian financial crisis, Islamic finance has been turned into one of the most important growth sectors of the Malaysian economy as a whole, generating employment and income for both Muslim and non-Muslim Malaysians and attracting business and funds from both Muslims and non-Muslims.

Global Ambitions and the Everyday Politics
of Islamic Finance in Malaysia

Islamic finance has made significant inroads in Malaysia, becoming an important area for a more market-oriented mode of governance to reassert itself. Political and commercial elites have used Islam as a tool of financial modernization and the financialization of the economy. While the rise of Islamic finance is clearly shaped by its non-Western context and thus demonstrates that convergence on particularly Anglo-American financial principles is not inevitably the dominant logic of financial system change, it nevertheless cannot be separated from Malaysian efforts to play a more important role in regional and global circuits of capital. Following efforts to consolidate Malaysia's financial system in the wake of the Asian financial crisis of 1997–8, Islamic finance first was identified as a regional then as an international ambition. Thus, for example, in a framework document to guide the development of Malaysia's financial sector in the first decade of the twenty-first century, Bank Negara envisioned as a major achievement to 'epitomize Malaysia as a regional Islamic financial centre' (BNM 2001: 79). A decade later, these ambitions have become global, namely to strengthen 'Malaysia's position as an international Islamic financial centre' (BNM 2011: 40). But at the same time, this took place against the background of a credit-fuelled domestic consumption boom in which Islamic financial products have come to play an increasingly significant source of consumer finance. This section will discuss these developments in turn.

Malaysia International Islamic Financial Centre Initiative

In its attempt to position itself at the top of the emerging international Islamic financial market, Malaysia has become very actively involved in developing domestic and international Islamic capital markets. Many of the efforts to further liberalize the Malaysian financial system can directly be linked to government efforts to promote Islamic finance as well as put itself at the forefront of international Islamic finance. In 2007, financial regulators eased foreign exchange administration and migration rules to this end. Indeed, endeavours initiated under Mahathir to establish Malaysia as a destination for Islamic funds were continued and intensified under his successors. Thus, high-level efforts have been put not only into creating the foundations for a thriving domestic sukuk market but also into achieving increasing international salience. Pivotal to these are Malaysia's ambitions to establish itself as a regional if not international financial centre for Islamic finance and its efforts to shape the processes of knowledge production that underpin the further development of Islamic finance.

In August 2006, the Malaysia International Islamic Financial Centre (MIFC) initiative was launched. Its overarching goal is 'to create a vibrant, innovative and competitive international Islamic financial services industry in Malaysia ... and to strengthen Malaysia's position as an Islamic finance hub' (BNM 2007, inside cover). This process of redefining and repositioning itself as a financial centre, be it regional or international, is a key element of market discourse, not just in Malaysia but also in other parts of the world. Indeed, it is hard to find a country which has not proclaimed itself, or one of its major cities, as a financial centre over the last decade. What is significant about this is how closely connected Malaysia's efforts to develop Islamic finance – something which could also be seen as a cultural phenomenon challenging processes of marketization – are to its self-understanding as a market state.

In a speech applauding the launch of the MIFC initiative, then Bank Negara deputy governor Dato' Razif further outlines its importance: 'The benefits of being a financial centre are tremendous. Besides enhancing services sector contribution to GDP, it will create job opportunities, contribute towards promoting greater cross border investment and trade flows, better quality and diversified products and services, and strengthen further the global economic and financial inter-linkages among countries' (Mohd Razif 2006). Thus, 'being a financial centre' is a key aspect of Malaysia's development strategy, both internally and externally. For example, Bank Negara's 2006 *Annual Report* identifies Islamic-based financial services as one of five emerging areas of growth in the services sector (20). This is particularly important given Malaysia's increasingly services-based economy (more than half of its GDP is generated in the service sector).

Malaysia has played a leading role in the development of both its domestic and international sukuk market. Over the last decade, the global sukuk market has experienced exponential growth from a volume of just over USD 1 billion in 2001 to more than USD 137 billion in 2012 (IIFM 2013). Indeed, sukuk has emerged as a global asset class, and the Malaysian market currently accounts for more than two-thirds of sukuk issuance globally. What started out in the 1980s as a niche market, dominated by government paper, has since become a big international market for corporate and sovereign sukuk. Moreover, sukuk are not only promoted to Muslim borrowers and investors. They are increasingly becoming accepted as regular financial instruments, also issued by large secular multilateral financial institutions and multinational corporations. This includes international financial institutions such as the World Bank (International Bank for Reconstruction and Development) and the International Finance Corporation (its private sector arm); regional financial institutions such as the Islamic Development Bank; and a number of companies such as Nestlé or Tesco (see Table 6.1). In Malaysia, the Islamization of the local bond market was closely followed by the internationalization of the Islamic bond market.

Table 6.1 *Malaysian sukuk issuance*

Date	Issuer (place)	Volume
Sovereign, sub-sovereign and multilateral		
2002	Government of Malaysia – first global sovereign sukuk	USD 600 million
2004	International Finance Corporation (World Bank group)	RM 500 million
2005	International Bank for Reconstruction and Development (World Bank group)	RM 760 million
2008	The Export-Import Bank of Korea	RM 3 billion (Islamic/conventional)
2008	Islamic Development Bank	RM 1 billion
Corporate		
1990	Shell (Malaysia)	RM 125 million
2001	Kumpulan Guthrie – first global corporate sukuk	USD 150 million
2003	Nestlé Foods (Malaysia)	RM 700 million
2004	Standard Chartered Bank (Malaysia)	RM 380 million
2004	Esso (Malaysia)	RM 300 million
2007	Tesco Stores (Malaysia) – guaranteed by Tesco (UK)	RM 3.5 billion (Islamic/conventional)
2008	UMW Toyota Capital (Malaysia)	RM 1 billion
2011	Khazanah Nasional – first renminbi multicurrency sukuk	RMB 500 million

Sources: MIFC initiative; Securities Commission Malaysia.

Moreover, Malaysian financial policymakers have played key roles not only in developing the domestic financial architecture but also in shaping the emerging global governance framework for Islamic finance. This includes hosting the Islamic Financial Services Board, created in 2002 to develop global capital requirement standards for Islamic financial institutions (Rethel 2011). In 2011 the International Islamic Liquidity Management Corporation (IILM) was created to facilitate the cross-border management of liquidity for Islamic financial institutions. Based in Kuala Lumpur, its founding shareholders are the central banks of Indonesia, Kuwait, Luxembourg, Malaysia, Mauritius, Nigeria, Qatar, Turkey and the United Arab Emirates and the Islamic Development Bank.[5] Malaysia already has a very well developed and liquid Islamic money market, and this initiative is clearly aimed at strengthening international linkages in Islamic finance.

Another important initiative was the launch of the International Centre for Education in Islamic Finance (INCEIF) in 2006 to 'fulfil the human capital needs of a rapidly expanding industry' (BNM 2007: 28). INCEIF offers postgraduate degrees in Islamic finance as well as courses for professionals such as the Chartered Islamic Finance Professional Programme. It also organizes

[5] The list of founding shareholders and further information about IILM is available at www.iilm.com

seminars that are attended by practitioners and financial regulators from both Muslim-majority and non-Muslim countries. There are clear indicators that Malaysia wants to shape the Islamic finance knowledge base by taking a lead in facilitating the production of those hybrid combinations of market and religious knowledge that underpin Islamic finance not just locally but globally. At the same time and adopting a more everyday perspective, it is apparent that the uptake of Islamic finance in Malaysia and its broader socio-economic impact have been uneven. Islamic finance in Malaysia is ubiquitous and, according to Rudnyckyj (2014: 76), this means that 'individual citizens now must make banking decisions commensurable with their religious practices'. Indeed, Malaysia's global Islamic financial ambitions are intimately connected to the everyday experiences of savers and borrowers in Malaysia. This is especially so as the government has explicitly linked its ambition of 'becoming the indisputable global hub for Islamic finance' to achieving the target of a 40 per cent Islamic share of domestic financing by 2020 (PEMANDU 2013).

Islamic Finance, Creditable Piety and Consumerist Development

A specific focus of inquiry of the everyday political economy literature is the multiple ways in which everyday savers and borrowers have become implicated in ongoing processes of financialization, understood here as the growing influence of financial markets over economic, political and social life (Pike and Pollard 2010; see also, e.g., Langley 2008; Seabrooke 2007). In Malaysia, Islamic finance has become an increasingly important pathway to credit, particularly where consumer finance is concerned. Indeed, the annual volume of loans disbursed by Islamic banks to (Muslim and non-Muslim) households has increased more than sixfold in the period from 2007 to 2012 from less than RM 8 billion to more than RM 50 billion (compared to a less than 1.5 times increase of loans disbursed by conventional commercial banks during the same period).[6]

Its advocates suggest that in expanding the credit choices of consumers, Islamic finance has contributed to a more inclusive financial development (Mohieldin et al. 2012). However, an analytically more challenging and normatively more demanding question to ask is not whether financial development in Malaysia has been inclusive but inclusion *in what* and *with what implications.* Between 2008 and 2012, Malaysian household debt in the formal financial system grew at an average annual rate of 12.5 per cent. Malaysia currently has one of the highest levels of household debt not only in the Asia-Pacific

---

[6] Author's calculation based on data from Bank Negara's monthly statistical bulletin, available at www.bnm.gov.my/files/publication/msb/2013/6/xls/1.15.xls, accessed 30 July 2013.

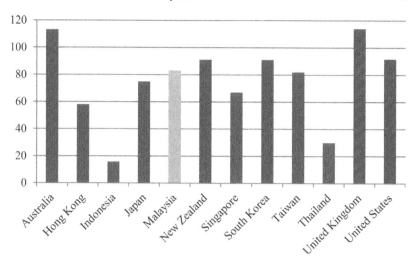

Figure 6.1 Malaysian household debt in cross-country comparison (percentage of GDP). *Source: The Malaysian Reserve*, 8 July 2013.

region (see Figure 6.1) but among emerging market economies more generally (Rethel 2012). While these comparative figures have to be taken with a certain amount of caution, given that they underplay the importance of informal credit especially in countries with less developed financial systems, they are nevertheless striking.

In terms of the usage of household credit provided by Islamic banks in Malaysia, the biggest share of financing goes into the purchase of passenger cars, followed by the purchase of residential property.[7] This is closely tied to the aspirations of Malaysia's emerging consumer society and growing middle class. Indeed, Chua (2009: 108) calls car ownership 'the emblem of economic success' and middle-class status in East Asia. However, what is potentially more worrisome is the rapid growth of credit/debt that is not directly linked to the purchase of assets. Thus, the volume of personal finance loans extended by Islamic banks grew more than sevenfold between 2007 and 2012. Similarly, the use of Islamic credit cards also increased during the same period. These developments are the more significant given Islamic injunctions on debt that also apply to the household level (Roza et al. 2012). According to Rudnyckyj (2014: 82), the proliferation of Islamic finance in Malaysia signifies that 'financial action becomes a site for the potential enactment of a religious identity and pious duties'. However, Islamic financial products are increasingly aggressively

---

[7] For a detailed breakdown of loans by purpose, refer to Bank Negara's monthly statistical bulletin, available at www.bnm.gov.my/files/publication/msb/2013/6/xls/1.19.xls, accessed 30 July 2013.

marketed, and at least one of the biggest Malaysian Shariah-compliant lenders offers Islamic financial products as the default choice.

In the wake of the Asian financial crisis of 1997–8, Malaysian financial policymakers deliberately encouraged banks to expand their loan books which contributed to a boom in household lending (Rethel 2010). Ambitious targets to expand the share of Islamic finance in the domestic economy seem to have further pushed this trend. This has led to a Malaysian citizenry increasingly directly exposed to the whims of financial markets. The dramatic rise in household debt levels has not gone unnoticed and led to a number of regulatory responses with the aim to tighten up the regulation of credit to the household sector. Measures included the implementation of a maximum loan-to-value ratio of 70 per cent for third homes in 2010; the shortening of the maximum tenure of personal finance and home loans extended by both conventional and Islamic financial institutions; and the prohibition of preapproved personal financing products in 2013 (BNM 2010, 2013b).

Moreover, in 2006 financial policymakers established the Credit Counselling and Debt Management Agency (Agensi Kaunseling dan Pengurusan Kredit, AKPK) in response to the growing numbers of households experiencing financial difficulties and struggling with their debt burden. Since its inception, AKPK has provided more than 265,000 individuals with credit counselling services (*Borneo Post*, 27 June 2014). Similarly, more than 100,000 individuals have sought to enrol in its debt management programme. As of February 2014, 22.8 per cent of those who had sought the help of the AKPK with managing their debts had gone bankrupt (*The Sun Daily*, 28 April 2014). On average, 41 Malaysians declare bankruptcy every day, with those under the age of 44 being particularly affected (*The Star*, 1 March 2013). Improving financial education and literacy has emerged as a core policy response in recent years (Di Castri 2011: 2). Thus, AKPK provides a range of financial education programmes delivered e.g. in collaboration with universities and government agencies. However, overall policy efforts clearly put the onus on individual financial consumer to 'be responsible for their own financial well-being' (Koid 2010). This understanding of household debt – or more specifically overindebtedness in combination with a consumerist growth regime – not as fundamentally questionable practice but as a problem to be managed is perhaps best summarized in the following statement by Visa Malaysia country manager Stuart Tomlinson: 'With sound knowledge on financial education, young people would become better consumers. They will be able to fully utilize their credit cards, manage their loans and avoid falling into the debt trap' (quoted in *The Star*, 1 March 2013).

This diagnosis of a lack of financial literacy as a root cause of overindebtedness is also evidenced by a renewed focus on financial education and planning pursued by consumer associations such as the Federation of Malaysian

Consumers Associations (FOMCA). Indeed, in 2011 FOMCA launched the annually held Financial Literacy Month, with the 2013 event tellingly entitled 'Financial Responsibility Begins with Me' (Consumers International 2013). FOMCA also collaborates with financial industry players to promote financial literacy in schools. However, a range of actors pursue a more progressive agenda with regard to both the diagnosis of the problem and potential solutions. In a recent documentary by civil society activists, rising levels of household debt are put in the context of Malaysia's ongoing socioeconomic transformation, where costs of living, especially in the urban centres, rise more rapidly than incomes. The documentary focuses, in particular, on the difficulties young Malaysians experience when it comes to affording housing, given the rise of urban house prices.[8] Along these lines, the Consumers Association of Penang lists – among its key recommendations for tackling the problem of growing household debt – increasing the provision of affordable housing, improving the public transport system to reduce dependence on privately owned vehicles and putting in place restrictions on the advertisement of credit and loans (CAP 2011). While there is some lively discussion of the drivers of rising household debt in online fora such as lowya.net,[9] the dominant portrayal of household debt as an individual problem, of financial well-being as the private responsibility of consumers, and of overindebtedness as the result of at best the foolishness of youth and at worst of personal failure rather than systemic pressures makes political mobilization around this issue inherently difficult.

How are tensions between a growing significance of Islamic consumer finance and rising levels of household debt negotiated in Malaysia? While Islamic finance contributes to the expansion of the credit economy and the ongoing financialization of Malaysian capitalism, it also provides challenges for exactly these processes, specifically by disrupting existing practices and introducing new ways of thinking. Two pathways in particular stand out: religiously informed moral appeals and deliberation of economic-commercial principles, and legal challenges in court. More specifically, in Malaysia religiously informed principles are turned to not only to draw out how unwise (and un-Islamic) it can be to incur debt but also as a basis for debt forgiveness. With regard to the former, for example, Khatijah et al. (2013: 37) suggest that from an Islamic standpoint debt should only be incurred 'in cases of real necessity'. They also make a case for more careful financial planning. With regard to the latter, we can look, for example, at the role of Shariah advisors

---

[8] This documentary can be accessed at: www.youtube.com/watch?v=hv9bWjgEXtc.

[9] See, for example, the thread on 'Are Malaysians spending beyond their means', which can be accessed at https://forum.lowyat.net/topic/2042526. This thread was sparked by a newspaper article in *The Sun* (22 September 2011) that branded Malaysians as 'Shopaholics' and the debate centred around the purchase of luxury consumer goods as a marker of status and personal financial management.

of Islamic banks in Malaysia. Not only do they determine which credit (and related) practices are permissible from an Islamic perspective and which are not, but they can also demand that financial institutions apply the principle of debt forgiveness in cases of hardship.[10] For example, in February 2008 Bank Islam announced that it was to introduce a payment holiday for housing finance payments for the months of November and December (a period with heavy financial commitments especially for families) (*The Star*, 22 February 2008; *Bernama*, 19 February 2008). Remember that the suspension of debt repayments at times where the borrower experiences financial strain is a core provision in the Quran for Islamic finance. Therefore, Islamic finance potentially has the scope to alter the trajectory of the current politics of debt and indebtedness in Malaysia.

Moreover, an interesting development in recent years has been the proliferation of legal action that involves Islamic financial products. Indeed, challenging Islamic financial products in court has become an important means to ensure that Shariah principles are adhered to in a progressive manner. Along these lines, studying legal rulings on Islamic financial transactions between 1987 and 2012, Apnizan and Hakimah (2012) report that disputes mainly arose over debt-based contracts, in particular with regard to housing finance. They suggest that Islamic financial institutions in Malaysia so far had shown a preference for debt-based instruments over profit-and-loss sharing products (Apnizan and Hakimah 2012: 57). However, this was being challenged in a growing number of lawsuits. Similarly, a recent survey conducted by researchers from the IIUM and USM indicates growing dissatisfaction, in particular, with debt-based home financing products structured according to the principle of *bai bithaman ajil* (Dzuljastri and Fauziah 2011).

Conclusion

Over the last thirty years, Islamic finance has made considerable inroads in the Malaysian financial system while also becoming an increasingly significant segment of global financial markets. Malaysian financial elites have fully embraced capitalist modernity. Yet, at the same time the development of Islamic finance in Malaysia shows that there is some flexibility in how a country engages with financial globalization and that in so doing there is some scope for it to choose its own developmental path. This does not so much amount to a binary decision of engagement or not with global circuits of capital, but rather the terms of this engagement and the ways in which integration is managed.

---

[10] Author's conversation with Shariah advisory board member of Malaysian Islamic bank, Kuala Lumpur, March 2013.

Adopting an everyday political economy approach can draw out some of the social challenges and economic ambiguities that lie behind this success story.

Elite efforts to promote Islamic finance have productively engaged its ambiguities. Malaysian financial policy elites have communicated different aspects of Islamic finance to different stakeholders, successfully playing off the various meanings associated with Islamic finance to increase its salience. To market players, such as big multinational corporations, international investors and multilateral financial institutions, they have pointed out the similarities of Islamic finance with conventional finance. To Muslims, whose strict belief prevented a participation in the conventional financial system, financial elites have emphasized the alternative character of Islamic finance, actively promoting, for example, the spread of anecdotes of the small stall-holder who always used to struggle and who can now expand his business rapidly due to the availability of Islamic financing. At times a similar rhetoric is employed by financial elites towards their counterparts in other Muslim nations. Finally, advocates of Islamic finance seek to attract both Muslim and non-Muslim investors and borrowers with the ethical and socially responsible character of Islamic finance and its potential developmental role (see, e.g., Zeti 2012).

In so doing, the development of Islamic finance in Malaysia has clearly been an integral part not just of government efforts to widen and deepen financial markets but more generally of a shift to an increasingly financialized and consumption-oriented political economy. Thus, for some ironically, Islamic finance in Malaysia seems to further entrench the market state and to reproduce existing notions of capitalist development rather than to represent a genuine alternative or site of resistance. Effectively, Islamic finance has served as a conduit for Malaysian commercial and financial elites to play a more prominent role in global circuits of capital. At the same time, Islamic finance has been reflective of the changing dynamics of inclusion and exclusion that have shaped Malaysia's political economy. While in its early days Islamic finance was a means to encourage rural Malays to save and engage with the formal financial system, more recently it has become the facilitator of an aspiring consumer society, with participants keen to purchase houses and cars. However, the development of Islamic finance and the broader socioeconomic effects of a financial development strategy fuelled by the expansion of domestic credit have not been uncontested. By looking at how tensions between the growing availability of Islamic consumer finance and rising levels of household debt are negotiated in everyday life, this chapter has illustrated how elite efforts to develop Islamic finance in Malaysia encounter local realities and are sustained, resisted and transformed in various ways by everyday actors such as borrowers and savers.

References

Al-Mamun, A., Wahab, S. A. and Malarvizhi, C. A. (2010) 'Impact of Amanah Ikhtiar Malaysia's microcredit schemes on microenterprise assets in Malaysia', *International Research Journal of Finance and Economics* 60: 144–154.

Apnizan, A. and Hakimah, Y. (2012) 'The Trend of Legal Suits Involving Islamic Financial Transactions in Malaysia: Evidence from the Reported Cases'. ISRA Research Paper No. 48.

Best, J. and Paterson, M. (eds.) (2010) *Cultural Political Economy*. London: Routledge.

BNM (1994) *Money and Banking in Malaysia*, 4th edition. Kuala Lumpur: Bank Negara Malaysia.

(2001) *Financial Sector Masterplan*. Kuala Lumpur: Bank Negara Malaysia.

(2007) *Malaysia International Financial Centre Initiative*. Kuala Lumpur: Bank Negara Malaysia.

(2010) 'Measures in Promoting a Stable and Sustainable Property Market and Sound Financial and Debt Management of Households', Press Statement, November 3, www.bnm.gov.my/index.php?ch=en_press&pg=en_press_all&ac=2159&lang=en.

(2011) *Financial Sector Blueprint*. Kuala Lumpur: Bank Negara Malaysia.

(2013a) *Financial Stability and Payment Systems Report 2012*. Kuala Lumpur: Bank Negara Malaysia.

(2013b) 'Measures to Further Promote a Sound and Sustainable Household Sector', Press Statement, July 5, www.bnm.gov.my/index.php?ch=en_press&pg=en_press_all&ac=2841&lang=en.

Camroux, D. (1996) 'State responses to Islamic resurgence in Malaysia: accommodation, co-option, and confrontation', *Asian Survey* 36(9): 852–868.

CAP (2011) 'Household debt in Malaysia – is it sustainable?', available at: www.consumer.org.my/index.php/personal-finance/debt/465-household-debt-in-malaysia-is-it-sustainable.

Chan, S. H. (2010) 'The influence of leadership expertise and experience on organisational performance: a study of Amanah Ikhtiar Malaysia', *Asia Pacific Business Review* 16(1): 59–77.

Chua, B. H. (2009) 'From small objects to cars: consumption expansion in East Asia', in H. Lange and L. Meier (eds.) *The New Middle Classes: Globalising Lifestyles, Consumerism and Environmental Concern*. Dordrecht: Springer, pp. 101–115.

Cizakca, M. (2011) *Islamic Capitalism and Finance: Origins, Evolution and Future*. Cheltenham: Edward Elgar.

Consumers International (2013) 'FOMCA launch financial literacy month in Malaysia', available at: http://www.consumersinternational.org/news-and-media/news/2013/10/fomca_literacy/

Crouch, H. (1996) *Government and Society in Malaysia*. Ithaca: Cornell University Press.

Di Castri, S. (2011) 'Empowering and Protecting Financial Consumers: Bank Negara Malaysia's Consumer and Market Conduct Framework', available at SSRN: http://ssrn.com/abstract=1843281.

Dzuljastri, A. R. and Fauziah, M. T. (2011) 'Consumers' perception on Islamic home financing: Empirical evidences on Bai Bithaman Ajil (BBA) and diminishing partnership (DP) modes of financing in Malaysia', *Journal of Islamic Marketing* 2(2): 165–176.

Gomez, E. T. and Jomo, K. S. (1997) *Malaysia's Political Economy: Politics, Patronage and Profits*. Cambridge: Cambridge University Press.

Hamayotsu, K. (2004) 'Islamisation, patronage and political ascendancy: the politics and business of Islam in Malaysia', in E. T. Gomez (ed.) *The State of Malaysia: Ethnicity, Equity and Reform*. London: Routledge, pp. 229–252.

Hamilton-Hart, N. (2002) *Asian States, Asian Bankers: Central Banking in Southeast Asia*. Ithaca and London: Cornell University Press.

Hobson, J. M. and Seabrooke, L. (eds.) (2007) *Everyday Politics of the World Economy*. Cambridge: Cambridge University Press.

IIFM (2013) *Sukuk Report: A Comprehensive Study of the Global Sukuk Market*, 3rd edition. Manama: IIFM.

Khatijah, O., Sapora, S. Z. A. G. and Kamaruzaman, J. (2013) 'Debt ridden behaviour and coping skill from an Islamic spectrum', *Middle-East Journal of Scientific Research* 13 (Special Issue on Research in Contemporary Islamic Finance and Wealth Management): 35–41.

Khoo, B. T. (1995) *Paradoxes of Mahathirism: An Intellectual Biography of Mahathir Mohamad*. Kuala Lumpur and Oxford: Oxford University Press.

Khoo, B. T. and Hadiz, V. (2011) 'Approaching Islam and politics from political economy: a comparative study of Indonesia and Malaysia', *The Pacific Review* 24(4): 463–485.

Koid, S. L. (2010) 'Financial Consumer Protection in Malaysia', presentation given to the AFI Global Policy Forum Bali, Indonesia, 28 September, available at: www.afi-global.org/sites/default/files/cp%2001%20-%20koid%20swee%20lian%20bnm%20malaysia%20-%20market%20place.pdf.

Lai, J. (2015) 'Industrial Policy and Islamic Finance', *New Political Economy* 20(2): 178–198.

Langley, P. (2008) *The Everyday Life of Global Finance: Saving and Borrowing in Anglo-America*. Oxford: Oxford University Press.

Lucock, D. A. (1990) 'Banking on the Rural Poor in Malaysia. Project Ikhtiar'. Gemini working paper 6, available at: http://pdf.usaid.gov/pdf_docs/PNABG674.pdf.

Martin, R. (2002) *Financialization of Daily Life*. Philadelphia: Temple University Press.

Maurer, B. (2008) 'Re-socialising Finance? Or Dressing it in Mufti? Calculating Alternatives for Cultural Economies', *Journal of Cultural Economy* 1(1): 65–78.

(2012) 'The disunity of finance: alternative practices to western finance', in K. K. Cetina and A. Preda (eds.) *The Oxford Handbook of the Sociology of Finance*. Oxford: Oxford University Press, pp. 413–430.

Mohd, R. (2006) 'Deputy Governor's Closing Keynote at the Malaysian Islamic Finance – Issuers and Investors Forum 2006', Mandarin Oriental Kuala Lumpur, 15 August, http://www.bnm.gov.my/index.php?ch=en_speech&pg=en_speech_all&ac=226&lang=en.

Mohieldin, M., Iqbal, Z., Rostom, A. and Fu, X. (2012) 'The role of Islamic finance in enhancing financial inclusion in Organization of Islamic Cooperation (OIC) countries', *Islamic Economic Studies* 20(2): 55–120.

Norma, M. S. (2012) 'Microfinance and prospect for Islamic microfinance products: the case of Amanah Ikhtiar Malaysia', *Advances in Asian Social Science* 1(1): 27–33.

PEMANDU (2013) 'Annual Report: Financial Services', available at: http://etp.pemandu.gov.my/annualreport2013/upload/ENG/05_NKEA03_ENG_FS.pdf.

Pike, A. and Pollard, J. (2010) 'Economic geographies of financialisation', *Economic Geography* 86(1): 29–51.

Rethel, L. (2010) 'Financialisation and the Malaysian political economy', *Globalizations* 7(4): 489–506.

(2011) 'Whose legitimacy? Islamic finance and the global financial order', *Review of International Political Economy* 18(1): 75–98.

(2012) 'Each time is different! The shifting boundaries of emerging market debt', *Global Society* 26(1): 123–143.

Rice, G. (1999) 'Islamic ethics and the implications for business', *Journal of Business Ethics* 18(4): 345–358.

Roza, H. Z., Radiah, A. K., Noor, I. J. and Sabitha, M. (2012) 'Burgeoning house-hold debt: an Islamic economic perspective', *Middle-East Journal of Scientific Research* 12(9): 1182–1189.

Rudnyckyj, D. (2013) 'From wall street to *Halal* street: Malaysia and the globalisation of Islamic finance', *The Journal of Asian Studies* 72(4): 831–848.

(2014) 'Islamic finance and the afterlives of development in Malaysia', *PoLAR: Political and Legal Anthropology Review* 37(1): 69–88.

Seabrooke, L. (2006) *The Social Sources of Financial Power*. Ithaca and London: Cornell University Press.

(2007) 'The everyday social sources of imperial and hegemonic financial power', in J. M. Hobson and L. Seabrooke (eds.) *Everyday Politics of the World Economy*. Cambridge: Cambridge University Press, pp. 83–102.

Thirkell-White, B. (2006) 'Political Islam and Malaysian Democracy', *Democratization* 13(3): 421–441.

Tripp, C. (2006) *Islam and the Moral Economy: The Challenge of Capitalism*. Cambridge: Cambridge University Press.

Venardos, A. M. (2006) *Islamic Banking and Finance in Southeast Asia: Its Development and Future*. Singapore: World Scientific Publishing.

Warde, I. A. (2000) *Islamic Finance in the Global Economy*. Edinburgh: Edinburgh University Press.

Zeti, A. A. (2007a) 'Malaysia's experience in strengthening its market for global sukuk activities', BIS Review 88/2007.

(2007b) 'The international dimension of Islamic finance', BIS Review 95/2007.

(2012) 'Internationalisation of Islamic finance – bridging economies', Welcoming address by the Governor of the Central Bank of Malaysia at the Global Islamic Finance Forum 2012, Kuala Lumpur, September 19, available at: www.bis.org/review/r120920d.pdf.

Resisting Marketization: Everyday Actors, Courts and Education Reform in Post–New Order Indonesia

Andrew Rosser

Introduction

A key debate in the recent literature on Indonesian politics has centred on the extent to which everyday actors, including citizens from poor and lower–middle-class backgrounds and their allies in the NGO movement,[1] have been able to participate effectively in the policy-making process since the fall of Suharto's authoritarian New Order regime in the late 1990s. On one side of this debate, scholars such as Vedi Hadiz, Richard Robison and Olle Tornquist have argued that policy making in the post–New Order period has remained just as exclusionary as it was under the New Order despite the fact that the country has become more democratic and decentralized (Hadiz 2003, 2010; Hadiz and Robison 2005; Robison and Hadiz 2004; Tornquist et al. 2004). Power relations, they have argued, have simply been reorganized rather than transformed: instead of fading from the scene, the politico-bureaucratic, business and criminal figures who dominated the New Order 'have been able to reinvent themselves through new alliances and vehicles, much like they have, for example, in parts of Communist Eastern Europe/Central Asia' (Hadiz 2003: 593). At the same time, they suggest, Suharto's rule left a powerful legacy in relation to the participation of everyday actors in policy making. The New Order's systematic pursuit of a policy of disorganizing civil society and repressing any form of political activity on the part of opposition groups, they suggest, has 'effectively paralyz[ed] most independent capacity for self-organization among groups like the urban middle class and the working class' (Hadiz and Robison 2005: 232).

---

[1] Hobson and Seabrooke (2007: 15–16) define everyday actors as 'those who are subordinate within a broader power relationship but, whether through negotiation, resistance or non-resistance, either incrementally or suddenly, shape, constitute and transform the political and economic environment around and beyond them'. I use the term here in a manner consistent with this definition.

Research for this chapter was made possible by a grant from the Australian Research Council through its Future Fellowship scheme (Grant number FT110100078).

On the other side of this debate, scholars such as Hans Antlov, Marcus Mietzner, Ed Aspinall and myself have argued that democratization and decentralization have opened up new opportunities for everyday actors to influence policy-making, resulting in a slightly more inclusive political system. For instance, in a paper co-authored with Kurnya Roesad and Donni Edwin (Rosser et al. 2005), I argued that the shift to a more democratic political regime has (i) removed key obstacles to organization by poor and disadvantaged groups and NGO activists, making it easier for them to engage in collective action aimed at achieving pro-poor change; and (ii) created an electoral incentive for politicians to promote policy changes that benefit these groups or at least appeal to them. Consistent with this, several scholars have noted that some national and local political leaders have used 'populist' policies effectively to get themselves elected or reelected (Mietzner 2009; Rosser and Wilson 2012; Aspinall and Warburton 2013; Rosser and Sulistiyanto 2013; Aspinall 2014). Finally, Mietzner (2013) has drawn attention to the fact that numerous civil society activists from New Order times have become active in political parties, the legislature and (to a lesser extent) the executive arm of government in the post–New Order period, giving them direct access to the policy-making process. While some 'activists-turned-politicians' have failed to produce change as a result, Mietzner argues, others 'have initiated ... legislation that led to ground-breaking reforms' (2013: 28). In no cases does this group of authors suggest that everyday actors now play a substantial role in policy-making. But they do suggest that these actors now matter politically.

This chapter contributes to this debate by examining the role of everyday actors in education policy-making during the post–New Order period. Since the fall of the New Order, the Indonesian government has introduced a range of neoliberal reforms to the country's education system, following closely policy prescriptions recommended by government technocrats and the World Bank. However, this shift towards a more marketized education system has been hotly contested. I argue here that while elite groups have constituted the main source of resistance to marketization of the education system, everyday actors have played an important role in challenging specific reforms, in particular through strategic use of the courts, especially the Constitutional Court. Their activism has not generally been effective in halting these reforms, but, in some cases, it has led to the watering down of reform. As such, I suggest that scholars of Indonesian politics need to give greater attention to the role of everyday actors both in policy-making and courts as a means for their participation. Writing everyday actors into our narratives about Indonesian politics is necessary to provide a more accurate and nuanced account of Indonesian politics and, to the extent that such analysis guides policy, improve the quality of policy-making.

In terms of locating the analysis presented in this chapter within a broader understanding of the everyday political economy of Southeast Asia, the research presented here raises particular issues about the role of everyday actors engaged in struggles to protect those marginalized from the region's economic development. In this sense, parallels can be drawn with the arguments presented in Nick Henry's chapter in this volume – specifically the emphasis on civil society activism. However, rather than positioning activist groups as conduits for the translation of progressive international norms into domestic political contexts, this chapter gives primacy to the role of activists motivated by the need to challenge processes of marketization and privatization (in this case the educational system) that are realized within a highly predatory political-economic system. In doing so, a domestic court system, rather than international norms/standards, emerges as the key site within which attempts at push back against statist and capitalist interests play out. In focusing on the agendas, interests and activities of everyday actors, the chapter also accords with Jonathan Rigg's argument, set out in Chapter 2 of this volume, that to understand ongoing processes of economic transformation in the Southeast Asian region, we cannot simply look at state actors' developmental policies without paying attention to how 'development as practice [i]s pursued and given meaning by people in their everyday actions'.

In presenting this argument, I draw on material derived from interviews with key informants; government laws, regulations and other documents; analyses by NGO activists and intellectuals; and media reports. The chapter is structured as follows. I begin by identifying the main political and social actors who have sought to influence Indonesia's education policies during the post–New Order period. I then examine the dynamics of education policy-making during this period focusing on three policy cases that illustrate clearly the role played by everyday actors in resisting neoliberal education policy reform. The final section of the chapter assesses the implications of the analysis for the study of Indonesian politics and maps out a future research agenda.

The Main Actors: Technocrats, Predatory Elites, Populists and Everyday Actors

In broad terms, four main sets of political and social actors have sought to influence Indonesia's education policies during the post–New Order period, each of which has had a distinct policy agenda, interests and means of accessing the policy-making process. The first of these has consisted of government technocrats and their allies at the World Bank and other donor organizations. Key individuals in this set have included Bambang Sudibyo (minister of national education from 2004 to 2009); Mari Pangestu (minister of trade from 2004 to 2011); Boediono (vice president 2009–2014); Fasli Jalal (various director general–level positions in the Ministry of National

Education (MoNE)/Ministry of Education and Culture (MoEC)[2] from 2001 and 2010 and then vice minister of national education from 2010 to 2011); and Satrio Soemantri Brodjonegoro (director general of higher education from 1999 to 2007).[3] In policy terms, this set of actors has promoted neoliberal reform of the education system and, in particular, school-based management (SBM), minimum service standards (MSS), teacher certification requirements, autonomy for educational institutions, prudent spending, competition between educational institutions for access to government funding, and opening of the education sector to foreign investment (World Bank 1998; Jalal and Mustafa 2001). A key theme of their agenda has been a need for Indonesia to respond to competitive pressures unleashed by globalization by reforming the education system to create 'smart and competitive Indonesians', a phrase used repeatedly in MoNE's 2005–9 Strategic Plan (MoNE 2005). To this end, they have also supported academic freedom as a basic tenet of institutional autonomy.

This set of actors has exercised influence over education policy because of donors' leverage over the state stemming from their control of mobile investment resources – the fact that its agenda has been congruent with demands from business to restrain government spending and enhance bureaucratic efficiency – and the presence of substantial numbers of in-house technocratic staff in key ministries, especially the MoEC and the National Ministry of Development Planning (Bappenas). In other words, its influence has been underpinned by both structural and instrumental power. It has exercised greatest influence during the predominantly intrabureaucratic phases of the policy-making process – the preparation of draft laws and implementing regulations following their passage by the national parliament (Dewan Perwakilan Rakyat or DPR) – when technocratic and World Bank officials have had greatest access to this process.

The second set of political and social actors who have sought to influence Indonesia's education policies during the post–New Order period has consisted of predatory political, bureaucratic and business figures. Key individuals and organizations in this set have included various members of the DPR's education and budget committees (which are responsible for approving government spending in the education sector), various senior bureaucratic officials (who initiate spending proposals), business groups with strong bureaucratic and political connections, and many staff members at public universities and schools. Members of this grouping have sought to maximize political and bureaucratic control over budgetary resources and procurement (whether at the national or educational institution level or points in-between) so as to

---

[2] The name of the ministry has changed over time.
[3] All of these individuals have held other appointments beyond those mentioned here. I list here those appointments most relevant to the discussion that follows.

generate opportunities for corruption and rent extraction. Their access to the policy-making process has stemmed from their direct occupation of the DPR and bureaucracy (in the case of predatory political and bureaucratic figures), access to policy-makers via 'brokers' or intermediaries (in the case of predatory business figures) and the control that this has given them over budget and procurement processes.

The third set of political and social actors that has sought to influence Indonesia's education policies during the post–New Order period has consisted of politicians who have pursued populist strategies as a way of enhancing their electoral popularity and promoting their political careers. Examples have included President Susilo Bambang Yudhoyono and Idham Samawi and I Gede Winasa, the former *bupatis* of Bantul and Jembrana, respectively (Mietzener 2009; Rosser and Wilson 2012; Rosser and Sulistiyanto 2013). In general, this set of actors has promoted education policies that redistribute resources to the poor and disadvantaged such as free education and the provision of cash subsidies to poor people to encourage them to send their children to school. This agenda has conflicted with the technocratic/World Bank agenda in two respects: it has prioritized improved access to education over improved educational quality – the latter being crucial to producing 'smart and competitive Indonesians' (compare with Tyson's discussion of 'talent' later in this volume) – and required the government to increase education spending beyond levels considered prudent in neoliberal circles. Politicians pursuing populist strategies have been able to promote this agenda by virtue of their occupancy of government positions, in particular within the Executive.

The final set of actors – and the one most important for this discussion – has been everyday actors such as poor and lower-middle-class parents, students and their allies in the NGO movement and nationalist intellectual circles. Key individuals in this set have included those associated with parent and teacher groups such as the Education Coalition, the Education Forum, Auditan and the Alliance of Parents Concerned about Indonesian Education; activists at Indonesia Corruption Watch (ICW) (a prominent anti-corruption NGO), the Institute for Policy Research and Advocacy (ELSAM) (a prominent human rights NGO) and the Jakarta Legal Aid Bureau (LBH Jakarta) (a prominent legal aid NGO); nationalist intellectuals such as Professor HAR Tilaar, Winarno Surakhmad and Professor Soedijarto; and figures associated with Taman Siswa (a nationalist educational organization)[4] such as Darmaningtyas.[5] Members of this set of actors have promoted a policy agenda that emphasizes citizens' rights to free education, equal access to quality education and the use of education to build national identity and resilience, although the relative emphasis placed

---

[4] On Taman Siswa's history and ideology, see McVey (1967) and Hing (1978).
[5] On these two organizations, see Rosser and Curnow (2014).

on these elements has varied from actor to actor with NGO activists tending to be stronger on rights and equal access, and nationalist intellectuals tending to be stronger on national identity and resilience. The common element in these groups' activism has been opposition to the commercialization or privatization of education, something they associate with neoliberal reform of the education system. Members of this coalition have generally been excluded from the education policy-making process[6] but, as we will see later, have been able to challenge government policies, particularly through the Constitutional Court.

The Political Economy of Education Policy-Making in Indonesia: Predation, Populism and Everyday Activism

During the New Order period, the Indonesian government neglected the education sector, reflecting the New Order elite's antipathy towards human rights concerns and dominant focus in development policy terms on natural resource exploitation, unskilled low-wage manufacturing and capital-intensive manufacturing, none of which required skilled labour. While it substantially expanded the geographical reach of the education system and improved access to education, it invested much less in education compared to neighbouring countries such as Malaysia, Korea and Thailand (World Bank 1998: 111). At the same time, it used the education system as a vehicle for propagating the state ideology, *pancasila*, enforcing political control and distributing patronage rather than encouraging independent and critical thinking (Leigh 1999; Nugroho 2005). The education bureaucracy and public schools and universities that dominated the education system[7] became part of the larger franchise structure that characterized the New Order, the key feature of which was the sale of public office for private gain (McLeod 2000). Captured by predatory bureaucrats, corruption and rent-seeking within the education system were rife (Irawan et al. 2004; Rosser and Joshi 2013).

Combined together, these three factors – underinvestment, a focus on political control, and corruption and rent-seeking – resulted in low educational quality, as reflected in the country's poor performance in international standardized tests such as PISA and TIMSS (World Bank 1998: 148). They also contributed to serious retention problems: even before the 1997–8 economic crisis (which led to a brief but sharp drop in enrolment rates), almost 20 per cent of primary school students did not finish primary school, and 1.5 million primary school graduates per year did not continue on to junior secondary school (World Bank 1997: 68–9, 1998: 46).

---

[6] Interviews with Ade Irawan (ICW), Lody Paat (Education Coalition), and Roi (Pattiro), all Jakarta, November 2012.

[7] Public schools currently account for roughly 80–90 per cent of enrolments depending on the level of education (Department of National Education 2008: Table 2).

The 1997–8 economic crisis and attendant collapse of the New Order provided an opportunity for government technocrats and their donor supporters to promote a shift away from this patrimonial, statist and authoritarian model of education and towards a freer, more market-driven system. On the one hand, the country's transition to democratic and decentralized rule created a political environment that was more compatible with the technocrats' emphasis on institutional autonomy, academic freedom and decentralized school management. On the other hand, the economic crisis dramatically enhanced the structural power of the World Bank, the International Monetary Fund and other donors by substantially increasing the government's need to attract additional aid resources. In this context, government technocrats and the World Bank mapped out a reform agenda (see especially World Bank 1998 and Jalal and Musthafa 2001) and moved to support this with donor-funded loans and grants. Subsequent pressure on the government to reform the education sector came during the 2004–5 World Trade Organization negotiations on trade in services where pressure was exerted on developing countries to encourage greater trade in educational services. Finally, competitive pressures unleashed by globalization have created further structural pressure on the government to improve both access to and the quality of education.

The result has been the introduction over the past fifteen years of a wide range of neoliberal education reforms including SBM, the formulation of MSS for the sector, the introduction of teacher certification requirements and the rationalization of the school curriculum. Efforts have also been made to increase the autonomy of educational institutions (particularly top-ranked public universities) by changing their legal status, establish 'international standard' schools to deliver high-quality school education, introduce competition between universities for government research funding, and open up higher education to foreign investment. Significantly, the technocrats and donors have also backed increased government spending on education, recognizing that government underinvestment in the sector was a key reason for its low quality and student retention problems. They have also backed moves to implement universal free basic education, reflecting the fact that UNESCO's Education for All goals call for universal free primary education, and the World Bank has made a partial shift away from support for education user fees, at least at primary school level (see World Bank 1998).[8]

However, this shift towards a more marketized education system has not proceeded smoothly. As we will see below, some reforms have been declared unconstitutional or have been otherwise successfully challenged in the courts, forcing the government back to the policy drawing board; other reforms have been pushed much further than government technocrats and donors have

---

[8] On the World Bank's shifting position in relation to user fees, see Klees (2008).

considered prudent; and other reforms again have run into problems in implementation. The overall result has been the emergence of an education system that, while increasingly market-oriented in nature, has stopped short of being fully neoliberal. On the one hand, the education bureaucracy and educational institutions have remained part of the larger 'franchise' structure that emerged under the New Order. On the other hand, education policy has, in some instances, had a stronger orientation towards rights than is consistent with the neoliberal model.

There have been three main reasons for this outcome.

Predation

The first of these has been that the predatory elements that dominated the education bureaucracy, public schools and public universities during the New Order have maintained their control over these institutions despite the transition to more democratic and decentralized rule. Education-related cabinet positions have continued to be given to members of the major Islamic organizations, Muhammadiyah and Nahdlatul Ulama, and senior positions in MoEC and the Ministry of Religious Affairs, the two government departments most directly responsible for education policy, to staff from the state universities under their control, entrenching established patronage networks.[9] Likewise, at the local level, district education offices continue to be staffed largely by former public school teachers and members of the Persatuan Guru Republik Indonesia or PGRI, a teachers' representative organization that is close to government.[10] Senior management positions in public schools and universities continue to be bought and sold in accordance with the New Order's franchise model (Irawan et al. 2004; Rosser and Joshi 2013). Finally, predatory business groups have continued to develop collusive relationships with political and bureaucratic officials involved in education policy-making.[11] The predatory elements in control of the education bureaucracy, public schools and universities have been able to subvert implementation of reforms that threaten their interests.

A clear example in this respect has been SBM. SBM sometimes involves the devolution of authority over school affairs to principals or teachers only, while in other cases it involves parental and community participation through

---

[9] Interviews with informed sources, Jakarta, November 2012.

[10] Interviews with informed sources, Jakarta, November 2012, and Yogyakarta, December 2012.

[11] Perhaps the best illustration of this is the Angelina Sondakh corruption scandal of 2011–12. At the heart of this scandal were allegations that Sondakh, a Democratic Party parliamentarian, took bribes from a company owned by the party's former treasurer to ensure that specific projects, including ones related to the purchase of university laboratory equipment, were included in the government's education budget and that the company won the relevant contracts. See Parlina (2012), Setuningsih (2012), *Jurnal Nasional* (2012) and Amelia (2012) for reports on this case.

school committees. With the issuance of Minister of Education Decree 44/2002 on Education Boards and School Committees, the policy document most centrally associated with SBM in Indonesia, Indonesia opted for the latter approach. However, school committees have tended to be dominated by school principals rather than act as vehicles for the articulation of parents' demands. Although Minister of Education Decree 44/2002 requires school committee members and chairs to be selected through a consultative selection process, school principals have often simply appointed them without consultation. Alternatively, principals have actively lobbied for the selection of particular candidates and used intimidation and other unfair practices to get their way. The fact that parents have often lacked the education, expertise and confidence to properly monitor school decision making, particularly in poor communities where education levels and levels of professional expertise among parents are low, has enabled school principals to dominate committee decision making regardless of the selection process and use them to promote school policies, especially on fees and procurement, that entrench corruption and mismanagement and harm the interests of parents and schoolchildren (Rosser and Joshi 2013: 9–10).

At the same time, predatory elements in regional governments have gained control over the central government grants introduced in 2005 to support SBM by providing schools with some degree of financial autonomy. Known as School Operational Assistance (BOS), the purpose of these grants was to reduce financial pressure on schools, and hence their need to charge school fees, by covering operational costs such as those related to the registration of new students, the purchase of textbooks, the production of report cards, stationery, teacher development and training, remedial teaching programmes, and examinations. When the BOS was first introduced in 2005, BOS funds were transferred directly from the central government to schools bypassing provincial and district governments (Rosser and Joshi 2013: 8). However, as the size of the BOS grew, predatory elements in district governments began to agitate for change in these arrangements, eventually securing a decision by the central government in 2011 to channel BOS funds to schools via district governments.[12] This led to widespread delays in the distribution of BOS funds and claims by anti-corruption activists that BOS funds were being withheld from schools until they paid bribes to district officials (*Jakarta Post* 2011). In the end, the central government decided to channel the BOS funds through provincial governments instead. But by maintaining a layer of bureaucracy in between the central government and schools, this policy still arguably undermines school financial autonomy and, in so doing, the principle of SBM.

---

[12] Interviews with informed sources, Jakarta, November 2012.

Another example of predatory elements subverting neoliberal education reform has been the national school exam (*ujian nasional*). Introduced in its current form in 2002, *ujian nasional* has been a feature of the country's education system for decades, although its name and nature have changed over time.[13] Government technocrats and their donor supporters have viewed *ujian nasional* (and its predecessors) as a potentially useful instrument for technocratic policy-making and determining progression through the education system (World Bank 1998: 37, 2004: 100; Triaswati et al. 2001: 96–9; Umar 2004). But its utility in this respect has been undermined by widespread cheating during the conduct of the exam, often involving whole classes or schools with the encouragement of teachers and principals[14] and corruption in its administration. With respect to the latter, the problem has been corrupt dealings between national education bureaucrats and private firms over the supply and distribution of exam papers and the leaking and sale of exam papers and their solutions before the conduct of the exam.

Populism

The second reason why the shift towards a more marketized education system has not proceeded smoothly is that democratization has created an incentive for politicians to promote populist or redistributive education policies, in particular free education, because of their electoral appeal, notwithstanding their often high cost to the government budget. While many politicians have not responded to this incentive, preferring instead to build political support through the cultivation of patronage networks and party machines, some have done so with positive electoral results (Mietzner 2009; Rosser et al. 2011). Indeed, there appears to have been a gradual ratcheting-up of politicians' promises in relation to free education over time with some electoral contests now involving commitments by candidates to extend free education beyond primary and junior secondary school (which has been national government policy since 2009) to include senior secondary school. Because of the high cost of free education, the result has been upward pressure on the education budget, generating concerns in technocratic and donor circles about its fiscal sustainability.[15] The introduction of free education has also entailed a greater concern with citizens' rights to education than is arguably consistent with the neoliberal agenda.

---

[13] For instance, it was known as the 'national final stage study evaluation' (Evaluasi Bejajar Tahap Akhir Nasional) between 1984 and 2001 and the 'national final exam' (*ujian akhir nasional*) between 2002 and 2004. It has only been known as the 'national exam' since 2005 (Darmaningtyas and Subkhan 2012: 174–175).

[14] For a personal account of this phenomenon, see Sarasvati (2012).

[15] Interview with a World Bank economist, Jakarta, November 2012.

Everyday Activism

The final reason why the shift towards a more marketized education system has not proceeded smoothly is that democratization and decentralization have increased opportunities for everyday actors to participate more in this process. Democratization has removed key obstacles to organization by groups such as NGOs and parents of schoolchildren, making it easier for them to engage in collective action in relation to education issues. It has also entailed the establishment of new entry points into the policy-making process for NGO activists and ordinary citizens such as the Constitutional Court, reflecting fractures within the elite in relation to the protection of human rights and a perceived need for a final arbiter (i.e., the Constitutional Court) on intra-elite disputes. This court has proven to be sympathetic to rights-related causes, reflecting the liberal outlook of its judges and the inclusion of a Bill of Rights in the 1945 Constitution and other rights-related provisions between 2000 and 2002 (Mietzner 2010). Finally, decentralization of political authority to the district level – enacted initially through two laws in 1999 that were revised in 2004 – has strengthened the ability of NGO activists, parents and other groups to access and monitor policy-making and implementation by bringing it closer to them (Antlov 2003).

Everyday actors have played an important role in contesting neoliberal education reform in three areas in particular. The first of these relates to the legal status of educational institutions. Government technocrats and their donor allies have argued that educational institutions, in particular higher education institutions (HEIs), which under the New Order were essentially part of the bureaucracy, should have greater autonomy from government in order to mobilize the funding they require, ensure intellectual freedom and respond effectively to the demands of students and other clients. In its 1998 report on Indonesia's education system, for instance, the World Bank (1998: 93) argued that 'a lack of autonomy and responsibility at the university level has led to a lack of accountability and transparency at the institutional level'. Similarly, government technocrats in a World Bank–Bappenas task force on higher education established around the same time argued that 'Centralized control especially control over financial management, has inhibited universities from taking the role as the driving force of community development' (Moeliodihardjo et al. 2001: 230).

To support this agenda, the World Bank funded a project under the directorate general of higher education to 'create an enabling environment for the evolution of autonomous and accountable public higher education institutions (HEIs) and to develop effective support mechanisms for the improvement of the quality, relevance, efficiency, and equity of higher education' (World Bank 2005: 5). The main outcome of this was the preparation of a draft law that proposed a change in the legal status of educational institutions at both the school and higher education levels to 'education legal entity' (*badan hukum pendidikan* or BHP), a status that entailed greater autonomy over their financial and managerial affairs. In March 2007, President Susilo Bambang Yudhoyono submitted the draft law to the DPR, initiating the enactment process.[16]

Throughout this time, parents groups, university student organizations and their allies in NGOs such as ICW and LBH Jakarta and nationalist intellectual circles lobbied hard against the draft law, holding public discussions on the issue of educational institution autonomy, making comments to the press and, in the case of student groups, organizing public protests (Darmaningtyas et al. 2009: 285–306). They also published widely on the issue in the mass media and books (see, e.g., Irawan 2007; Surakhmad 2007; Darmaningtyas et al. 2009). Their main arguments were that educational institution autonomy would enable the government to avoid its obligations to fund education; that school and university fees would skyrocket, making education unaffordable for many people; and that autonomy would thereby worsen inequality. Following passage of the law in December 2008, they responded by taking the matter to the Constitutional Court, claiming that the law was unconstitutional. In 2010, the Constitutional Court ruled in their favour, declaring the law both unconstitutional and null and void.

The effect was to force the government back to the policy drawing board and ultimately to water down its reforms. As a stop-gap measure, it made changes to existing regulations to provide a legal basis for the continued operation of several elite state universities that had changed their status to state-owned legal entity, a legal status constructed as a precursor to BHP. In conjunction with the DPR, MoEC then produced a new law on higher education (Law 12/2012) that reaffirmed the principle of autonomy, but only for HEIs. This law was subject to an unsuccessful challenge in the Constitutional Court during 2012 and 2013. But although it has survived, it only provides autonomy for HEIs, not other educational institutions, most notably schools.

The second area in which everyday actors have played an important role in contesting neoliberal education reform has been that related to so-called international standard schools (SBIs). These schools had their origins in concerns about the quality of Indonesian education and recommendations by the World Bank–Bappenas task force on education financing in the late 1990s that the government consider privatizing the country's 'best' public schools and redirecting the subsidies they received to schools lower down the quality hierarchy or, alternatively, giving these schools 'more autonomous' status, 'so that they can finance themselves by doing their own income generating activities' (Triaswati et al. 2001: 117). In the 2009 government regulation providing for the establishment of SBIs, they were defined as public and private national schools that 'have already fulfilled all national education standards

---

[16] Jadual Acara Pembahasan RUU BHP.

[and which are] enriched with certain quality superiorities that originate from Organisation for Economic Co-operation and Development (OECD) member countries or other developed countries'.[17] Specifically, they were required to follow curricula used in OECD or other developed countries; use information and communication technology (ICT) and English in the delivery of these curricula; employ teaching staff who are fluent in English and a minimum proportion of whom have postgraduate qualifications (they were permitted in this respect to employ foreigners if no qualified Indonesians are available); provide international standard facilities (particularly with regard to ICT); and create sister school programmes with either leading domestic schools or schools in developed countries. Students who enrolled in these schools also had to meet demanding minimum academic performance requirements and score well on an intelligence test.[18] Most controversially, schools selected for the SBI programme were granted permission to charge fees, effectively exempting them from adhering to the national policy on free basic education, and were provided with much higher levels of government funding than 'regular' schools.

This policy was widely criticized on several grounds: (i) that SBI breached constitutional requirements for free basic education because they charged fees; (ii) that these schools' fees often disappeared into the pockets of education bureaucrats and school officials rather than contributing to improvements in educational quality and facilities; (iii) that SBI generally failed to come good on their commitment to provide scholarships to students from poor backgrounds; (iv) that schools which segregated students into international and regular classes often used government support for and fees from regular students to subsidize the provision of international standard classes and associated new facilities; and (v) that, by effectively excluding students from poor backgrounds from attending SBI/international standard classes and favouring the provision of international standard classes over regular ones, these schools created a two-'caste' education system, thereby worsening inequality (Auditan nd; Seputar Indonesia 2007; Winarti 2008; Metrotvnews.com 2012; Wedhaswary 2012).

In early 2012, a group of parents and activists from ICW, ELSAM and other NGOs launched a Constitutional Court case challenging the constitutionality of Article 50(3) of Law 20/2003 on a National Education System, the legal foundation for SBIs. As in the BHP Constitutional Court case, sympathetic nationalist intellectuals, including Darmaningtyas and Professor HAR Tilaar, testified in support of their side.[19] In January 2013, the Constitutional Court

---

[17] See *Minister of Education Regulation 78/2009 on the Implementation of International Standard Schools in Primary and Secondary Education*, Article 1(8).

[18] See *Minister of Education Regulation 78/2009 on the Implementation of International Standard Schools in Primary and Secondary Education*, especially Articles 4, 5, 6, 10, 16 and 20.

[19] Personal communication with Andi Muttaquien, an ELSAM lawyer involved in the case, June–July 2012.

ruled that Article 50(3) was unconstitutional, effectively bringing an end to SBI.[20] In its judgement, the Court was particularly critical of SBIs' unequalizing social effects and detrimental cultural impact stemming from the use of English as the primary language of instruction.[21] The government has responded to the decision by indicating a desire to maintain the SBI programme in a revised form, using the term 'autonomous schools' (*sekolah kategori mandiri*) as a replacement (Damarjati 2013). But it seems unlikely that it will be able to simply reinvent the programme under a different name given the Constitutional Court's expressed concern for quality education to be available to all and for schools to cultivate a sense of national identity and pride, in particular via the use of *Bahasa Indonesia* as a medium of instruction.

The third area in which everyday actors have played an important role in contesting neoliberal education reform has been the national exam. On the one hand, NGO activists and nationalist intellectuals have been active in raising awareness about problems of cheating and corruption in the national exam through engagement with the media and publication of research and opinion on the topic (see, e.g., Ridho 2007; Arifin 2012; Darmaningtyas and Subkhan 2012: 168–214). On the other hand, a group of 58 parents and school children supported by activist lawyers from LBH Jakarta have pursued reform of the national exam through the court system. In 2006, they filed a citizens' lawsuit at the Central Jakarta District Court requesting that the government change various aspects of the exam and issue a public apology for failing to protect citizens' rights to education and children's rights, especially those of children who had failed the exam and were consequently unable to continue their education. In 2007, the Court ruled in their favour, forcing the government to appeal to the Jakarta High Court in 2008 (where it lost again) and then to the Supreme Court in 2009 (where it lost for a third time). The government continued to carry out the national exam in the aftermath of the Supreme Court decision, reflecting Supreme Court advice that it could do so legally because it had instituted various reforms to the exam in the years since the Jakarta District Court case began (Pratisto et al. 2009). But NGO and nationalist intellectual criticism of the national exam continued. Eventually, in May 2013, after widespread media coverage of delays and irregularities in that year's exam, the head of MoEC's research and development unit (*balitbang*), which was responsible for timely printing of the exam papers, resigned from his position and the government withdrew responsibility for managing the primary school exam from the National Education Standards Board (Jakarta Globe 2013; Radio Australia 2013). At the time of this writing (May 2013), it seemed that the government had decided to go

---

[20] See *Tempo English* (2013).
[21] See Mahkamah Konstitusi, Putusan Nomor 5/PUU-X/2012, pp. 189–195.

back to the drawing board in relation to the primary school exam and that it was considering not holding it altogether.

Conclusion

This chapter has shown that efforts by government technocrats and their donor supporters to promote neoliberal reform of the country's education system in the post–New Order period have been hotly contested with the result that the shift towards a more marketized education system has proceeded slowly. At the same time, it has suggested that this slowness has been due not just to resistance from predatory bureaucrats, populist politicians and other elite actors but also everyday actors such as parents, students, NGO activists and nationalist intellectuals. The latter have played an important role in the education policy-making process in large part because they have made effective use of the court system, especially the Constitutional Court. By taking key reform measures to court and winning, they have forced the government back to the policy drawing board on these issues and promoted a watering down of reform efforts. This activism and its effectiveness stand in marked contrast to the New Order period when everyday actors were almost entirely excluded from the policy-making process and the courts were entirely unreceptive to their interests and concerns. As such, the chapter provides evidence to support the view of those scholars who have argued that the fall of the New Order has ushered in an era of more inclusive policy-making even if it remains dominated, as Hadiz and others have argued, by elements nurtured under the New Order's predatory rule.

These findings have two broad implications for the way in which we analyse post–New Order politics. First, they suggest that scholars of Indonesian politics need to give greater attention to the role of everyday actors in the policy-making process. Studies of New Order politics focused overwhelmingly on elite actors in the military, bureaucracy, political parties, religious organizations and major corporations. Analysis of post–New Order politics has to a large extent continued in this mould. While everyday actors may play only a modest role in the policy-making process, they are nevertheless part of the story. Ignoring their role risks an incomplete and potentially misleading analysis. As Indonesia has shifted away from authoritarian rule towards consolidated democracy and as the economy has transitioned from economic crisis to solid growth, the issues at the centre of Indonesian politics have begun to change fundamentally. In particular, matters of social policy – health, education, water supply, sanitation and electricity – have become increasingly salient. Accordingly, we need to know more about how everyday actors mobilize around these issues and engage with the policy-making process.

Second, these findings also suggest that we need to give greater attention to the role of courts as a forum in which policy-making occurs. As a number of scholars have pointed out (e.g., Mietzner 2010; Butt 2012) and as the analysis here confirms, the Constitutional Court has clearly emerged as an important policy-making forum. But the national exams case suggests that even established courts can play an important role in this respect, including the Supreme Court, long considered to be government-dominated and unsympathetic to rights-related causes (Pompe 2005). Is the national exams case an anomaly, or are established courts now a viable means by which everyday actors can challenge government policy? If the latter, why have these courts changed their orientation?

We also need to understand better which everyday actors have access to the court system, under what conditions and on what terms. This is a concern that is raised again in Tan's discussion of domestic workers from Southeast Asia seeking legal redress in Hong Kong courts. For Indonesia, Mietzner (2010) and Butt (2012) have drawn attention to the importance of judicial activism within the Constitutional Court in ensuring rights-friendly judgements and the way this has been facilitated by the court's institutional design. At the same time, scholars associated with Leiden's Van Vollenhoven Institute have shown how justice-seekers' capacities and strategic judgements shape their choice of avenues through the legal repertoire (see, e.g., Berenschot et al. 2011). There is no doubt that judicial activism and accessible court design are important preconditions for rights-friendly court decisions, as is a certain degree of heroism on the part of justice-seekers. But other than via individual heroism, we know little about how rights-related cases make it to court in the first place. In particular, we need to know more about who has access to NGOs capable of launching and sustaining court cases, how these NGOs choose cases to support and how their ideological and political orientations shape their approaches to these cases. In general, we need to know more about the institutional arrangements that mediate access to courts, not just in Indonesia, and everyday actors' ability to participate in the policy-making process.

These analytical changes are needed not simply to enhance the quality of academic analysis for its own sake but also to enhance policy-making. This chimes in with Hobson and Seabrooke's (2007: 4) commitment to 'capture real world changes' as a core ambition of the Everyday Political Economy project. Political analysis is increasingly becoming an input into policy-making processes within international development organizations (Carothers and de Gramont 2013) and in relation to aid programmes to Indonesia in particular (Datta et al. 2011). Over the past few years, a number of donors have commissioned or carried out political economy studies of Indonesia's education sector. There is some evidence to suggest that these are promoting a rethink within donor circles about their approaches to development in this sector, particularly in relation to quality enhancement through teacher certification (see, e.g., Chang et al. 2014). Most of these organizations are formally committed to empowering the poor. To the extent that they are genuinely able to do this by enhancing poor peoples' participation in policy-making processes, it is important that they understand well the role of everyday actors in these processes and the scope and avenues for change.

References

Amelia, R. (2012) 'Angelina faces 20 years in jail as bribery trial begins', *Jakarta Globe*, 7 September.

Antlov, H. (2003) 'Not enough politics! Power, participation and the new order democratic polity in Indonesia', in E. Aspinall and G. Fealy (eds.) *Local Power and Politics in Indonesia: Decentralisation and Democratisation*. Singapore: Institute of Southeast Asian Studies, pp. 72–86.

Arifin, H. (ed.) (2012) *Buku Hitam Ujian Nasional*. Yogyakarta: Resist Book.

Aspinall, E. (2014) 'Health care and democratization in Indonesia', *Democratization* 21(5): 803–823.

Aspinall, E. and Warburton, E. (2013) 'A healthcare revolution in the regions', *Inside Indonesia* 111, January–March, www.insideindonesia.org/current-edition/a-healthcare-revolution-in-the-regions.

Auditan (nd) 'Mengenal Perkumpulan Auditan', www.antikorupsi.org/id.

Berenschot, W., Bedner, A., Laggut-Terre, E. and Novrianti, D. (2011) *Akses Terhadap Keadilan: Perjuangan Masyarakat Miskin dan Kurang Beruntung Untuk Menuntut Hak di Indonesia*. Jakarta: KITLV Jakarta.

Butt, S. (2012) 'Indonesia's constitutional court: conservative activist or strategic operator', in B. Dressel (ed.) *The Judicialization of Politics in Asia*. London: Routledge, pp. 98–116.

Carothers, T. and de Gramont, D. (2013) *Development Aid Confronts Politics: The Almost Revolution*. Washington, DC: Carnegie Endowment for International Peace.

Chang, M., Shaeffer, S., Al-Samarrai, S., Ragatz, A., de Ree, J. and Stevenson, R. (2014) *Teacher Reform in Indonesia: The Role of Politics and Evidence in Policy-making*. Washington, DC: World Bank.

Damarjati, D. (2013) *Mendikbud Belum Putuskan Status Sekolah Kategori Mandiri Pasca RSBI*. http://news.detik.com/read/2013/01/13/131732/2140683/10/mendikbud-belum-putuskan-status-sekolah-kategori-mandiri-pasca-rsbi.

Darmaningtyas and Subkhan, E. (2012) *Manipulasi Kebijakan Pendidikan*. Yogyakarta: Resist Book.

Darmaningtyas, Subkhan, E. and Fahmi-Panimbang (2009) *Tirani Kapital Dalam Pendidikan: Menolak UU BHP (Badan Hukum Pendidikan)*. Yogyakarta: Pustaka Yashiba and Damar Press.

Datta, A., Jones, H., Febriany V., Harris, D., Dewi R., Wild L. and Young J. (2011) *The Political Economy of Policy-making in Indonesia: Opportunities for Improving the Demand For and Use of Knowledge*. ODI Working Paper 340, London: Overseas Development Institute.

Department of National Education (2008) *Ikhtisar Data Pendidikan Nasional Tahun 2007/2008*. Jakarta: Department of National Education.

Hadiz, V. (2003) 'Reorganizing political power in Indonesia: a reconsideration of so-called 'democratic transitions', *Pacific Review* 16(4): 591–611.

(2010) *Localising Power in Post-Authoritarian Indonesia: A Southeast Asian Perspective*. Stanford: Stanford University Press.

Hadiz, V. and Robison, R. (2005) 'Neoliberal reforms and illiberal consolidations: the case of Indonesia', *Journal of Development Studies* 41(2): 220–241.

Hing, L. (1978) 'The Taman Siswa in Postwar Indonesia', *Indonesia* 25: 41–59.

Hobson, J. and Seabrooke, L. (eds.) (2007) *Everyday Politics of the World Economy*. Cambridge: Cambridge University Press.

Irawan, A. (2007) 'Ancaman RUU Badan Hukum Pendidikan', *Seputar Indonesia*, 18 September.

Irawan, A., Eriyanto, Djani, L. and Sunaryanto, A. (2004) *Mendagangkan Sekolah*. Jakarta: Indonesia Corruption Watch.

Jakarta Globe (2013) 'Education Ministry to Clean House after National Exam Fiasco', 13 May, www.thejakartaglobe.com/news/education-ministry-to-clean-house-after-national-exam-fiasco/.

Jakarta Post (2011) 'Minister "Has to Explain" BOS Delay', 4 April.

Jalal, F. and Mustafa, B. (2001) *Education Reform in the Context of Regional Autonomy: The Case of Indonesia*. Jakarta: MoEC and the World Bank.

Jurnal Nasional (2012) 'KPK Kaji Keterlibatan Rektor', 3 November, http://kpk.go.id/id/nukpk/id/berita/berita-sub/120-kpk-kaji-keterlibatan-rektor.

Klees, S. (2008) 'A quarter century of neoliberal thinking in education: misleading analyses and failed policies', *Globalisation, Societies and Education* 6(4): 311–348

Leigh, B. (1999) 'Learning and knowing boundaries: schooling in new order Indonesia', *Sojourn: Journal of Social Issues in Southeast Asia* 14(1): 34–56.

McLeod, R. (2000) 'Soeharto's Indonesia: a better class of corruption', *Agenda* 7(2): 99–112.

McVey, R. (1967) 'Taman Siswa and the Indonesian national awakening', *Indonesia* 4: 128–149.

Metrotvnews.com (2012) 'RSBI Cekik Leher Kelas Menengah ke Bawah', 7 April.

Mietzner, M. (2009) *Indonesia's 2009 Elections: Populism, Dynasties and the Consolidation of the Party System*. Sydney: Lowy Institute.

(2010) 'Political conflict resolution and democratic consolidation in Indonesia: the role of the Constitutional Court', *Journal of East Asian Studies* 10: 397–424.

(2013) 'Fighting the hellbounds: pro-democracy activists and party politics in Post-Suharto Indonesia', *Journal of Contemporary Asia* 43(1): 28–50.

Ministry of National Education (2005) *Strategic Plan: 2005–2009*. Jakarta: Ministry of National Education.

Moeliodihardjo, B., Wirakartakusumah, M. Aman, Benu, Agustinus, Wibisono, Kunto, Mochtar Mas'oed, Siswomihardjo, Ahmad, Muchtar, Setyawan, Palgunadi T. and Pusposutardjo, Suprodjo. (2001) 'New paradigm in higher education', in F. Jalal and B. Musthafa (eds.) *Education Reform in the Context of Regional Autonomy: The Case of Indonesia*. Jakarta: MoEC and the World Bank, pp. 164–281.

Nugroho, H. (2005) 'The political economy of higher education: the University as an Arena for the struggle for power', in V. Hadiz and D. Dhakidae (eds.) *Social Science and Power in Indonesia*. Singapore and Jakarta: ISEAS and Equinox, pp. 143–165.

Parlina, I. (2012) 'Angelina Sondakh: from beauty queen to suspect', *The Jakarta Post*, 2 April.

Pompe, S. (2005) *The Indonesian Supreme Court: A Study of Institutional Collapse.* Ithaca: Southeast Asia Program, Cornell University.

Pratisto S., Anthony and Turido, S. (2009) 'Guru Ditekan, Soal Ujian Bocor', *Gatra*, 9 December: 86–87.

Radio Australia (2013) 'Pemerintah Siapkan Format Baru UN Untuk Siswa SD', 16 May, www.radioaustralia.net.au/indonesian/2013-05-16/pemerintah-siapkan-format -baru-un-untuk-siswa-sd/1132028

Ridho, I. (ed.) (2007) *Menggugat Ujian Nasional.* Jakarta: Teraju.

Robison, R. and Hadiz, V. (2004) *Reorganising Power in Indonesia: The Politics of Oligarchy in an Age of Markets.* London: Routledge.

Rosser, A. and Curnow, J. (2014) 'Legal Mobilisation and Justice in Indonesia: Insights from the Struggle Over International Standard Schools', *The Asia-Pacific Journal of Anthropology* 15(4): 302-318.

Rosser, A. and Joshi, A. (2013) 'From user fee to fee free: the politics of realising universal free basic education in Indonesia', *Journal of Development Studies* 49(2):175–189.

Rosser, A., Roesad, K. and Edwin, D. (2005) 'Indonesia: the politics of inclusion', *Journal of Contemporary Asia* 35(1): 53–77.

Rosser, A. and Sulistiyanto, P. (2013) 'The politics of universal free basic education in Indonesia: insights from Yogyakarta', *Pacific Affairs* 86(3): 539–560.

Rosser, A. and Wilson, I. (2012) 'Democratic decentralisation and pro-poor policy reform in Indonesia: the politics of health insurance for the poor in Jembrana and Tabanan', *Asian Journal of Social Science* 40(5–6): 608–634.

Rosser, A., Wilson, I. and Sulistiyanto, P. (2011) 'Leaders, Elites and Coalitions: The Politics of Free Public Services in Decentralised Indonesia', DLP Research Report No. 16.

Sarasvati, D. (2012) 'The national examination and how it determines student futures: a case study through personal experience in working with children who failed the national examination', in H. Arifin (ed.) *Buku Hitam Ujian Nasional.* Yogyakarta: Resist Book, pp. 225–259.

Seputar Indonesia (2007) 'Pungli Marak di Sekolah Unggulan', 27 May. Setuningsih, N. (2012) 'KPK Calls University Heads in Investigation Linked to Angelina, Nazaruddin', *Jakarta Globe*, 21 June.

Surakhmad, W. (2007) 'Kriminalisasi Pendidikan', *Kompas*, 2 May. *Tempo English* (2013) 'Education Unplugged', 20 January: 26–30.

Tornquist, O., Priyono, A., Edwin, D., Samadhi, W., Pradjasto, A., Prabawati, D., Kariadi, S., Yulianto, O. and Widjaja, A. (2004) *Executive Report: 1st Round Study of the Problems and Options of Indonesian Democratisation.* www.asianettverket .uio.no/pdf04/Indonesia_demos_report.pdf.

Triaswati, N., Oey-Gardner, Mayling, Alisjahbana, Armida S., Elfindri, and Nazara, Suahasil. (2001) 'Financing education: implications for decentralization', in F. Jalal and B. Musthafa (eds.) *Education Reform in the Context of Regional Autonomy: The Case of Indonesia.* Jakarta: MoEC and the World Bank, pp. 33–130.

Umar, J. (2004) 'Pendidikan Nasional Dalam Ujian', *Media Indonesia*, 4 April and 5 May.

Wedhaswary, I. (2012) 'Kemdikbud Harus Evaluasi RSBI', *Kompas.com*, 4 January, http://tekno.kompas.com/read/2012/01/04/13395796/Kemdikbud.Harus.Evaluasi .RSBI

Winarti, A. (2008) 'State Schools Found Favoring Wealthier Students', *The Jakarta Post*, 27 June: 5.

World Bank (1997) *Indonesia: Sustaining High Growth with Equity*. Washington, DC: World Bank.

(1998) *Education in Indonesia: From Crisis to Recovery*. Washington, DC: World Bank.

(2004) *Education in Indonesia: Managing the Transition to Decentralization*. Washington, DC: World Bank.

(2005) 'Project Appraisal Document on a Proposed Loan in the Amount of US$50.00 million and a Proposed Credit of SDR19.85 million (US$30.00 million equivalent) to the Republic of Indonesia for a Managing Higher Education for Relevance and Efficiency Project', http://documents.worldbank.org/curated/en/2005/05/5816828/ indonesia-managing-higher-education-relevance-efficiency-project.

Part IV

People, Mobilities and Work

8   From Formal Employment to Street
     Vending: Malaysian Women's Labour
     Force Participation over the Life Course

Anja K. Franck

Introduction

Since gaining its independence from the United Kingdom in 1957, Malaysia has undergone rapid economic development. For Malaysian women, this development has also signified their large-scale entry into the formal labour force. Throughout the 1970s and 1980s, women in Malaysia entered waged employment, particularly within the manufacturing sector, in unprecedented numbers (Lim 1993). During these decades, female labour force participation rates increased dramatically (Noor 1999). However, despite the expansion of the economy, declining fertility rates (Razak 2011) and increased educational attainment of women (UN and Malaysia 2011), female labour force participation rates in Malaysia have never reached above 50 per cent (Fernandez 2011). In fact, World Bank data suggests that Malaysian women have the lowest participation rates in the entire Southeast Asian region.[1]

A closer examination of Malaysian labour force data reveals a strong 'one peaked pattern' (Horton 1996) of female labour force participation. This suggests that women tend to be active in the formal labour market when they are younger, but around the average age of marriage and childbirth, their participation rates decline quite rapidly. As a result, over half of the women of working age in Malaysia (4.9 million out of 9.4 million women) are found 'outside the labour force', with over three million stating 'housework' as their main reason not to enter waged work (Malaysia 2012: 15–6, 21). It is, however, highly unlikely that such a large share of women in Malaysia are 'housewives' – with no other income-earning activities. Instead, a more likely explanation is the lack of recognition for (Loh-Ludher 2007) and inadequate coverage of women's informal work in labour data (Franck 2012). This expectation, that women 'outside the labour force' continue to work informally, is also put forward in several official documents (see, e.g., Malaysia 2006: 290, 2012: 16). While official labour force data is generally agreed to provide inadequate coverage of women's

---

[1] This data can be accessed at data.worldbank.org/indicator/SL.TLF.CACT.FE.ZS/countries

work (Benería 1999; Chen 2001), it can nonetheless provide some indications regarding women's informal work – notably through the labour reported as own account and contributing family work. In the Malaysian case, such data shows that women seem to move from formal to informal types of work over the life course. This chapter engages with the fairly straightforward question: *Why?*

In approaching this question, it needs to be noted that *women* are clearly not a single category – in Malaysia or elsewhere. Instead, their identities intersect other structures of social hierarchy such as class, ethnicity, religion, locality, age and so on. The women in focus here largely belong to the Malaysian working class. They (mostly) lack higher education, and the majority used to work as machine operators in global factories or in low-skilled jobs in the tourism industry. Today, they run small-scale informal businesses in Penang's urban *kampungs* (villages). The majority are also Malay, and above forty years of age. In many aspects, the political economy of their everyday lives is situated at the intersection of the global and the local – between the development strategy pursued by government elites and the place-based gender power relations of their society. It is set at the interstices between the interests and practices of major (national as well as transnational) employers and alternative means of income earning – notably the presence of a large informal local economy. This chapter will focus on their labour market experiences and decisions. As such, the chapter directs attention towards the conditions under which women in Malaysia are able to access and sustain work during different periods in their lives. The objective here is, however, not only to provide empirical accounts of how the economic transformations in Malaysia over the past decades are 'played out' in the everyday lives of working-class women. Instead, adopting an Everyday Political Economy perspective, the chapter also suggests that people's actions are important for sustaining, contesting and reshaping economic processes (see Elias and Rethel in the introduction to this volume). And, as will be illustrated throughout this chapter, these women are not 'passive receivers' of elite economic policy but active agents whose everyday actions, strategies and decisions have an impact on the political economy (Hobson and Seabrooke 2007).

The first part of this chapter provides a brief overview of the feminization of export industry employment in Asia and women's work in the informal economy. Drawing from the latest Malaysian labour force survey (LFS) report (Malaysia 2012), the subsequent sections provide an overview of current labour market trends for women in Malaysia, before discussing women's experiences and decisions in the labour market.

The Feminization of Export Industry Employment

During the 1960s and 1970s, transnational corporations (TNCs) increasingly outsourced labour-intensive production to low-wage locations in the Global

South. In the Asian region, countries like South Korea, Taiwan, Hong Kong and Singapore, followed by Malaysia, Thailand and Indonesia, became preferential destinations. The initial stages of the export-oriented development model pursued in many of these countries rested upon the access to 'cheap' labour – and notably upon the access to 'cheap' *female* labour (Caraway 2007). However, the jobs created in these first stages were not made available to all segments of the female labour force. Instead, there has been a selective interest in hiring certain groups of women workers. In the Malaysian and Asian context, this has largely implied an interest in hiring young and unmarried women (Pearson 1998). Kabeer (2000: 5) describes how women became the ideal labour force in export industries 'on grounds which reflected an intersection of the "economics of demand" and the "culture of supply"'. This is important as it indicates that we can understand women's integration into these industries as reflecting a dialectic relationship between the interests and workings of capital and gender place-based power relations. A whole array of studies have shown how the feminization of factory work has been facilitated by discourses around young (Asian/oriental/Southern) women as 'particularly suitable' for assembly-type work because of their 'nimble fingers' (Elson and Pearson 1981), docility, discipline, non-militancy and patience with monotonous work (Chant and McIlwaine 1995; Ong 2010). The poor labour conditions for women workers in these factories – where full-time and secure forms of employment have increasingly been replaced with insecure, casual and informal types of work (Standing 1999) – have further been justified by ideas around women's waged work as 'secondary' to their 'main' (read: reproductive) duties (Blomqvist 2004). Whereas governments actively utilized gender-based stereotypes in attracting TNC activities (Kaur 2000; Ng et al. 2006), Elias (2005) points out that multinationals themselves also took an active part in shaping the emergence of a low-waged and feminized labour force in receiving countries.[2]

Beyond highlighting the conditions of work in export industries, the above studies have made an important contribution to the understanding of how different groups of women are encouraged or discouraged to engage in waged labour during different periods in time (Basvalent and Onaran 2004). An Everyday Political Economy perspective offers the opportunity to take this analysis one step further through the suggestion that *the struggles and actions* of working women influence broader political economic processes. In this chapter, this is made visible through a focus upon women's decisions to leave export industry work – and opt for work in the informal economy.

---

[2] Studies of feminization have been much preoccupied with low-skilled factory work. However, women (in Malaysia and other parts of the Asia-Pacific) are also increasingly engaged in work in trade-related services (notably the tourism industry), which characteristically display a similar demand for young and temporary female labor (ILO 2001).

The Informal Economy

Contrary to early accounts of the informal economy, in which it was expected to diminish and be formalized in the phase of modernization and development (Benería and Floro 2005), informal work remains a permanent and growing feature of the global economy. In fact, the informal economy (especially in developing and emerging economies) plays a key role in employment creation, production and income generation (OECD 2002) – and has a particularly important role for the everyday lives of women (ADB and ILO 2011). Informal workers are engaged in a wide range of occupations, in both informal *and* formal enterprises within and outside the agricultural sector (Chen 2007). They can be casual and temporary workers, employees, own account, unpaid family and home-based workers. While 'precarious work' can be identified through its uncertain, unpredictable and risky nature from the view of workers (Kalleberg 2009), 'informal work' is characterized by its lack of legal recognition, regulation and protection (Lloyd-Evans 2008). The two are, however, inherently connected as the increase in precarious types of work (regulated, semi-regulated or unregulated) in the formal economy (Standing 1999) influences the ongoing 'informalization' of formal economy work (Pearson 2007) as well as the increasing mobility of workers between the formal and informal economy. Given these trends, studies suggest that the traditional approach towards the formal and informal economy as two separate spheres fails to capture the way in which the formal and informal economies have evolved (Chant and Pedwell 2008). Chen (2007), therefore, proposes that we approach the relationship between the two as a continuum of economic relations.

While employment 'precariarity' is linked to loss of job security and diminishing opportunities to obtain or sustain employment (Standing 1999), studies of the informal economy have also received criticism for its depiction of informal work as merely resulting from poverty, oppression or 'the product of involuntary exclusion' from the formal labor market (Williams and Gurtoo 2011: 5). Several studies have, however, pointed out that women enter informal work for a wide variety of reasons, including increased autonomy, flexible working hours, the possibility to balance home and work responsibilities, proximity to economic activities, dissatisfaction with conditions and wages in formal jobs (Franck 2011b, 2012; Jütting et al. 2008). Acknowledging this does not deny that the work they perform – in both the formal and informal economy – is framed and often restricted by norms and practices around women's work and mobility, access to resources and disproportionate responsibility for reproductive work (Franck 2011b). It does, however, award women informal workers *agency* in the global economy – their actions and decisions have a significant outcome for the broader economic development (for more on the need to include labour and the agency of workers in International Political

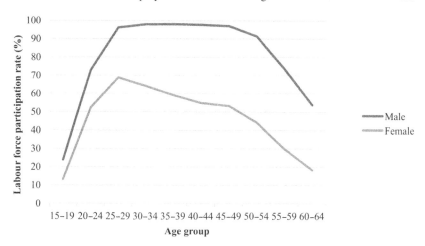

Figure 8.1 Female and male labour force participation rates by age (2011). *Source*: LFS report, Malaysia (2012: 25).

Economy [IPE] analysis, see Herod 2007). Precariarity is, however, relevant for such reasoning as it can feed into our understanding of why women decide to opt for informal rather than formal work.

Women's Labour Force Participation in Malaysia

The export-oriented development model pursued in Malaysia since the early 1970s has been strongly associated with a feminization of manufacturing labour. Female shares of manufacturing labour increased steadily between the 1970s and the 1990s (Malaysia 1990) and were particularly high in export industries such as electronics, textiles and clothing (Ahmad 1998). While there has since been a decline in women's share, manufacturing remains the largest industry of employment for women in Malaysia, accounting for around 18 per cent of women's total employment (Malaysia 2012: 80). Other important industries of employment are wholesale and retail trade, education, accommodation, food and beverage, service activities, and agriculture, forestry and fishing.

As illustrated in Figure 8.1, female labour force participation in Malaysia shows a distinct one-peaked pattern (Horton 1996). Male participation, on the other hand, plateaus around 90 per cent for most of men's working lives. Due to the increased educational attainment of women and delayed age of marriage, the peak in female participation has shifted from the age group of 20–24 in 1990 to the current 25–29 age group (UNDP and Malaysia 2015). However, there is still a permanent decline in women's participation around the average age of marriage and first child. While the need to facilitate the reentry of women to the labour force after childbirth through provisions of childcare facilities is emphasized in the latest Malaysia Plans (2006–10, 2011–15), progress remains slow. According to Pillai (2011: 30), only 1 per cent of children aged 0–4 years in Malaysia are enrolled in registered childcare centres. In terms of fulfilling the promises of childcare, the Malaysian government's greatest response has been to liberalize the market for foreign domestic workers (Elias 2009). However, hiring a domestic worker, although their wages are (appallingly) low, is largely impossible for Malaysian working-class families. The potentially positive relationship between the systems of overseas domestic worker employment and women's possibilities to work outside the home is, therefore, restricted to the middle and upper classes. Apart from that, questions can certainly be raised regarding the conditions and rights of foreign domestic workers in Malaysia, as is discussed in more detail in the chapter by Elias and Louth in this volume.

Another visible characteristic in the labour force data is that Chinese women have higher participation rates (averaging at around 50 per cent) relative to Malay and Indian women (where the rate is 46.5 and 43.4 per cent, respectively). There is, however, need for caution in making generalized assumptions around how ethnicity (and religion) intersects with women's engagement with waged labour. While Malay (and thus Muslim) women are often portrayed as the least likely to work, the LFS data indicates that it is, in fact, Indian women who have the lowest labour force participation rates. Further, while the role of Malay women has no doubt been influenced by Islamization projects in Malaysia (see Ong 1990; Stivens 2006), their roles as *economic agents* can be situated at the intersection of Islam and Malay culture. Despite a strong male breadwinner norm, Malay women have historically played an active role in the economy of families, communities and society (Lie and Lund 1994: 32), and studies indicate that Islam provides both an incentive as well as a restriction with regard to Malay women's income earning (Yusof 2010). Finally, as Figure 8.2 shows, all three main ethnic groups have a similar one-peaked pattern of participation, with high participation rates in the younger age groups followed by a permanent decline. We should, therefore, not downplay the challenges faced also by Chinese and Indian women when it comes to combining work and family.

As indicated above, the work–family relationship needs to be further examined at the intersection with class. If we use educational attainment as a proxy for socioeconomic class, we find that women with tertiary education have significantly higher labour force participation rates (59.4 per cent) – relative to those with secondary (45.7 per cent), primary (40.5 per cent) or no formal education (36.6 per cent). Using occupational categories, the pattern revealed is that the highest skilled occupations, such as managers, do not exhibit the same one-peaked pattern as can be seen among, for example, plant and machine

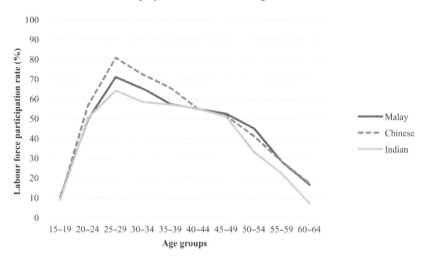

Figure 8.2 Female labour force participation rates by age and ethnicity (2011). *Source*: LFS report, Malaysia (2012: 28).

operators or service and sales workers (Malaysia 2012: 77). Women with higher education, therefore, have a higher labour force participation rate and those in higher skilled professions seem to be better able to sustain these over the life course. An important explanation for this is likely that women in the upper and middle classes are better able to negotiate the work–family relationship – for example, they are better able to access and afford different types of childcare. However, the age composition of the key industries of employment for women in Malaysia shows great variation. While women in the lower income groups work in occupations which typically have a young composition of the labour force, they also work in industries where the pattern is different. Figure 8.3, for example, illustrates the age composition of the female labour force in manufacturing and agriculture. It shows that while manufacturing work is associated with a strong peak at the age group of 25–29, agricultural work peaks at the age group of 45–49.

The reversed one-peaked pattern in agriculture is related to employment status. In agriculture there is a high share of women in unpaid family work, which is typically associated with informal employment relationships. Moreover, *own account* and *unpaid family work* are often used as a proxy for informal work. However, note that this represents an underestimation of women's total informal work given the large number of informal workers also found in the category *employees* (ILO 2007) and women's tendency to not report informal work in labour force surveys (Franck and Olsson 2014). Figure 8.4 shows the status of employment in Malaysia by age and illustrates that women seem to move

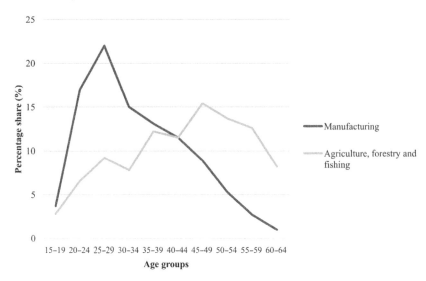

Figure 8.3 Age composition of the female workforce by sector (2011). *Source*: LFS report, Malaysia (2012: 96).

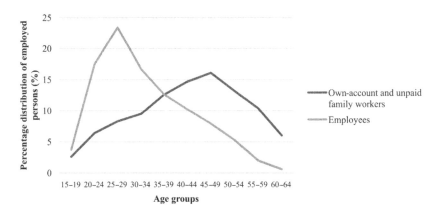

Figure 8.4 Women employees and own account and unpaid family workers by age. *Source*: LFS report, Malaysia (2012: 110).

from formal to informal employment over the life course. Importantly, however, it also illustrates that the pattern which emerges is no longer one-peaked. Therefore, while previous scholarship has emphasized that if the magnitude of women's informal work was fully covered in the data this would increase women's share of informal workers *and* the total workforce (Chen et al. 1999: 604), this chapter suggests that, in the Malaysian case, it would also alter the pattern of participation from a strong one-peak to more of a two-peaked pattern of participation.

I conducted the fieldwork for this chapter in the state of Penang between 2009 and 2011. The purpose of the fieldwork was to study the continuum of formal and informal work among Malaysian women. I, therefore, set out to interview women who were currently engaged in the informal economy regarding their labour market experiences and decisions. In an attempt to find women informal workers in a public and accessible location, women who worked in and around Penang's local markets (hawkers and street vendors) were approached. After conducting a small pilot study, eighty interviews were conducted with women in four main locations in Penang Island, as well as a group in a small mainland town, Bukit Mertanjam.

The interviews were semi-structured using an interview guide which contained (apart from basic data such as the respondents' age and education level, etc.) open-ended questions around work life history, labour market decisions, the work–family relationship, current status of employment and conditions of work. Among the respondents, fifty-two are Malay and the remaining are Chinese (fifteen), Indian (seven) and migrant (six). The majority were also above forty years of age. The majority (fifty-four women) had some form of secondary education, nineteen women had primary education, five had no formal schooling and one had higher education. Although all of the women interviewed are engaged in small-scale informal businesses (in markets, food-courts, streets or homes), they occupy different employment categories. Around 69 per cent were *own account workers*, followed by *employee*, *employer* and *unpaid family worker*.

Previous Labour Market Experiences

Conclusive with official data on women's labour force participation in Malaysia, a common feature in the stories told by the women in Penang was that they had left waged employment in the formal economy at a relatively young age – around the time of marriage and first child. As revealed in Table 8.1, the vast majority had, prior to marriage, held employment in manufacturing and services, most commonly in factories, hotels and restaurants. Around 25 per cent of the respondents stated that they had previously not held formal employment. Among this latter group, the majority had, however, previously worked in the informal economy and only a very limited number (five) stated that they had no previous experience from remunerative activities at all. For Malay women, in particular those above the age of 50, manufacturing had been the most important industry of employment, while services had been the most important for women below the age of 40. This is consistent with the way that services have increased its importance to the Malaysian economy (Ng 2010).

Table 8.1 *Previous labour market experience of respondents by ethnicity*

	Agriculture	Manufacturing	Services[a]	No formal experience	Total
Malay	0	23	20	9	52
Chinese	1	2	6	6	15
Indian	1	3	1	2	7
Migrant	0	1	2	3	6
Total	2	29	29	20	80

[a] Using the UN-based International Standard Industrial Classification system, services include construction, trade, transport, professional business services and public services.

The women were asked to specify why they had left their former jobs. The question was open-ended, but four main factors were detectible from their answers.[3] The most common was 'marriage and childbirth'. Many women simply exclaimed 'I got married!' as a response to the question of why they left their former jobs. However, when asked why marriage made them leave, it became clear that this answer instead implied: I got married – hence I had a baby.[4] Secondary factors were 'retrenchments' and 'disliked the conditions in the former job'.[5] Both of these were largely related to conditions of work in export industries (i.e., factories and hotels). Some of the women in these two categories had left work involuntarily (although they had been offered a so-called *voluntary* retrenchment), while others had made their own decision to leave. Not seldom, the latter was the simultaneous effect of marriage, child-birth and (unsustainable, precarious) labour conditions. In other words, once the women got married and/or had children, the conditions of work were experienced as incompatible with their roles as wives and/or mothers. For some women this was linked to the low wages; for others it was the shift work and long working days (including compulsory overtime). However, as will be discussed later, an issue that stood out – both for women's decisions to leave as well as for their ability and willingness to reenter formal work – was the impact of locational patterns of export industries to special zones or areas. In many cases, the work–family conflict experienced in formal types of employment had been resolved by the woman resigning from her job to, at a later stage, work informally in closer proximity to the house. Although the income earned from informal activities varied significantly, very few women seemed to view

---

[3] It should be noted that these categories represent my interpretation of how their statements could be categorized.

[4] Marriage and children have, therefore, been treated as one factor here, although it needs to be noted that not all married women had children.

[5] Apart from the factors named here as reasons for leaving previous employment, individual or several women also stated: wanted to try making a business, retirement, 'take care of other family members' and migration.

'not working' as a feasible option. Their labour market decision was, therefore, not one of 'working' versus 'not working' (Pearson 2007) but rather one of 'working in the formal waged labour force' versus 'working in the informal economy'. Among this group of women, the latter had clearly prevailed. In the following sections, I will look at some of the reasons why.

The Decision to Not Reengage with Formal Work but to Opt for Informal Work

Of central importance to why many women did not regard a (re)entry to formal employment as a feasible option was the difficulties associated with being a working mother (and/or wife). This is summarized quite clearly by one Chinese respondent: 'I have no time to work! And even if I did, who is going to take care of the children?' This chapter, therefore, constitutes no departure from the general agreement that there is a lack of fit between the demands of the family and institutional support offered to working women in Malaysia (Abdullah et al. 2008). There seemed to be a sort of general agreement among the women that factory or hotel work was their only available option in terms of formal work. This is not surprising considering that employment in manufacturing and hotels and restaurants accounts for close to 50 per cent of women's total employment in Penang (Malaysia 2012: 210) – and for those who lack higher education, this share is most likely even higher. Work–family conflicts are experienced by women in all sectors of employment, especially in lower income families who have a more limited access to childcare facilities. However, there are conditions associated with work in trade-related industries in Penang which make such industries inaccessible and/or undesirable for many working mothers. From the interview material, it is possible to detect three key (although interrelated) factors relating to why they would not pursue formal work: unwillingness or inability to handle working conditions, the place/location of workplaces and gendered (spatial) norms.

Conditions of Work

While working conditions in export industries are diverse (depending on skill levels and so on), for the respondents of this study employment in such industries was associated with both a temporary and precarious nature. Many of the women, for example, stated with certainty that they were far too old to be hired already around the age of 40 – and sometimes even younger (see also Franck 2011a). While the practices of hiring young women in factories have been well documented (Ng et al. 2006), a number of women commented that hotels in Penang applied similar practices. One woman, for example, laughingly explained that after childbirth she was no longer beautiful enough to work at the front desk in a hotel. While she stated this with a certain degree of sarcasm, it was clear that age was an important factor wherein many believed they were no longer 'hireable'.

Apart from the hiring practices of employers, the actual labour conditions in these industries were continuously brought up during the interviews. Both factory and hotel jobs involve shift work, and several women commented that the long shifts were both physically and mentally straining. One former electronics factory worker, for example, stated: 'It's terrible to work in a factory! You work twelve hours and you have to stand up for twelve hours!' For most women, however, the biggest challenge when it came to shift work was the difficulties it produces for balancing work and family. Another concern for some women was the way that basic wages in factories and hotels were set at a too low level, requiring workers to rely on tips, commissions or overtime pay to make a decent salary. Several women with experience of factory work had, therefore, been forced to take up informal work to make ends meet. A related issue to that of the low (and unsecure) wages was the issue of jobs security. The many recent retrenchments from factories and hotels in Penang made some women cautious to return to such jobs. As an informal employee in a wedding shop, one of the respondents had an average income of RM 480 (around US$ 150) per month. Prior to being retrenched from a factory, she had earned roughly double that amount (RM 980), yet she perceived the informal job as more *secure* compared to returning to factory work: 'It's not that I don't want to [work in a factory again]. I am just afraid that the same thing might happen again and that they [the factory] would shut down too.' Precarious working conditions in the formal economy thus influenced the decision to opt for informal work. Finally, a number of women also made reference to the hierarchy in formal workplaces, and several of the more elderly women commented that they found being shouted at and corrected by the younger management uncomfortable and even shameful. By contrast, own account work granted freedom from abusive employers and thus provided a greater sense of freedom.

Place/Location of Formal and Informal Jobs

An issue which kept resurfacing during the interviews was the geographical distance to formal jobs. Several women responded to the open-ended question of whether they would like to have a formal job by stating that they did not want to 'go that far'. The explanation for this is likely that they equated the question of 'formal jobs' with 'factory' or 'hotel' jobs, as they saw this as the only feasible jobs for them. As in many other places in Asia, a defining feature of export industry manufacturing in Malaysia is the geographic concentration of production in export processing or industrial zones. In Penang, the export processing zone (the Bayan Lepas) is located in the southern part of the island

and the industrial estates located in the mainland area around Butterworth. Hotels are, on the other hand, concentrated along the northern coastline and in the urban centre George Town.

For the women interviewed for this study (apart from those living in the main tourist resort of Batu Ferringhi), all required considerable commuting time as well as access to transportation. Among the respondents, less than 50 per cent of the women had access to their own vehicle (motorbike or car), and some also expressed concerns around travelling on public transportation on their own. For others, prevailing norms around married women's mobility were an even bigger concern, and several women stated that their husbands did not find it appropriate for them to travel alone to work in places outside the home or village. The geographic concentration of export industries in special zones or areas has gained much scholarly attention (particularly within my own academic discipline, economic geography: see, e.g., Dicken 2011). Such studies have emphasized the advantages of geographic concentration to producers and buyers, but have paid scant attention to the outcome for the (predominantly female) workforce. Based on the findings of this chapter, it can, however, be argued that while the geographic concentration of activities may suit the needs of employers and consumers, it effectively restricts many women's ability to sustain such employment over the life course.

As a central difference, informal employment can be accessed in close proximity to the home, and for women without access to transportation or childcare, this provides a clear incentive to engage with such work. Among the respondents of this study, the vast majority (close to 90 per cent) lived within walking distance to their current place of work. This allowed the women to uphold their family obligations while securing access to their own income. As stated by one woman: 'If you work in a factory you will spend less time with your children. When you are here [in the market] you have time with the children. If you are here you can come and you are close by.' Some also mentioned the advantage of being 'free' as a self-employed worker where working time could be adjusted according to the needs of their families, such as following school opening hours and having the possibility to stay home with sick children.

Normative Constructions around Gender, Work and Place

As illustrated in several examples above, the reproductive roles awarded to women had a significant impact upon their decisions to leave and not reenter formal work. For the most part, this decision was their own. However, there were also women who stated that it was a decision taken by the husband or another family member. As married women, regardless of previous experiences in the labour market, the respondents were largely expected to conform to traditional gendered roles within the household. This was visible in the stories of women of all ethnicities, although some of the Malay women were articulate that this was in accordance with their religion (i.e., according to Islam). It was also among Malay women that the answer 'my husband won't let me work anymore' featured in the most straightforward manner. While this answer was in many cases related to the 'housewife-norm', the unwillingness of husbands to let the wife uphold formal work was in many cases also directly linked to the way that childcare was unavailable, unaffordable or not perceived as trustworthy. As stated by this former factory worker:

I want to work but my husband won't let me anymore! I have to look after the baby. It's not worth it if you send them to the baby sitter. For one child it costs RM400 and for two it's RM800! You work and you get 1200 and then you give 800 to the sitter! Maybe at 600 it would be worth it.

Without access to affordable and dependable childcare, it was difficult for many women to make it a plausible option that they should leave the home (or village/community) for waged employment. Many of the respondents had, therefore, stayed at home until their children had reached school age and then opted for informal work which, in their own as well as their husband's view, provided better opportunities to combine earning an income with their roles as mothers. Among the women, there were significant differences in how they perceived decision making within the household as well as the way in which they handled the restrictions it placed on their ability to leave the home for public remunerative work. Some women stated that they accepted the man as the decision maker in the family because this was in accordance with Malay culture or Muslim beliefs. In other cases, the women expressed discontent with the way that the husband took on the role of decision maker – or the way that he had enforced his decisions. One woman, who was now a widow, stated that her husband had not let her work, adding: 'In the past we were stupid! When the husband didn't like it then we didn't argue or fight back … My husband didn't want me to work [because] he was jealous. He wouldn't even let me out of the house. In modern times this doesn't happen.'

Interestingly, while some women faced resistance from husbands and families with regard to formal work, informal work performed in closer proximity to the home was largely perceived as acceptable by their families. This finding is consistent with the argument made by Loh-Ludher (2007) that the work women do in the informal economy is constructed – by the women themselves as well as by their families – as something of an extension of their domestic work. However, this chapter contributes two further points to this argument. The first is that women themselves actively participate in such constructions, not due to 'victimization' but as a way to secure self-interest. Asked about their job title, a number of women stated that they were 'housewives' who did not 'really work'. Describing their informal work as 'non-work' may be interpreted as a way to minimize and domesticate the work women perform (Domosh and Seager 2001). However, it could also be that women use these titles as a means to (re)negotiate and extend their room to manoeuvre. By labelling their own working activities as 'just helping out' or 'for pocket money only', they are, in other words, seemingly complying to the male breadwinner norm while at the same time securing their own access to remunerative activities both within and outside the household. As such, it could also be viewed as a covert form of everyday resistance. Second, when markets or street-vending sites become constructed as 'female' spaces, they also become considered 'safe places' for women to work in. To several women, where work outside the household was inaccessible or even unacceptable by the husband or other family members, the market area represented an *accessible* and *acceptable* public place of work – a place 'in-between' traditional Western notions of public and the private space (Yasmeen 2006). As such, informal work not only represents an important economic activity, but it is also a means by which women can renegotiate their access to public places of work.

Conclusion

There is no doubt that the export-oriented development model pursued in Malaysia has been successful in terms of creating economic growth and employment. But, it has not been equally successful when it comes to sustaining women's long-term engagement in the labour force. Instead, as is clearly illustrated by the official data, women's formal labour force participation is transitory, with many leaving the formal labour market at a relatively young age. As women leave formal employment, they tend to go statistically 'missing' from the official labour force data. However, the introduction to this chapter raised doubts regarding the accuracy of the labour force data, as many women in Malaysia continue to work informally although their labour may not be reported in the LFS. This study, therefore, proposes that while women's formal labour force participation has one peak (Horton 1996), women's full work participation over the life course can be more accurately described as two-peaked.

Approaching women's work as a continuum of formal and informal work is not foreign to contemporary scholarship (see Chen 2007). This chapter enhances knowledge around *why* this pattern occurs. Previous literature around the feminization of export industry employment has made important contributions in terms of highlighting the conditions of work for women in these industries. This chapter has, however, attempted to show how these conditions influence women's own decisions to uphold or leave formal work. The interviews showed that export industry employment (typically in factories and hotels) exhibits distinct characteristics (such as shift work, low and insecure wages, a preference for young women workers and the geographic concentration of activities in special zones or areas) which makes it difficult or undesirable for women to sustain after marriage and childbirth. The interviews also revealed that for many women the move from formal to informal work was a deliberate choice, one which reflected women's unwillingness to (re)engage in exploitative work in the formal economy, on the one hand, and the desire for more freedom and flexibility in order to meet their double role as breadwinners and mothers, on the other. Informal work also enabled them to secure access to income and public places of work in spite of norms that suggest that they are not 'supposed to' work outside the home.

The above findings provide an illustration of how the elitist economic development project in Malaysia over the past six decades plays out within the everyday lives of working-class women. However, the chapter also illustrates the need for perspectives which recognize that the actions of ordinary people have ramifications for the international political economy (Hobson and Seabrooke 2007). Such perspectives reveal that women workers are not just passive receivers. Instead, as they find the conditions of formal work incompatible with their everyday lives, they act to find income-generating activities elsewhere. The fact that so many working-class women – upon whose backs the export growth of the Malaysian economy has been built (Ng et al. 2006) – opt out of the formal labour market has implications beyond the household and local community. Instead, as the Malaysian government increasingly recognizes, the low female labour force participation rates represent a problem. This is so not only in terms of the underutilization of resources but also because it hampers economic growth and development. As such, the everyday actions and strategies of women workers are inherently related to the international political economy.

References

Abdullah, K., Noor, N. M., and Wok, S. (2008) 'The perception of women's roles and progress: A study of Malay women', *Social Indicators Research* 89(3): 439–455.

ADB and ILO (2011) *Women and Labour Markets in Asia: Rebalancing for Gender Equality*. Bangkok: International Labour Organization and Asian Development Bank.

Ahmad, A. (1998) *Women in Malaysia: Country Briefing Paper*. Manila: Asian Development Bank, http://www.adb.org/documents/women-malaysia-country-briefing-paper

Basvalent, C. and Onaran, Ö. (2004) 'The effect of export-oriented growth on female labor market outcomes in Turkey', *World Development* 32(8): 1375–1393.

Benería, L. (1999) 'The enduring debate over unpaid labour', *International Labour Review* 138(3): 287–309.

Benería, L. and Floro, M. (2005) 'Distribution, gender, and labour market informalization: A conceptual framework with a focus on homeworkers', in Kudva and

Benería (eds.) *Rethinking Informalization: Poverty, Precarious Jobs and Social Protection*. Ithaca: Internet-First University Press, pp. 9–27.

Blomqvist, G. (2004) *Gender discourses at work: export industry workers and construction workers Chennai, Tamil Nadu, India*. PhD Dissertation, Department of Peace and Development Research, Gothenburg University, Gothenburg.

Caraway, T. L. (2007) *Assembling Women: The Feminization of Global Manufacturing*. New York: Cornell University Press.

Chant, S. and McIlwaine, C. (1995) 'Gender and export manufacturing in the Philippines: Continuity or change in female employment', *Gender, Place and Culture* 2(2): 147–176.

Chant, S. and Pedwell, C. (2008) *Women, Gender and the Informal Economy: An Assessment of ILO Research and Suggested Ways Forward*. Geneva: ILO.

Chen, M. A. (2001) 'Women in the informal sector: A global picture, the global movement', *SAIS Review* 21(1): 71–82.

(2007) *Rethinking the Informal Economy: Linkages with the Formal Economy and the Formal Regulatory Environment*. DESA Working Paper No. 46, ST/ESA/2007/DWP/46.

Chen, M. A., Sebstad, J. and O'Connell, L. (1999) 'Counting the invisible workforce: The case of homebased workers', *World Development* 27(3): 603–610.

Dicken, P. (2011) *Global Shift: Mapping the Changing Contours of the World Economy*, 6th edition. London: Sage.

Domosh, M. and Seager, J. (2001) *Putting Women in Place: Feminist Geographers Make Sense of the World*. London and New York: Guilford Press.

Elias, J. (2005) 'Stitching-up the labour market: Recruitment, gender and ethnicity in the multinational firm', *International Feminist Journal of Politics* 7(3): 90–111.

(2009) 'Gendering liberalisation and labour reform in Malaysia: Fostering "competitiveness" in the productive and reproductive economies', *Third World Quarterly* 30(3): 469–483.

Elson, D. and Pearson, R. (1981) 'Nimble fingers make cheap workers', *Feminist Review* 7(Spring): 87–107.

Fernandez, J. (2011) 'Gender differentials in the Malaysian labour market', in C. Ng, N. Endut and R. Shuib (eds.) *Gender Studies: A Malaysian Reader*. Penang: USM Press, pp. 107–125.

Franck, A. K. (2011a) '"I am too old! Who is going to give me a job?" Women Hawkers in Teluk Bahang, Penang, Malaysia', *Journal of Workplace Rights* 15(1): 111–132.

(2011b) 'Factors motivating women's informal micro-entrepreneurship: Experiences from Penang, Malaysia', *International Journal of Gender and Entrepreneurship* 4(1): 65–78.

(2012) *From Formal Employment to Street Vending: Women's Room to Maneuver and Labor Market Decisions under Conditions of Export-Orientation – the Case of Penang, Malaysia*. PhD Dissertation, Department of Human and Economic Geography, University of Gothenburg, Series B, No. 121.

Franck, A. K. and Olsson, J. (2014) 'Missing women? The under-recording and under-reporting of women's work in Malaysia', *International Labour Review* 153(2): 209–222.

Herod, A. (2007) 'The agency of labour in global change: Reimagining the spaces and scales of trade union praxis within a global economy', in Hobson and Seabrooke (eds.) *Everyday Politics of the World Economy*. Cambridge: Cambridge University Press, pp. 27–44.

Hobson, J. M. and Seabrooke, L. (eds.) (2007) *Everyday Politics of the World Economy*. New York: Cambridge University Press.

Horton, S. (1996) 'Women and industrialization in Asia: Overview', in S. Horton (ed.) *Women and Industrialization in Asia*. London and New York: Routledge, pp. 1–42.

ILO (2001) *Human Resources Development, Employment and Globalization in the Hotel, Catering and Tourism Sector*. Geneva: ILO.

(2007) *Labour and Social Trends in ASEAN 2007: Integration, Challenges and Opportunities*. Bangkok: ILO Regional Office for Asia and the Pacific.

Jütting, J., Parlevliet, J. and Xenogiani, T. (2008) *Informal Employment Re-loaded*. OECD Development Centre Working Paper No. 266, OECD Development Centre, Paris.

Kabeer, N. (2000) *The Power to Choose: Bangladeshi Women and Labour Market Decisions in London and Dhaka*. London and New York: Verso.

Kalleberg, A. L. (2009) 'Precarious work, insecure workers: Employment relations in transition', *American Sociological Review* 74(1): pp. 1–22.

Kaur, A. (2000) 'Working on the global conveyor belt: Women workers in industrialising Malaysia', *Asian Studies Review* 24(2): 213–230.

Lie, M. and Lund, R. (1994) *Renegotiating Local Values: Working Women and Foreign Industry in Malaysia*. Richmond: Curzon Press.

Lim, L. L. (1993) 'The feminization of labour in the Asia-Pacific rim countries: From contributing to economic dynamism to bearing the brunt of structural adjustments', in N. Ogawa, G. W. Jones and J. G. Williamson (eds.) *Human Resources in Development along the Asia-Pacific Rim*. New York: Oxford University Press, pp. 175–209.

Lloyd-Evans, S. (2008) 'Geographies of the contemporary informal sector in the global south: Gender, employment relationships and social protection', *Geography Compass* 2(6): 1885–1906.

Loh-Ludher, L. (2007) 'Homeworkers online: Utilization of ITC for home-based work in Malaysia', *The Electronic Journal of Information Systems in Developing Countries* 32(5): 1–14.

Malaysia (1990) *Sixth Malaysia Plan 1990–1995*. Kuala Lumpur: Government of Malaysia.

(2006) *Ninth Malaysia Plan 2006–2010*. Putrajaya: Department of Statistics Malaysia.

(2012) *Labour Force Survey Report Malaysia, 2011*. Putrajaya: Department of Statistics Malaysia.

Ng, C. (2010) *Gender Equality and Women's Rights: Analysis for Action*. Report submitted to the United Nations Country Team Malaysia.

Ng, C., Mohamad M. and Beng Hui, T. (2006) *Feminism and the Women's Movement in Malaysia: An Unsung (R)evolution*. Oxon and New York: Routledge.

Noor, N. M. (1999) 'Roles and women's well-being: Some preliminary findings from Malaysia', *Sex Roles* 41(3/4): 123–145.

OECD (2002) *Measuring the Non-Observed Economy: A Handbook*. Paris: OECD.

Ong, A. (1990) 'State versus Islam: Malay families, women's bodies, and the body politics of Malaysia', *American Ethnologist* 17(2): 258–276.

(2010) *Spirits of Resistance and Capitalist Discipline: Factory Women in Malaysia*, 2nd edition. Albany: State University Press of New York.

Pearson, R. (1998) '"Nimble fingers" revisited: Reflections on women and third world industrialization in the late twentieth century', in C. Jackson and R. Pearson (eds.) *Feminist Visions of Development: Gender Analysis and Policy*. London and New York: Routledge, pp. 171–188.

(2007) 'Reassessing paid work and women's empowerment: Lessons from the global economy', in A. Cornwall, E. Harrison and A. Whitehead (eds.) *Feminisms in Development: Contradictions, Contestations and Challenges*. London and New York: Zed Books, pp. 201–213.

Pillai, V. G. A. (2011) 'The changing family dynamics in Malaysia and its effects on children', in A. M. Baginda (ed.) *Social Development in Malaysia*. Kuala Lumpur: Malaysian Strategic Resource Centre, pp. 25–47.

Razak, R. A. (2011) 'Malaysia demographics: Overview and prospects', in A. M. Baginda (ed.) *Social Development in Malaysia*. Kuala Lumpur: Malaysian Strategic Resource Centre, pp. 1–23.

Standing, G. (1999) 'Global feminization through flexible labor: A theme revisited', *World Development* 27(3): 583–602.

Stivens, M. (2006) '"Family values" and Islamic revival: Gender, rights and state moral projects in Malaysia', *Women's Studies International Forum* 29(4): 354–367.

UN and Malaysia (Economic Planning Unit) (2011) *Malaysia: The Millennium Development Goals at 2010*. Kuala Lumpur: United Nations Country Team, Malaysia.

UNDP and Malaysia (Ministry of Women, Family and Community Development) (2015) *Study to Support the Development of National Policies and Programmes to Increase and Retain the Participation of Women in the Malaysian Labour Force*. Putrajaya: Department of Statistics Malaysia.

Williams, C. C. and Gurtoo, A. (2011) 'Women entrepreneurs in the Indian informal sector: Marginalisation dynamics or institutional rational choice', *International Journal of Gender and Entrepreneurship* 3(1): 1–28.

Yasmeen, G. (2006) *Bangkok's Foodscape: Public Eating, Gender Relations, and Urban Change*. Bangkok: White Lotus Press.

Yusof, R. (2010) 'Interpreting How Religious Values Affect Entrepreneurial Behaviour among Muslim Businesswomen: the Case of Businesswomen from the District of Pendang, Kedah in Malaysia'. Paper presented at 2nd Congress of the Asian Association of Women's Studies (CAAWS), 9–11 December, Penang.

9 Everyday Identities in Motion: Situating Malaysians within the 'War for Talent'

Adam Tyson

Introduction

Southeast Asian elites seeking to manage complex processes of political and economic transition as part of the desire to build and sustain national economic competitiveness are increasingly preoccupied with the issue of talent. The cultivation and retention of skilled workers, innovative entrepreneurs and corporate protégés is considered essential for countries seeking to maximize their regional comparative advantage. Talented individuals are expected to use their metacognitive skills and influence to contribute to national development and, by extension, enhance the performance legitimacy of the regime in power. This chapter draws on evidence from Malaysia in order to examine the disjuncture between state efforts to cultivate and retain talent, and the ways in which people interpret and respond to heavily instrumentalist talent enhancement projects. The Everyday Political Economy approach adopted here looks beyond broad determinants of the brain drain, focusing instead on the critical nuances – specifically pertaining to identity politics – that help explain why individuals emigrate and how talent initiatives become enmeshed with politicized expressions of power.

The country's recent economic transformation plans have focused on the need to propel Malaysia towards high-income country status, creating a knowledge economy infused with entrepreneurial spirit and producing, no less, a new generation of geniuses and Nobel laureates. To this end, private as well as state-owned enterprises are said to be embroiled in a global 'war for talent' (EIU 2011). This now highly globalized narrative posits that the war can only be 'won' if companies and governments affirm the worth of each individual employee and citizen while at the same time investing differentially in them in order to maximize their potential (Thrift 2010: 199). Comprehensive policies designed to achieve this goal, such as the Tenth Malaysia Plan (2011–15) and the Economic Transformation Programme (2010) are at odds, however, with Malaysia's conservative and reactionary politics, where the language of *ketuanan Melayu* (Malay supremacy) has entered the mainstream and the politics of ethnoreligious insult has become routinized in order to preserve the ruling party status of the United Malays National Organization (UMNO). As a consequence, government efforts to retain and recapture Malaysian talent – considered so vital for economic transformation – are faltering.

The modern political economy of ethnicity in Malaysia began with the 1971 New Economic Policy (NEP), implemented in a period of martial law following the 13 May 1969 race riots in Kuala Lumpur that claimed at least 200 lives. Ethnic quotas were introduced in order to reduce income disparities by empowering the Malay majority through the expansion of *bumiputera* (indigenous) equity ownership, guaranteed university admissions and public sector jobs, and ease of access to business licences, bank loans and bailouts.[1] An elaborate system of clientelism emerged, and a shift in priorities took place in the 1980s as the number of Malay millionaires increased while only modest socioeconomic uplift targets were maintained for the majority of Malays in politically dependent heartland states such as Kedah, Kelantan and Terengganu. These are just some of the distortions introduced by the NEP (1971–90) and carried forward through the National Development Policy (1991–2010) and the current New Economic Model. Moreover, as conceded by Mustapha Mohamad, the current minister for international trade and industry, the government's expansionist race-based economic policies remain a key determinant of Malaysia's brain drain (Zachariah and Palansamy 2013).

Having set ambitious targets in order to achieve developed country status by 2020, requiring annual GDP growth rates of at least 7 per cent, factions within the Malaysian government have explicitly called for the reversal of discriminatory practices, and reformers openly acknowledge the need for interethnic reconciliation and greater social integration.[2] This chapter contends that, as part of a broad agenda of inclusivity, these imperatives clash with the everyday politics and political economy of exclusion and antagonism so salient in contemporary Malaysia. It seems as if – as part of Malaysia's increasingly marketized ambitions and discussion of the middle-income trap – the language of talent is deliberately individualistic (neoliberal even) and stripped of reference to ethnicity or difference. However, in reality the fixation with talent rubs up against not just those interests within the political elite that seek to preserve ethnic quotas but, more importantly, the way in which the political economy of

---

[1] *Bumiputera* (literally 'sons of the soil') is a post-independence administrative category applied to the supposed original inhabitants of the land. To formally qualify, one must speak, dress and live as a Malay-Muslim, although in practice the category also applies to indigenous peoples in Sabah and Sarawak, many of them Christian, and the Christian Portuguese community in the state of Malacca. The 1971 NEP introduced a *bumiputera* compliance regime that continues to shape the political economy of ethnicity in Malaysia.

[2] In February 1991, the Vision 2020 policy – designed to achieve advanced industrialized country status – was announced by Mahathir Mohamad (Prime Minister of Malaysia 1981–2003) in order to navigate the country towards a post-industrial, post-racial society.

ethnicity has taken root within everyday life in Malaysia. Writers such as Thrift (2010) point to the rise of talent in terms of processes of commodification (how 'intangible assets' such as creativity and innovation come to be marketized, not least by human resource specialists and talent 'gurus' themselves). But this process of commodification has exposed the deeply contentious politics at the heart of Malaysia's political economy of ethnicity – a stark illustration of a point raised by Rudnyckyj (2008: 77) concerning how neoliberal ideas are never straightforwardly transplanted into postcolonial settings. In focusing on the issue of talent, this chapter provides a lens through which we can examine the tensions that exist between the country's everyday racialized politics and the economic transformation agenda of certain political and commercial elites. In stark contrast, then, to the focus in Franck's chapter in this volume on working-class lives, the focus of this chapter is on those relatively privileged workers identified as 'talent'. And yet, just as Franck observed the emergence of resistant economic subjectivities (as workers joined the informal labour market), in this chapter we see how the identity of workers as 'talent' itself comes into friction with both state-sanctioned and everyday forms of ethnic politics. In this sense, both chapters identify modes of everyday resistance to the Malaysian modernity project – and yet these are forms of resistance that result in oftentimes contradictory and complex outcomes.

Recent work by Tajuddin (2011) and Raquiza (2012) highlights the structural conditions within which the political economy of ethnicity in Southeast Asia has emerged. This chapter will examine the ways in which broad structural shifts are reproduced within localized political economic processes by focusing on the case of peninsular Malaysia, where there is a growing disjuncture between state talent policies and everyday grounded practices. Evidence for this chapter derives from nondirective interviews and observations conducted in public universities, civil society organizations, government ministries and private talent recruitment agencies operating in Malaysia between 2009 and 2011, supplemented by interviews with the Malaysian diaspora in the United Kingdom in 2013. Online Malaysian sources such as One Brain Blog, Outstation, Mobile Malaysians, Plugging the Brain Drain, the Nutgraph, and the Wake Up Call Malaysia Facebook page were also consulted. The first section of this chapter focuses on the nationwide debate around talent in relation to Malaysians living overseas, highlighting the importance of ethnicity and identity politics in relation to discussions of the 'brain drain'. The second and third sections of the chapter examine how local efforts to build 'talent' take shape within the context of wider ethnic politics. These sections situate 'brain drain' and the 'war for talent' vis-á-vis concrete local practices. The second section examines talent recruitment and retention initiatives, entrepreneurial enhancement strategies and small retailer support schemes. The final section views talent through the lens of education and the arts, where segregation and censorship ensure that the loss of talent will remain a concern for generations to come.

Talent, Identity and Mobility

According to the 2010 Housing and Population Census of Malaysia, *bumiputera* (Malays and other 'sons of the soil') constitute a 67.4 per cent national majority, followed by Chinese-Malaysians at 24.6 per cent and an Indian-Malaysian minority of 7.3 per cent. From identity cards to school transcripts, hospital records to dietary obligations, it is clear that Malaysians continue to be differentiated in everyday settings according to ethnicity and religious background, and that many have internalized these differences. Scholars such as Ty and Goellnicht (2004) attempt to look beyond hyphenated identities in order to understand processes of negotiation undertaken by successive generations of migrants hoping to participate more fully in social and political life. However, in the case of Malaysia it is observable that such hopes are undermined by long-standing, heavily politicized tensions between reified groupings of *pendatang* (immigrants, sojourners) and *bumiputera* – divisions that are central to the modes of 'graduated sovereignty' (Ong 2000) based fundamentally on officially sanctioned manipulations of social identities that characterize state rule in Malaysia (Chin 2000).

As Lim (2008) has identified, there is a passion for race in Malaysia, one that gives rise to overt forms of political intimidation as well as more subtle, everyday forms of racist language, symbolism and imagery. Prime Minister Najib Razak's allusion to a 'Chinese tsunami' just days after the May 2013 general election is a recent example of calculated political intimidation (Hamzah 2013).[3] Forms of racism continue to radiate throughout Malaysian society. One of the consequences – and the focus of this chapter – is the movement of highly skilled and educated non-Malays overseas, creating a 'brain drain' that is increasingly viewed as impacting on Malaysia's chances of achieving high-income status by the end of this decade.

According to World Bank (2011b) figures, the emigration rate of tertiary educated Malaysians, standing at 11 per cent, compares favourably with Southeast Asian neighbours such as Laos (37.4 per cent) and Vietnam (27.1 per cent). As many as 1.5 million Malaysian nationals currently live abroad, however, and at least one-third are tertiary educated individuals destined for high-income countries (see Table 9.1), thus constituting a significant talent haemorrhage in a country of only 29 million people (ADIC 2012).

---

[3] On 5 May 2013, the thirteen-party Barisan Nasional coalition led by the UMNO lost the popular vote by a margin but still managed to secure 133 out of 222 parliamentary seats. UMNO has formally been in power since Malaysia gained independence in 1957.

Table 9.1 *Bilateral estimates of migrant stocks from Malaysia as of 2010 (above 10,000)*

1.	Singapore	1,060,628
2.	Australia	119,197
3.	Brunei Darussalam	81,576
4.	United Kingdom	65,571
5.	United States	55,007
6.	Canada	25,477
7.	New Zealand	15,912
8.	India	12,945
	Worldwide	*1,481,202*

Source: World Bank (2011a).

Table 9.2 *Bilateral estimates of migrant stocks to Malaysia as of 2010 (above 10,000)*

1.	Indonesia	1,397,684
2.	Philippines	277,444
3.	China	125,584
4.	Bangladesh	122,912
5.	India	106,880
6.	Singapore	103,318
7.	Thailand	79,604
8.	Japan	19,595
9.	Myanmar	17,034
10.	Pakistan	16,477
11.	United Kingdom	12,803
	Worldwide	*2,357,603*

Source: World Bank (2011a).

Of the 1,060,628 Malaysians residing in Singapore, approximately 400,000 (or 37.7 per cent) qualify as skilled migrants. This is in clear contrast to the state-sanctioned programmes of labour outmigration seen in countries such as the Philippines, Indonesia and Cambodia (see Elias and Louth, this volume). As the reverse bilateral flow chart (Table 9.2) demonstrates, Malaysia receives a disproportionately large number of immigrants from low-income countries. Many of the Indonesians arriving in Malaysia, for instance, are employed as *pembantu* (domestic workers) and *kuli bangunan* (low-skilled construction workers, menial labourers).

The result of these bilateral migration flows is a combined loss for Malaysia of potential leadership, entrepreneurial innovation, managerial nous and aesthetic creativity. In response to this real but indeterminate threat, the CEO of Talent Corporation Malaysia, Johan Merican, has promised to stop the leakages in Malaysia's 'talent pipeline'.[4] Directors from the NES Global Talent office in Malaysia, a private talent agency with a mandate to plug gaps in key economic sectors such as oil and gas, have joined in the effort by creating a 'platform for talent'. This means that NES Global is looking for ways to discourage promising young graduates from leaving the country, for instance by ensuring that they are absorbed into Malaysian industry on a competitive, meritocratic basis.[5] There are also circumstances in which the lost externalities caused by the brain drain can be offset by positive feedback effects such as remittances, knowledge and technology transfers, investment and trade opportunities (EIU 2011). With this in mind, the Malaysian government encourages skilled migrants with a low probability of return to view themselves as 'talent ambassadors' playing a role in the country's development regardless of their whereabouts (PEMANDU 2013).

Malaysian policymakers started to formally address the brain drain in 1995 with the establishment of the Returning Scientist Programme under the Ministry of Science, Technology and Innovation. This initiative proved unsatisfactory and was superseded by the first-generation Returning Experts Programme in 2001 and the launch of Brain Gain Malaysia in 2006. Poor results prompted the prime minister's office to establish Talent Corporation Malaysia as a special unit in 2011, cross-cutting government and private sectors. Talent Corporation's flagship policies are the second-generation Returning Experts Programme, offering tax incentives and other concessions, and the Talent Roadmap 2020 dedicated to optimizing domestic talent, attracting global talent and building sustainable talent networks. Johan Merican, the CEO, estimates that 1,800 Malaysians were repatriated under the Returning Experts Programme as of June 2013, although he concedes that more needs to be done to understand why people are leaving and how Talent Corporation can reengage the diaspora (Pak 2013).

Global economic imbalances and asymmetries, coupled with domestic political factors, offer compelling explanations as to why tertiary educated individuals emigrate. Foo (2011) found the main determinants of the brain drain to be high levels of income, liveability and religious diversity, geographical

---

[4] Interview with Johan Merican in Kuala Lumpur, 14 December 2011. Talent Corporation Malaysia began operating in January 2011 in order to reverse the brain drain as well as to compete with neighbouring Talent Capital Singapore.

[5] Interview with a senior director from NES Global in Kuala Lumpur, 4 July 2011. Analysts from the Socio-Economic Development and Research Institute, interviewed in Kuala Lumpur on 7 February 2011, argued that more skilled Malaysians will stay if they can be convinced that wages are commensurate with qualifications and career trajectories are determined by merit rather than religion or race.

proximity, and English as the national language in the destination countries.[6] Based on data gathered from her Mobile Malaysians PhD project, Koh (2012) found the key drivers to be educational opportunities, family, identity (belonging) and the political impressions derived from new social media. During my time working for a public university in Malaysia (December 2009 to September 2011), I found that, in the absence of coercion, students and professionals leave their birthplaces on the basis of pragmatic calculus, or romantic idealism, or indeed any number of psychosocially complex personal reasons.

Decisions made by self-initiated migrants are informed, to a large extent, by sets of differentials. Beyond rational economic and resource differentials (comparing earnings abroad, or the quality of facilities and infrastructures in destination countries), there are important 'residual differentials' worth considering (Portes 1976). Residual differentials take into account everyday political experiences and, in the case of Malaysia, reflect the changing attitudes of (usually young, upwardly mobile) citizens with political or professional grievances linked to racism or a lack of integrity in classrooms and workplaces. The story of Tan Chye Ling, a researcher in molecular biology, reinforces this point. Tan felt 'suppressed' as a postgraduate student in Malaysia and was compelled to ask why – given that pay is not everything – people choose to work overseas, away from their loved ones, enduring high stress levels and loneliness (*Malaysiakini* 2008). Tan laments the barriers to career advancement in Malaysia, using the example of higher education to demonstrate that expertise is no substitute for loyalty or passivity in Malay-dominated sectors of the economy. In everyday life, Tan concludes, Malaysians are disillusioned with the corruption, the red tape and the blasé attitude of officialdom (*Malaysiakini* 2008).

Focusing on the diaspora, the determinants of outmigration and return migration are situational and highly contingent. For instance, given the recent uncertainty facing the UK National Health Service, many Malaysian physicians are contemplating a return 'home'. There are hundreds of Malaysian physicians currently working in the UK, constituting a significant brain bank that both the Malaysian Academy of Surgeons as well as Talent Corporation Malaysia are keen to draw upon. The majority of UK-based physicians who I interviewed, however, are church-going Chinese-Malaysians for whom regular reports of ethnoreligious tensions in Malaysia create a sense of antipathy and reinforce the view that the Malaysian government aims to retain power at all costs.[7]

---

[6] Foo's (2011) sample (N = 194) does not represent the view of the Malaysian diaspora as a whole. The majority of those surveyed were unmarried Chinese-Malaysian students in their twenties.

[7] Interviews with Malaysian ophthalmologists and dermatologists working in the UK, 20–25 July 2013.

Talent Corporation hosts a number of outreach events in the UK each year in order to address these concerns and to try to inspire professional Malaysians to repatriate. Noor Hisham Abdullah, the director general of health, was guest of honour at a Talent Corporation healthcare professionals networking session held at the Crowne Plaza Hotel in Birmingham in August 2013. The session was attended by some thirty early-career healthcare professionals who raised issues related to the recognition of their qualifications and work experience, as well as Malaysian Medical Council registration criteria. From my observations, Abdullah held progressive views on Malaysian healthcare and was able to address the concerns of the audience in a relatively candid manner. I found, however, that Abdullah's audience of highly talented prospective returnees preferred to express their most critical views and political concerns during private or informal conversations with the director general and Talent Corporation representatives.

The anxieties surrounding religious freedoms and crime rates voiced by Malaysian physicians in the UK chime with those of other prospective Malaysian returnees. Back in Malaysia, religious and interethnic tensions are often aggravated by the editors of national dailies such as *Utusan Malaysia* and *Berita Harian*, firebrand leaders of Malay associations, government spokespersons, errant members of parliament and political aspirants. Talent Corporation executives acknowledge that the national political situation complicates their efforts to lure talented Malaysians home and to assist in their reintegration.[8] Chinese-Malaysians are most obviously in the firing line, although ethnic and religiously charged provocations touch the lives of many of Malaysia's Hindu, Shia, Ahmadiyah and *orang asli* (indigenous, animist) minority communities. Abdullah Badawi (Prime Minister of Malaysia 2003–9), Lee Kuan Yew (Prime Minister of Singapore 1959–90) and opposition leader Anwar Ibrahim are among the latest high-profile figures to criticize Malaysia's approach to ethnic relations. Abdullah Badawi has expressed concern over the government's fixation with *bumiputera* equity targets, whereas (rather more predictably) Lee Kuan Yew has blamed the shrinking talent reservoir in Malaysia on the government's determination to maintain ethnic Malay dominance, with institutionalized as well as everyday forms of discrimination fuelling the talent exodus (Welsh and Chin 2013; Yew 2013). Anwar Ibrahim has called for an end to race-based policies that enrich cronies and hopes to replace these policies with competitive open tenders and needs-based access to microcredit to help Malaysia regain its competitive edge (Ariffin 2012).

---

[8] Interviews with Talent Corporation executives in Kuala Lumpur, 20 June-14 July 2011.

Talent Enrichment

In a motivational book written by the current Prime Minister Najib Razak (2011: 88), we are told that the nurturing of intelligence and the cultivation of talent is essential for the future leadership of Malaysia. This future hinges on interethnic goodwill (but not necessarily integration), as suggested by the narrative illustration on the front cover of the book. Set in the capital city, the Malays of Kampung Baru are placed front and centre of the illustration, the focal point of Najib's *Satu Malaysia* (One Malaysia) national unity project. The Malays are flanked by Chinese on Petaling Street and Tamils from the Brickfields neighbourhood in the artist's depiction of everyday rush-hour experiences in Kuala Lumpur.[9] Cultivating and nurturing the next generation of talented Malaysians is expected to enhance productivity and innovation as the country rises out of the so-called middle-income trap (Razak 2011). Concerns about social cohesion and ethnic preferentialism must also be accounted for, however, as they are key residual differentials with the potential to undermine gains made under the government's highly instrumentalist talent reclamation and retention policies.

Malaysia's economic competitiveness agenda – and specifically its war for talent – has become a site of interagency struggle where competing agendas for the development of the country as a whole and for specific ethnic groupings are played out in various ways. Under the Najib administration, new 'clusters of excellence' policies and financial master plans have been announced, along with promises of triple crown business schools, high performing small and medium enterprises, and the discovery of *permata negara* (national gems) and future Nobel laureates. Nevertheless, the prime minister's top economic advisors warn that the human capital situation in Malaysia is reaching a critical stage, with talent deficits jeopardizing government plans to become global leaders in key knowledge-intensive economic sectors such as those identified in the 2010 Economic Transformation Plan (NEAC 2010; PEMANDU 2013). Members of the influential National Economic Advisory Council (NEAC) argue that too little is being done to cultivate or develop new talent, finding fault in 'education policies saddled with socio-political goals [that] have stymied the national objective of producing the best talent to meet the country's needs' (NEAC 2010: 55).

Thus, 'talent enrichment' projects do not merely involve combatting 'brain drain' but are viewed as complementing long-standing initiatives to build

---

[9] Kuala Lumpur has a number of ethnic precincts and enclaves. Kampung Baru began as an urban Malay settlement (or 'reservation') in 1900, witnessed the worst of the 13 May 1969 ethnic riots and is now an integral part of the modern city centre. The Petaling thoroughfare runs through the core of Chinatown and accommodates all types of traders, whereas the Indian-Malaysian community is concentrated in the Brickfields and Sentul areas of Kuala Lumpur.

local (specifically Malay) entrepreneurialism. And yet, such strategies are so enmeshed within the country's political economy of ethnicity that they operate more as mechanisms for delivering largesse to political cronies or for guaranteeing political support for the ruling party that they largely fail to deliver. Thus, we see that Malaysia's economic planning and performance management units, along with the Ministry of International Trade and Industry (MITI), the Ministry of Higher Education, the Public Services Department and the Council of Trust for Indigenous Peoples, are preoccupied with the development of *bumiputera* entrepreneurialism in response to domestic skills shortages, underperforming Malay businesses and, more tellingly perhaps, the beleaguered prime minister's political agenda (MITI 2013). The MITI manages as many as 247 citizen enhancement projects supported by the efforts of eight ministries and thirty-one government agencies tasked with the development of competitive *bumiputera* entrepreneurs (MITI 2013). These efforts are guided by the MITI's Bumiputera Entrepreneurial Development Roadmap and supported by the Council of Trust for Indigenous Peoples.

Politicians, policymakers and bureaucrats alike have either wilfully ignored or failed to take notice of the rhetorical question first posed by Kamal Salih in 1992 and repeated many times since: 'Can entrepreneurs be trained or is entrepreneurship acquired through learning by doing'? Or, put another way, are entrepreneurs 'born' rather than 'made'?[10] Some Malaysian agencies maintain that successful *bumiputera* entrepreneurs can be created through the right combination of stimulants and inducements, thus serving to mitigate the loss of talent that (somewhat ironically) occurs as a result of the ethnocentric, pro-*bumiputera* policies detailed in this chapter. Malaysian 'talent' seems to be far removed from its neoliberal cousin promoted in the business study literature (e.g., Hacker 2001; Michels, Handfield-Jones and Axelrod 2001) in that rather than being the apogee of individual potential traced by Thrift (2010), here it is deeply enmeshed in the country's racial politics. As Montsion (2012) discovered in Singapore, there is a continuous interplay between the production of desirable citizens (neoliberal or otherwise) and their own struggles with state enhancement projects.

The expansion of *bumiputera* compliance measures creates opportunities for millions of entitled (or 'special') citizens while reinforcing the divisive everyday political economy of ethnicity in Malaysia. It has been more than four decades since restructuring began under the NEP, and yet, year on year, the government announces costly new pump-priming initiatives in order to 'narrow disparities' and foster inclusiveness between *bumiputera* and non-*bumiputera* Malaysians (PEMANDU 2013). The MITI, for instance,

---

[10] Kamal Salih (1992) worked for the Malaysian Institute for Economic Research when he first posed this question. In the same year, Salih gained notoriety by co-founding Malaysia's International Medical University in order to fill a major skills gap in the country.

launched a 'smart partnership' with Unit Peneraju Agenda Bumiputera (TERAJU), which operates explicitly under the Prime Minister's Economic Planning Unit to enhance the socioeconomic status of Malays. TERAJU receives billions of dollars in public and private financing in order to manage a veritable wonderland of projects designed exclusively for *bumiputera* citizens, the largest being the High-Performing Bumiputera Companies Programme aiming to support thousands of companies. The Bumiputera Education Foundation expects to fund 12,000 *bumiputera* students between 2011 and 2016, whereas the *Skim Jejak Jaya Bumiputera* ('last mile' scheme) serves to increase *bumiputera*-owned corporate equity by getting companies listed on the Bursa Malaysia stock exchange.

When it comes to performance delivery, TERAJU bosses have been known to deliver paradoxical messages. For instance, a video entitled *Terajui Minda Anda* (*Steer Your Minds*) screened on 20 July 2011 as part of a two-day 'Driving Bumi Agenda' event stressed that *bumiputera* who aspire to be successful entrepreneurs have only themselves to blame if they fail (Hamsawi 2011). With this in mind, the MITI continues to generously fund top-down economic initiatives driven by the likes of TERAJU to sponsor and groom successive generations of Malay entrepreneurs and industrialists. Unofficially the hope seems to be that, even if successive generations of ordinary Malays do not 'succeed', the compliance measures and top-down initiatives created on their behalf will engender a sense of obligation and loyalty towards the government. Talent enrichment initiatives, especially (although not exclusively) among Malay citizens, can be viewed in terms of an apparent desire to foster neoliberal enterprising economic subjectivities ('the entrepreneur') that nonetheless serve a primary purpose of maintaining the political power base of the ruling party. In the following discussion, we can also observe how such desires, or logics of discipline more broadly, are also central to the development of education policy – a discussion that returns the focus much more squarely to ordinary Malaysians experiencing everyday life at the intersection of entrenched ethnic politics and marketizing economic agendas.

Learning to Be Exceptional

Global 'talent gurus' such as Karl-Heinz Oehler from the Hertz Corporation argue that the exceptional personality traits required to cope in a rapidly changing world – resilience and adaptability, intellectual agility and versatility – are in short supply and that Asia and Latin America suffer from acute shortages of creative individuals capable of overcoming the most pressing corporate challenges (EIU 2011). Reflecting the widespread concern among the country's economic managers with the country's international educational standing and economic competitiveness, prognoses such as these are taken seriously in

Malaysia. The government has conjured up a master plan known as the National Higher Education Strategic Plan (PSPTN) to steer the country towards excellence and nurture talent. Chen May Yee (2012), editor of the blog Outstation, reflects on education ('so important that we will even uproot the family to a distant land, all so our kids can go to a good school') and the government's latest master plan.

The Education Ministry is a top-heavy behemoth that rolls out schemes and programmes with little co-ordination. Teachers are swamped with administrative duties. Heads of school are picked on seniority not ability. Our schools are less racially diverse than ever. [And yet] we were pleased that the government – instead of insisting that we have the best education system in the world – is acknowledging [through the PSPTN] that we don't. So many of us – parents of young children – live in limbo, plotting moves to Australia, the UK, Canada, the US or Singapore, just so our kids can get a good education without sending us into debt. Our lives are a relentless calendar of looming education decision deadlines, beginning with primary school, with no let-up until university. If we could fix Malaysian education, we'd go a long way to fixing the brain drain. (Yee 2012)

Education is a cultural priority in Malaysia, and for non-*bumiputera* students the absence of entitlements pushes them to excel, either by outperforming their relatively tourniqueted Malay compatriots at home (a source of mutual animosity) or by choosing to study abroad (provoking fears of a growing talent exodus). During their formative years, young Malaysian students experience degrees of physical and cognitive separation, their social 'otherness' reinforced by classroom experiences and the future prospect of a job market replete with *bumiputera* compliance regulations. The government has responded with a number of plans, including the Student Integration Plan for Unity, designed to foster interaction across different school types through co-curricular activities, although the Ministry of Education admits that these initiatives are severely underfunded (MOE 2012). The initiatives are also relatively ineffective as students still tend to gravitate towards their 'natural' ethnic groupings when carrying out classroom assignments, joining social clubs, selecting halls of residence or participating in extracurricular activities (Tyson et al. 2011).

Generally speaking, Malay primary schoolchildren attend state or Islamic boarding schools, whereas some 650,000 Chinese and Indian-Malaysians attend private vernacular schools (CPPS 2012). It is estimated that as many as 95 per cent of Chinese children and 55 per cent of Indian children are enrolled in vernacular schools, where their own languages, cultures, religions and heritage are prioritized, raising concerns about national unity, social integration and future career trajectories (CPPS 2012). This same report found after six years of study that over 30 per cent of primary students from vernacular schools fail to obtain even a minimum level of proficiency in the national language, *bahasa Melayu*. In what they refer to as 'damage control', NES Global Talent Malaysia representatives occasionally serve on school advisory panels and provide input to curriculum development committees.[11] These representatives are concerned about the negative, often self-defeating impact of ethnic quotas and preferential policies, as well as the politicization of the national curriculum. It is quite telling that a senior Malaysian director at NES Global sent all five of his children to Australia and Singapore to study and find employment.

Malaysian universities continue to slip in global rankings, and the ongoing exodus of domestic talent creates a situation where the country 'faces a shortage of skilled professionals, including bankers, researchers and engineers' (Ng 2013). According to a local source, this decline was exacerbated by the events surrounding a conference concerning 'the bumiputera policy' held at University Sains Malaysia (USM) in Penang in September 2003.[12] The vice chancellor at the time hoped to raise the profile of USM and supported the conference, which was hosted by the School of Humanities. My source suggested that 'the VC got more than he bargained for' and gave an account of the conference and its aftermath which led to the exodus of some of that institution's most high-profile academics.

Malaysian academics are required, on paper at least, to pledge their loyalty to the government, while all university students with sponsorship in Malaysia are registered for compulsory National Civics Bureau (BTN) orientation and induction programmes. Shah (2010) argues that these publicly funded programmes – run like camp retreats, usually over four days – deliberately serve to 'disunite' Malaysians.[13] This is the result of the emphasis placed on the imperative of Malay dominance as well as overt warnings by BTN facilitators that Malays must never be *hamba* (slaves) in their own country. Many students attend BTN courses in Ulu Sepri, in the State of Negeri Sembilan, where games, outdoor activities, psychoanalytical challenges, film screenings, lectures and seminars are organized around themes of social justice, affirmative action, constitutional rights and international affairs. Reflecting the general mood surrounding civics training, one student recalled that BTN coaches and facilitators frequently distinguished between entitled *bumiputera* and ungrateful *pendatang* (immigrants), adding, with regret, that this malicious message resonated with many of her fellow inductees.[14]

---

[11] Interview with a senior director from NES Global in Kuala Lumpur, 4 July 2011.

[12] Personal correspondence with a Malaysian academic, 19 May 2014.

[13] A similar critique has been levied against Malaysia's National Service Training Programme (PLKN) by an anonymous source close to the Department of Defence, interviewed on 13 July 2011. Over 150,000 Malaysians have been drafted for PLKN since 2003 in an effort to 'boost their patriotism'.

[14] Interview with a student from the state of Kedah following her BTN orientation in Ulu Sepri, June 2011.

As an alternative to the existing structured learning environment in Malaysia, one that tends to reinforce the divisive imagery and practice of ethnic 'otherness', it is useful to turn to accounts of how top-down narratives are challenged through civil society projects, including art projects (see also Rethel's discussion in this volume of art as a resource for the development of counternarratives and critical reflection in her discussion of the 15Malaysia film project). One such example is Instant Café Theatre's parallel education project based on the play *Parah*.[15] However, permissions for this parallel project, detailed below, were not granted, constituting a lost opportunity for Malaysian students and their families to reflect upon the ways in which racial fixations affect their daily lives. Written by Alfian Sa'at and directed by Jo Kukathas, the play *Parah* was inspired by Abdullah Hussain's 1971 novel *Interlok* as well as the 2009 film *Talentime* by Yasmin Ahmad.[16] The play debuted in Singapore in June 2011, followed by three showcase performances at The Annexe Gallery in Kuala Lumpur, a full staging at Kuala Lumpur Performing Arts Centre in February 2012, and performances at the World Theatre Festival in Brisbane, Australia, in February 2013. *Parah* deals with friendship and adversity between four secondary school students after the discovery of a single word, *pariah* (Tamil, referring to a low untouchable caste), forces them to confront ethnic stereotypes and question their own identities and sense of belonging in Malaysia. The playwright captures the tensions and narratives surrounding ethnic identity and a migratory pattern dating back to the British colonial era and compels audiences to ask: how can young Malaysians better equip themselves to deal with ethnically divisive issues without resorting to hate speech and racist attitudes?[17]

Given the director's firm belief in the positive developmental role the arts can play in people's everyday lives, a *Parah* parallel education project was created in order to reach out to wider audiences in Malaysia, particularly students. Had the project been approved by the Ministry of Education, students would have engaged in open, creative dialogue about ethnic relations with the goal of transcending dominant (and highly damaging) stereotypes. According to Jo Kukathas, using art creatively was supposed to provide young people with new opportunities to learn how to discuss differences of opinion, belief and attitude in a mature fashion. In short, the parallel project was about getting students to

---

[15] Instant Café Theatre was founded in 1989 with the goal of examining the complexities of multiculturalism in Malaysia through cultural production and the arts.

[16] Yasmin Ahmad is credited with the first serious cinematic attempt to grapple with interracial romance in Malaysia (Gabriel 2011).

[17] Personal correspondence with Jo Kukathas, director of *Parah*, 9 January 2012. From my observations as a visiting lecturer in Malaysia between 2009 and 2011, discrimination and racist behaviour among university students is fuelled by the following negative stereotypes: Malays are lazy and entitled, Chinese are greedy and pork-contaminated, and Indians are thuggish and untrustworthy.

think seriously and critically about who they are as Malaysians, and this has strong implications for the development and retention of future talent cohorts.

A critique by Malaysian filmmaker Amir Muhammad featured prominently in the *Parah* parallel project proposal. Muhammad (2011) argued that, with a well-structured lesson plan, readings and discussions of Abdullah Hussain's *Interlok* would present a 'wonderful chance for students to relearn some of the basic empathy that we [Malaysians] have lost over the past four decades'. It has been over four decades since the 13 May 1969 race riots took place in Kuala Lumpur, leading to the establishment of the racially fixated NEP. As a result, Muhammad (2011) concludes that 'we [Malaysians] have been made so aware of what countries our ancestors came from that we have lost sight of what country we are creating for our descendants'. While the Ministry of Education announces new education and talent roadmaps and professional quality assurance regimes and deploys auditors to check that key performance indicators are being met, the essence of critical, creative learning is in decline.

Conclusion

The economic subject of the talented individuals has gained a spectacular level of attention in government agendas and policies aimed at addressing the country's economic competitiveness. What the analysis presented in this chapter shows are the very real limitations of importing this global policy framework ('the war for talent') into a divisive and fractious local political economy in which the concept of talent enhancement is often more easily aligned with the state's continuing commitment to ethnic privilege. Moreover, this chapter found that broad-brush, often highly fashionable, economic ideas and developmental policies can also be explored through a focus on everyday experience. How, for example, do ideas such as the 'brain drain' or the 'middle-income trap' serve to bring about particular understandings of what it means to be modern or dynamic in contemporary Malaysia? Economic reformers in Malaysia have largely bought into marketized visions of modernization in which a modern, dynamic Malaysia, flush with national and global talent, attains the status of high-income economy. And yet, as this chapter illustrates, the construction of certain groups as 'talent' takes place within the context of a marketizing economy that nonetheless remains deeply embedded in a localized political economy of ethnicity.

Thus, initiatives discussed in this chapter, such as the Returning Expert Programme and the National Higher Education Strategic Plan, focus on rational incentives and material enticements but fall short of their targets because of the failure to address the political and aesthetic issues at the heart of the brain drain. In particular, the everyday experiences of segregation in the workplace and school system, as well as by censorship in the media and the arts, increase the likelihood that, given the opportunity and the means, young skilled Malaysians will continue to leave the country. More generally, Malaysians continue to experience intrusive ethnic profiling and coding in everyday settings. Broken into its component parts, the NEP-inspired *bumiputera* agenda infiltrates all levels of the state (be it national education policy or the bureaucracy) and influences the production and consumption of music, media, film and the visual arts. It filters into printing and publications, influences campaigns and elections, laws, legislation and constitutional amendments, economic policy and development goals, rural–urban planning, and architecture. Moreover, and perhaps more importantly, *bumiputera* compliance measures affect a plethora of seemingly private issues and choices, including gender, family, marriage, sexuality, religious belief, career choices and, consequently, migration pathways.

References

ADIC (2012) *Country Profile Malaysia.* Australian Government Department of Immigration and Citizenship. www.immi.gov.au/media/statistics/country-profiles/.

Ariffin, L. J. (2012) 'Race-based policies must end, says Anwar', *The Malaysian Insider*, 26 September. www.themalaysianinsider.com/malaysia/article/race-based-policies-must-end-says-anwar.

Chin, C. B. N. (2000) 'The state of the "state" in globalization: social order and economic restructuring in Malaysia', *Third World Quarterly* 21(6): 1035–1057.

CPPS (2012) *Vernacular Schools in Malaysia: A Heritage to be Celebrated or a Hindrance to Nation Building?* Kuala Lumpur: Centre for Public Policy Studies.

EIU [Economist Intelligence Unit] (2011) *The Global Talent Index Report: The Outlook to 2015.* Chicago, IL: Heidrick & Struggles.

Foo, G. (2011) 'Quantifying the Malaysian brain drain and an investigation of its key determinants', *Malaysian Journal of Economic Studies* 48(2): 93–116.

Gabriel, S. P. (2011) 'Translating bangsa Malaysia: toward a new cultural politics of Malaysian-ness', *Critical Asian Studies* 43(3): 349–372.

Hacker, C. A. (2001) *How to Compete in the War for Talent.* Sanford, FL: DC Press.

Hamsawi, R. (2011) 'Teraju all set to steer ambitious Bumi SMEs', *New Straits Times*, 21 July: 4.

Hamzah, Z. (2013) 'Mengurus tsunami Cina PRU-13', *Utusan Online*, 12 May. www.utusan.com.my/utusan/Rencana/20130512/re_11/Mengurus-tsunami-Cina-PRU-13.

Koh, S.-Y. (2012) 'Everyday lives of the Malaysian diaspora', *New Mandala*, 11 January. http://asiapacific.anu.edu.au/newmandala/2012/01/11/everyday-lives-of-the-%e2%80%98malaysian-diaspora%e2%80%99/.

Lim, D. C. L. (2008) 'Introduction', in D. C. L. Lim (ed.) *Overcoming Passion for Race in Malaysian Cultural Studies.* Leiden: Brill, pp. 1–12.

Malaysiakini (2008) 'The leaving of the suppressed', 16 May. www.malaysiakini.com/letters/82998.

Michels, E., Handfield-Jones, H. and Axelrod, B. (2001) *The War for Talent.* Boston, MA: Harvard Business School Press.

MITI (2013) *MITI Report 2012*. Kuala Lumpur: Ministry of International Trade and Industry Malaysia.

MOE (2012) *Malaysia Education Blueprint 2013–2025: Preliminary Report*. Putrajaya: Ministry of Education.

Montsion, J. M. (2012) 'When talent meets mobility: un/desirability in Singapore's new citizenship project', *Citizenship Studies* 16(3–4): 469–482.

Muhammad, A. (2011) 'How we failed Interlok', 30 January. http://amirmu.blogspot.co.uk/2011/01/how-we-failed-interlok.html.

NEAC (2010) *New Economic Model for Malaysia: Part 1 – Strategic Policy Directions*. Putrajaya: National Economic Advisory Council.

Ng, J. (2013) 'Singapore is winning the talent battle', *The Wall Street Journal*, 8 October. http://blogs.wsj.com/searealtime/2013/10/08/in-talent-battle-malaysia-loses-to-singapore/.

Ong, A. (2000) 'Graduated sovereignty in Southeast Asia', *Theory, Culture and Society* 17(4): 55–75.

Pak, J. (2013) 'Will Malaysia's brain drain block its economic ambitions?', *BBC News*, 5 June. www.bbc.co.uk/news/world-asia-22610210.

PEMANDU (2013) *Economic Transformation Programme Annual Report 2012*. Putrajaya: Performance Management and Delivery Unit.

Portes, A. (1976) 'Determinants of the brain drain', *International Migration Review* 10(4): 489–508.

Raquiza, A. R. (2012) *State Structure, Policy Formation, and Economic Development in Southeast Asia: The Political Economy of Thailand and the Philippines*. Abingdon: Routledge.

Razak, N. (2011) *Perkhidmatan Awam: Meneraju Perubahan, Melangkau Jangkaan*. Putrajaya: Razak School of Government.

Rudnyckyj, D. (2008) 'Worshipping work: producing commodity producers in contemporary Indonesia', in J. Nevins and N. L. Peluso (eds.) *Taking Southeast Asia to Market: Commodities, Nature, and People in the Neoliberal Age*. Ithaca, NY: Cornell University Press, pp. 73–87.

Salih, K. (1992) 'Issues in creating the ultimate entrepreneur', *New Straits Times*, 18 April: 16.

Shah, S. (2010) 'Biro Tata Negara's real message', *The Nut Graph*, 3 February. www.thenutgraph.com/btns-real-message/.

Tajuddin, A. (2011) *Malaysia in the World Economy (1824–2011): Capitalism, Ethnic Divisions, and 'Managed' Democracy*. Plymouth: Lexington Books.

Thrift, N. (2010) 'A perfect innovation engine: the rise of the talent world', in J. Best and M. Paterson (eds.) *Cultural Political Economy*. Abingdon and New York: Routledge, pp. 197–221.

Ty, E. and Goellnicht, D. C. (eds.) (2004) *Asian North American Identities: Beyond the Hyphen*. Bloomington, IN: Indiana University Press.

Tyson, A., Jeram, D., Sivapragasam, V. and Azlan, H. N. (2011) 'Ethnicity, education and the economics of the brain drain in Malaysia: youth perspectives', *Malaysian Journal of Economic Studies* 48(2): 175–184.

Welsh, B. and Chin, J. (eds.) (2013) *Awakening: The Abdullah Badawi Years in Malaysia*. Kuala Lumpur: SIRD.

World Bank (2011a) *Bilateral Migration Matrix 2010*. http://go.worldbank.org/JITC7NYTT0.

(2011b) *Migration and Remittances Factbook 2011*, 2nd edition. Washington, DC: The International Bank for Reconstruction and Development/The World Bank.

Yee, C. M. (2012) 'Fix education, fix the brain drain', *The Malaysian Insider*, 21 September. www.themalaysianinsider.com/sideviews/article/fix-education-fix-the-brain-drain-chen-may-yee/.

Yew, L. K. (2013) *One Man's View of the World*. Singapore: Straits Times Press.

Zachariah, E. and Palansamy, Y. (2013) 'Putrajaya's race-based policies not the only reason for brain drain, say BN leaders', *The Malaysian Insider*, 8 August. www.themalaysianinsider.com/malaysia/article/malaysian-leaders-give-their-views-on-kuan-yews-scathing-remarks.

10 Regional Disputes over the Transnationalization of Domestic Labour: Malaysia's 'Maid Shortage' and Foreign Relations with Indonesia and Cambodia

Juanita Elias and Jonathon Louth

Introduction

Employing domestic workers from a variety of less developed countries in Asia has, in recent years, become widespread practice among middle-class Malaysian households. This normalization of domestic employment reflects both the unwillingness of the state to take on some of the social reproductive burdens needed to support increases in women's labour force participation, as well as the symbolic value that employment of a domestic worker plays in cultural perceptions of middle-class status. Indonesian women, in particular, have tended to dominate paid domestic work. This dependency of the Malaysian middle classes on low-paid Indonesian domestic workers was, however, thrown into flux in June 2009 when Indonesia placed an embargo on formalized flows of domestic workers into Malaysia. The actions of the Indonesian government were a reaction to ongoing cases of abuse against Indonesian migrants and, specifically, the death of an Indonesian domestic worker at the hands of her employer. Subsequently, the Indonesian government sought to engage in bargaining strategies with Malaysia in order to leverage better working conditions for its citizens. As negotiations with Indonesia appeared to falter, alternative sources of cheap domestic work were sought out. In particular, private recruitment brokers in Cambodia sought to bring in large numbers of women to be employed as domestic workers in Malaysia. Prior to the Indonesian ban on domestic workers, the trend of Cambodian women migrating to Malaysia for work was only just beginning to be registered (the more established pattern of female migration was from Cambodia to Thailand). The withdrawal of Indonesian domestic labour resulted in marked increases in the number of Cambodian women arriving in Malaysia (Kuppusamy 2012). However, a series of high-profile media reports of abuse and exploitation both in Malaysia by employers and in Cambodia by recruitment agencies called into question the regulatory measures supposedly in place to protect workers (Holliday 2012). In

October 2011 a complete ban on the sending of Cambodian women as domestic workers to Malaysia was announced (LICADHO 2011).

We explore the contours of these disputes between Malaysia, Indonesia and Cambodia. On face value, the disputes can be seen as manifestations of regulatory failures: failures to manage migration flows appropriately; failures to protect workers from abuses; and failures to agree basic terms and conditions of domestic worker employment. In such a perspective, these failings are best overcome via a response known as 'managed migration' (i.e., the better coordination of flows and protections of migrant workers by sender and host states). However, as will be argued in this chapter, more is going on than simply debates over how best to oversee short-term flows of migrant workers. Thus, this chapter seeks to contextualize the high-level policy negotiations and disputes that have come to characterize systems of temporary return migration for domestic work in Asia – drawing attention to the everyday political economies (be it of social reproduction, everyday agency or work) that constitute the conditions of possibility within which bilateral disputes and labour agreements between Southeast Asian states take shape. Indeed, regulatory shifts governing the supply of migrant domestic workers emerge in response to everyday processes associated with the reproduction of a deeply exploitative system of short-term labour migration that serve to draw new actors such as women migrants or formal and informal labour brokers into bilateral forms of labour governance.

We adopt a feminist everyday political economy approach emphasizing the role of gendered and racialized power relations that take shape within households as central to understanding the functioning of return migration systems. We link this understanding of the everyday to the recent resurgence in feminist thinking that emphasizes how the social relations of reproduction that take place within the household are a critical, yet widely overlooked, component of the functioning of the global economy (Bakker 2007; Steans and Tepe 2010). Furthermore, as the example of the booming market for migrant domestic workers illustrates, the social reproductive sphere itself has very much gone 'global' (Douglass 2009; Safri and Graham 2010; Elias and Gunawardana 2013). Decisions to migrate to take up domestic employment, as well as decisions to employ domestic workers, draw households into transnationalized webs of social reproductive relations and serve to reconfigure care relations in both host and sender states (Arat Kroc 2006). These social relations are fundamental to the production of neoliberal spaces (or the politics of 'market building'; Carroll and Jarvis 2014) that serve to extend market relations into the sphere of everyday life – and specifically into the household. It is an understanding of these relations and processes that we contend need to be understood in order to make sense of how and why states in Southeast Asia have become increasingly embroiled in disputes involving migrant domestic workers.

In terms of chapter structure, we open this chapter with an account of what a feminist everyday approach to political economy brings to the study of migrant labour regimes. We then, in a second section, provide a brief account of the domestic worker disputes between Malaysia, Indonesia and Cambodia. The third section of the chapter focuses on the underexamined socially reproductive tensions that underpin these labour disputes looking first at the gendered political economy of remittances in Indonesia and Cambodia and then to the transformations in social reproduction and cultures of domesticity that are taking shape in Malaysia. The final section explores questions of everyday agency – be it that of labour recruiters, workers or households – and its role in the active construction of markets for migrant domestic work and the modes of resistance that are possible. The analysis undertaken in this chapter draws upon a range of sources: media sources (print and online), primary documents and reports and academic studies of domestic worker migration (as well as some interviews with relevant organizations undertaken in Cambodia and Malaysia) in order to provide an account of what a feminist everyday political economy perspective brings to the study of migration politics in Southeast Asia. It is a contribution that is exploratory in nature, and there is certainly much scope for an expanded and more in-depth study into this topic. Although it should also be noted that in highlighting the role of media sources and publically available reports in our analysis we also recognize the role that these sources themselves play in the construction of ideas and narratives of everyday life.

Domestic Work and Everyday Life in Southeast Asia

This chapter is concerned with developing an understanding of how a group of non-elite actors (domestic workers) emerged as a major bilateral issue between these states. It should be noted, however, that it is our intention to avoid a purely actor-centric account of the everyday political economy – that is, one centred on the presentation of the voices and/or resistance strategies of migrant domestic workers and/or their civil society allies (see, e.g., Tan, this volume; Ford and Piper 2007; Elias 2008; Briones 2009). In contrast to this more agent-centric literature on migrant domestic work (while also recognizing the value and importance of this literature) we ground our analysis within an understanding of everyday life in which agency *does* matter but is not the *only* marker of what constitutes 'everydayness'. This need to bring back 'everydayness' into everyday political economy analysis is the focus of a recent critical essay by Davies (2014) who has argued for the need to look beyond the exercise of (oftentimes extraordinary) acts of agency in favour of an understanding of everyday life as it is experienced on a daily basis by ordinary people – as characterized by mundane daily rhythms and routines (see, in particular, the work of Lefebvre 2004 [1992]). However, Lefebrve's writings on everyday life that emphasize the household as an 'innately' feminized realm cannot be easily accommodated within a feminist political economy approach. While his emphasis on the cultures and practices of household life as part of a wider political economy critique is important (and is a theme that we pick up in later sections of this chapter), it is a perspective that feminists have widely critiqued (see Olsen 2011; Green 2012)[1]. Rather, as Felski (2000) argues, the practices of everyday life within households should be studied in terms of how they serve to *produce* gender; that is those scalar hierarchies rooted in the non- or underrecognition of the socially reproductive sphere and sustained by forms of oppression, injustice and even violence.

Turning to studies of everyday politics in Southeast Asia, it is notable that in Kerkvliet's conception of everyday politics – understood as the unconscious practices of people 'who probably do not regard their actions as political' (2009: 232) – politics is also described as including 'resource production and distribution within households and families' (230). It would appear then that the household is not absent in accounts of everyday life and everyday politics in Southeast Asia, rather, we would suggest, it is undertheorized and there is a risk that this undertheorization could (re)produce the silences that exist in political economy analysis when it comes to gender relations (including the silence of gender found in much Southeast Asian political economy scholarship – Teo 2013: 16–17). In developing a *feminist* everyday political economy, we point to both the material processes of social reproduction and the cultural production of norms regarding female subjectivities and cultures of domesticity. Household labour, understood as a routine and mundane aspect of everyday life, is thus recognized as fundamental to processes of capital accumulation (Fortunati 1995 [1981]) and is shown to be sustained by sets of cultural practices and habits relating to domesticity and class status as well as the intended and unintended consequences of state policies and practices.

We also do not want to suggest that the household is some sort of unchanging site of the everyday political economy, a place of endless repetition and routine. In terms of the cases discussed in this chapter, routines of everyday

---

[1] As useful as we find Lefebvre's ideas, the lack of critically aware agency he ascribes to women is detrimental (see Olsen 2011; Green 2012). Add to that Lefebvre's lazy critique of the 'modern women' who is portrayed as trapped and unreflective – as in 'control of production, of the household, children's education, social and cultural life, romance and love' (1995: 153) and little else. Lefebvre is attempting to critique modernist bourgeois construction of the (empowered) woman, but in as much as he deems the project doomed to ultimate failure, so too is his analysis.

life are invariably challenged and transformed by the presence (and then the sudden absence) of migrant domestic labour, while migrant domestic labourers themselves engage in a multiplicity of householding strategies (be it remittance sending or forms of long-distance mothering) that serve to reconfigure household relations in the sites that they have temporarily left behind. Thus, households are understood as sites of transformation and change. A feminist everyday political economy must take into account the deepening of market relations into the household that has occurred in terms of the expansion of private sector provisioning of social reproduction, the huge expansion of household indebtedness (in both the global north and mid- to low-income regions of the world such as Southeast Asia – see Rethel, this volume), or the growth of microfinance and microenterprise schemes that frequently serve to incorporate (and, oftentimes, adversely incorporate) poor households into the global economy. What is of particular interest to us in this chapter is the way in which household labour has become increasingly commodified as the challenges of meeting the socially reproductive needs of states are met by the growing market for paid domestic work. As LeBaron (2010) argues, the household has become a prime site through which more top-down marketizing agendas play out in the sphere of everyday life. Indeed, LeBaron's emphasis on the household in political economy analysis is a direct response to scholars of everyday political economy such as Hobson and Seabrooke (2007) who have tended to neglect the significance of gender relations in developing their analysis of the everyday political economy.

Nonetheless, migrant domestic workers do engage in modes and practices of resistance of the type described by authors such as Scott and Kerkliviet. But this is not to suggest that everyday political actions can simply be viewed as mere 'weapons of the weak'. Everyday forms of political agency are enacted by a range of actors (e.g., labour brokers, migrant sending households and employers) in ways that frequently reproduce those gendered hierarchies and broader systems of structural inequality that sustain the commodification of domestic work. In other words, although no agent is ever utterly confined within a 'structural straightjacket', agency is enacted within the 'repressive "confines"' (Hobson and Seabrooke 2006: 14) of the dominant social space (which, in our analysis, must include the confines of the household). The agency of everyday actors is mediated via a nexus of state, capitalist and household practices that themselves constitute new spaces of everyday political economy (Davies 2006). For example, as will be shown in later sections of this chapter, the regimes governing the flow of migrant domestic workers between states also serve to reproduce everyday cultures of surveillance and control (within households and within 'training centres') that construct the 'ideal maid' as the docile and subservient simple rural 'girl' and limit the scope and potential for worker agency let alone organizing.

Regulatory States and Managed Migration

State interventions and attempts to better manage migratory flows (and to engage in high-level foreign policy disputes over migrant labour issues) can be understood in relation to debates about the nature and character of state rule in Southeast Asia – specifically in terms of the emergence of more 'regulatory' forms of state rule (Jayasuriya 2005). Although the focus of this volume is on the everyday political economy, these political-economic transformations centred on the state remain relevant. This is because our analysis is not one in which we seek to reify the importance of the everyday as the only sphere/set of actors that matter – the regulatory context matters and, indeed, is integral to the production of everyday life itself. In what follows, we provide a brief outline of the labour disputes between Malaysia, Indonesia and Cambodia before turning to contextualize the disputes within broader debates concerning the transformation of state rule in Southeast Asia.

The large-scale movement of domestic workers within Asia is largely made up of formal flows of migrant workers under return migration systems – that are often governed by bilateral agreements known as memorandums of understanding (MOUs). The 2009 dispute between Indonesia and Malaysia honed in on what Indonesia viewed as inadequacies in the terms on which its workers enter Malaysia under the existing MOU (e.g., there were no guarantees of rest days or minimum rates of pay). In May 2011, with a view to ending the freeze on official flows of domestic workers from Indonesia, a new MOU was agreed and signed. However, despite stipulations in the MOU that rates of pay be set by 'market forces', Indonesia continued to press for an increase in the minimum monthly rate of pay. By mid-2012, only very small numbers of Indonesian domestic workers had entered Malaysia under the new MOU and the dispute has been further complicated by the 2012 announcement that Indonesia was seeking to end formal systems of return migration for unskilled workers by 2017[2]. By contrast, in the dispute with Cambodia where there was no MOU, it quickly became apparent that Cambodian private sector recruitment agencies were able to operate with complete disregard for the (inadequate) labour regulations that governed this sector leading to significant abuses against workers in training centres, in the transit phase and leaving workers especially vulnerable to abuses once in Malaysia (Human Rights Watch 2011; Holliday 2012). Prior to the ban, the Cambodian government had acknowledged a need to update the

---

[2] In Indonesia, such concerns were fuelled by increased democratic pressures on the state as members of the parliaments' Commission IX (that covers issues of transmigration) often coming from social activist backgrounds and a free press that sought to pressure the government into action (Elias 2013). Indeed, Indonesia's foreign policy agenda has increasingly asserted the importance of protecting its workers overseas (known as Tenga Kerja Indonesia).

ministerial order that regulated the employment of Cambodians overseas. A new sub-decree, no. 190,[3] issued a month before the ban came into place, makes certain overtures, yet it remained a 'skeletal' document (LICHADO 2011; Holliday 2012) and reflected Cambodia's much weaker bargaining position in international labour diplomacy[4].

In Rodriguez's work on the Philippine state, the management of migration takes the form of labour brokerage regimes whereby sender states effectively accommodate themselves to the demands of host states, taking on some of the regulatory functions associated with the supply of migrant workers (such as medical screening, overseeing transportation and guaranteeing a well-trained 'quality product') in return for more favourable terms and conditions of work for its citizens compared to other, lower income, and newly emerging labour sending states (Rodriguez 2010). Akin to writings on the regulatory state (the state as meta-regulator) (Jayasuriya 2005), Rodriguez's 'labour brokerage state' acts to license the role of private and semi-private actors (licensing recruitment agents and setting up semi-autonomous labour brokerage institutions such as Indonesia's National Agency for the Placement and Protection of Overseas Labor (BNP2TKI)[5]) to oversee and regularize the return migration systems for domestic work. In Cambodia, the label 'regulatory state' is less easily applied. Nonetheless, Springer's analysis of Cambodia's neoliberal transformation provides important insights into the 'microregulatory interventions' (such as union crackdowns and forced evictions) that ensure the persistent 'job readiness' of its population (2009: 142). Central to this perhaps more 'proto-regulatory' form of state rule are high levels of violence committed in the name of economic development, complemented by deeply opaque networks of corruption and nepotism (see also Heder 2012). Indeed, Cambodia's 'unregulated' labour recruitment industry is one in which the lines between the state and the private actors as well as between formal recruitment agency and informal networks of brokers are exceptionally blurred.[6] Although beyond the scope of this chapter, these blurred lines

---

[3] This replaced the 1995 sub-decree no. 57 that put forth certain minimum conditions for workers, the role of recruitment agencies and a general policy to 'to generate national revenue through foreign earnings' (UNIFEM 2006). However, the sub-decree was vague, lacking in specifics and, by the government's own acknowledgement, limited (Hing et al. 2011).

[4] This point was raised in a personal interview (Louth) with a National Project Officer, United Nations Inter-Agency Project on Human Trafficking, Phnom Penh, 4 March 2014.

[5] The fall of the authoritarian Soeharto regime following the 1997 Asian financial crisis saw democratically elected governments put legislation in place that increased the state's regulatory oversight of the return migration system (e.g., via the establishment of the BNP2TKI) yet also served to sanction the role of the private sector as the primary actor involved in organizing the official flow of migrants.

[6] A point raised in a personal interview (Louth) with Country Director, ActionAid Cambodia, Phnom Penh, March 3, 2014

between state and private authority involved in the regulation of the movement of people would make for a very interesting study of what both Ismail (2006) and Lewis (2011: 104–5) have termed the 'everyday state'.

Economic Development and the Production and Social Reproduction of Migrant Domestic Work

The discussion now turns to focus on the productive–socially reproductive tensions that underpin domestic worker disputes in Southeast Asia. We focus our attention in particular on the specific role that migrant domestic labour plays within increasingly transnationalized systems of social reproduction within these two states. As the feminist political economy literature on social relations of reproduction describes, gendered patterns of poverty and inequality are reproduced within an economic system in which social reproductive work even when it is paid for is rendered 'invisible' – not recognized as central to the functioning of the productive economy (Bakker 2007). The lack of value (both financially and culturally) accorded to socially reproductive work thus ensures that processes of global economic restructuring serve to further reproduce and exacerbate gendered inequalities and forms of poverty, inequalities that invariably intersect with other axes of inequality such as race, class and geography.

In analyzing migrant domestic work, it is important to emphasize how this form of work is constructed within the context of a capitalist economic system conceptualized here as a set of gendered spatial relations that serve to reproduce poverty and inequality. More specifically, the emergence of domestic workers as one of the largest and most feminized migratory flows in the Southeast Asian region reflects: (a) spatially organized patterns of poverty and inequality across the region (not just across states but also within states); (b) the ongoing incorporation of the region into a globalizing market economy as states increasingly embrace forms of neoliberal developmentalism that significantly expand the scope and reach of the market into all spheres of social life; and (c) the increased marketization and transnationalization of established patterns of social reproductive relations centred on the household. Indeed, it is this third point relating to the need to recognize the way in which patterns and practices of social reproduction centred on the household have gone global that is central to the feminist everyday political economy approach adopted in this chapter. That is to say, the scalar relations that underpin the subordination of the household, which mark it as 'outside' and separate from the market, have been thrown into flux as the space of the household economy expands across borders and the household itself emerges as a site for the production of commodified labour (Safri and Graham 2010)

Indonesia and Cambodia: Remittance-Led Poverty Alleviation and Women's Migration

A focus on social reproduction sphere brings to light important gendered assumptions that underpin the development of formalized/ing systems of return migration in Southeast Asia. In this section, we focus on the sender countries – Indonesia and Cambodia – in order to examine the remittance economies that have emerged due to the growth of a highly feminized form of employment. In doing so, it is important to recognize that an understanding of these remittance economies must take account of the extremely adverse terms upon which women enter into migrant domestic work. Remittances do, of course, constitute an important source of foreign exchange in much of the developing world, and writings on the migration–development nexus emphasize the positive impacts that remittances bring to both states and individual households. However, more nuanced, in-depth analyses of remittances tend to highlight the fairly minimal impact of remittances on household poverty levels[7] and point to the wider social costs associated with having household members working overseas (Parreñas 2005). Research on remittances has also pointed to their role in the reconfiguration and transformation of household relationships – not least in terms of how the rapid growth in temporary labour migration regimes is leading to the emergence of forms of 'global householding' (Douglass 2006) strategies that significantly challenge the ways in which we understand both the dynamics of household life and the nature of social reproduction (especially when the migration is for the purpose of taking up paid domestic work).

Research on the gendered impacts of migration not only points to the reconfigured household relations and daily practices that stem from the increased reliance of poor households on remittances but has also looked at the gendered logics and assumptions that underpin this social transformation. As writers such as Rahel Kunz (2008) argue, there is a persistent failure within international financial institutions to recognize the significant ways in which migratory flows are gendered beyond some rather dubious assertions concerning how women are more reliable (even 'rational') economic subjects in that they are more likely to remit a higher proportion of savings and when 'left behind' are better able to manage household finances. States in Southeast Asia have also tended to echo these 'heroic' narratives concerning women's contribution to remittance flows (Gibson et al. 2001) – a theme that, as we will see in the final section of this chapter, is further reproduced in the role of the recruitment industry in producing the subject of the 'ideal maid'.

---

[7] See, for example, Painduri and Thangavelu (2008) for a good analysis of the impacts of remittances on household spending patterns and household living standards in Indonesia.

Outward migration was, and continues to be, seen in both Indonesia and Cambodia as a mechanism to alleviate the negative impact of high levels of unemployment, especially in rural areas. In the Indonesian case, the 1997 financial crisis hit the country especially hard and, intersecting with increased demand for female migrants in wealthier states to work in both care-related and manufacturing employment, saw huge numbers of rural women migrants leave the country on temporary employment contracts. By 2007, women made up 79 per cent of Indonesian contract workers deployed overseas with most of these women taking up employment as domestic workers (Bank of Indonesia 2010). Invariably, wages remitted by migrants play an important role in Indonesia's attempts to ensure economic stability and development. It needs to be noted, however, that Indonesia is not a country overwhelmingly dependent on migrant worker remittances (Hugo 2008: 51; Bank Indonesia 2009). Cambodia too is not a remittance-dependent state – remittances in Cambodia are still quite low at 3 per cent of GDP in 2009 (Holliday 2012).

Nonetheless, both states have sought to enact policies and systems that aim to encourage overseas migration as a mechanism to bring in foreign exchange and, moreover, to alleviate poverty. In Indonesia, for example, it is significant that worker remittances since 2005 have been higher than inflows of official development aid. Furthermore, there is a spatial organization of migration at work with certain, largely impoverished, regions of the Indonesian archipelago overwhelmingly dependent on migrant remittances. The Cambodian government is actively encouraging migration as a stated policy aim as a means also to combat poverty, alleviative unemployment and bring in foreign earnings (Kingdom of Cambodia/ILO 2010). The global financial crisis compounded the situation with the highly feminized garment manufacturing industry, Cambodia's single largest export industry, being forced to lay off 10 per cent of its workforce – representative of some 30,000 job losses (World Bank 2009). Migration, then, becomes an attractive 'choice' for individuals experiencing economic hardship (and the decision to migrate is frequently influenced by enticements from agencies or brokers that might include bags of rice, cattle or cash loans; HRW 2011), and it presents an opportunity for a state looking for solutions to a range of economic and social problems. Unsurprisingly, remittances in Cambodia have increased dramatically from the early 2000s, more than doubling from the 2003 figure of US$ 138 million to US$ 335 million in 2009 (World Bank 2013).

The expansion of Malaysia's market for low-cost domestic work is dependent upon a particular spatial organization of labour whereby groups of economically marginalized women living in some of the poorest, usually rural, parts of Southeast Asia are drawn into the market economy. This spatial organization is one of the main mechanisms through which poor women come to be adversely incorporated into the market for domestic work and intersects with popular portrayals in Malaysia of Indonesian and Cambodian domestic workers as simple rural 'girls' struggling to cope in the modern urban Malaysian household environment. We now turn to examine these Malaysian households, drawing attention, in particular, to the role that domestic workers play in shoring up not just middle-class Malaysian women's ability to engage in the formal economy but also a vision of middle-class domestic well-being that underpins the Malaysian modernity project.

Malaysia: Socially Reproductive Workers and Reproducing Class Status

The demand for low-cost foreign domestic workers has emerged as a core feature of the dynamic transformation of social reproduction within several middle- to high-income Asian economies such as Malaysia. Given the patchy availability of childcare and elderly care services, migrant domestic labour is conventionally viewed as playing an important role in meeting the socially reproductive needs of middle-class Malaysian citizens and, ultimately, boosting the participation of educated Malaysian women in the formal labour market (Elias 2011). The deeply exploitative nature of this policy solution has, however, been well documented (Human Rights Watch 2004). Domestic workers are employed directly by households with their work permit tied to their employer and their freedom of movement restricted. They are subject to high levels of control and surveillance by employers, are not granted rest days, frequently experience difficulties such as non- or underpayment of wages, or are expected to perform additional household labour for employers' friends or neighbours.

The rise of migrant domestic worker employment in Malaysia should not be seen simply in terms of the pressures on households that stem from women's participation in the formal labour market. As Chin's (1998) work makes clear, employment of domestic workers also serves as a significant marker of social status. Cultures of domesticity, themselves often an outcome of a particular vision of modernity, intersect with the desires of a consumerist and aspirational urban middle class fuelling the demand for paid domestic work. Intimate practices of labouring *inside* the home are thus similar to practices of consumption or production that take place *outside* of the home in terms of their role in the production of class subjectivities. Not only are domestic workers, marked as different to their middle-class employers on the basis of their race and nationality, but their subordinate status within the household is also underscored by their association with the 'domestic' and the 'intimate'. An ongoing 'commodification of intimacy' (Boris and Parreñas 2010) – that is, the rise of affective forms of labour that appear to further marketize skills and behaviours traditionally associated with everyday domestic life – is thus characterized by the reproduction of gendered and class-based inequalities and hierarchies within the home.

Even with the ban in place, Indonesian women continued to dominate this sector of employment, and workers were still able to arrive into Malaysia on short-stay visas which could be converted into work visas. Nonetheless, the imposition of the moratorium did lead to significant labour shortages. Malaysian maid agencies suggested that domestic worker arrivals fell from around 1,000 per month prior to the ban to just 200 per month by January 2011, leading to a situation in which up to 35,000 Malaysian families were awaiting domestic workers, with 'waiting list' times averaging seven months (AsiaOneNews 2011). Given the association of class status and employment of domestic workers, it is interesting that the 'maid shortage' has produced certain anxieties about the 'stalling' of the Malaysian modernity project (or Malaysia's status as 'stuck' in the middle-income 'trap'). One extreme example of this comes from a dystopian vision of Malaysia in 2020 published by a popular online alternative Malaysian media outlet. In this account, Malaysia's economic decline is contrasted with that of a, by then, prosperous (and democratic) Indonesia which is now importing domestic workers from Malaysia:

As Siti walked pass [sic] the huge poster recruiting Malaysian maids for Indonesia she wondered what went wrong. 'We voted for BN [*Barisan Nasional* – the ruling party], we believed their promises of high income but now we can barely survive with the stagnant income and ever increasing cost of living ['], she thought bitterly ... It is the year 2020[8] and Tun Mahathir had just flagged off the first batch of Malaysian maids for Indonesia. There is no lack of eager women willing to take on domestic drudgery in a foreign land to escape the poverty in rural Malaysia. Reports of maids horrifically abused in Jakarta did not faze them. They are able to earn twice what a teacher earns and save most of it. Indonesia had progressed fast in the last decade and outstripped Malaysia in economic performance and income while Malaysia went backwards. (Gan 2012)

In the short story 'MH72', the Malaysian writer Krish Ram (2012) presents a similarly dystopian perspective in which the collapse of the Malaysian economy under their weight of a housing bubble leads to an educated middle-class Malaysian woman 'Susan' having to take up employment as a domestic worker in Hong Kong. The character of Susan, the stay-at-home highly educated wife and mother, is reflective of how women have come to play a symbolic role in the production of a specifically Malaysian modernity – the trappings of which include employment of an Indonesian domestic servant (Chin 1998). Indeed it is only with the rise of concerns about the middle-income trap that state policies have sought to emphasize the need for women to return to the workforce in order to support the country's knowledge economy (Elias 2011). The character's lifestyle quickly falls apart when her husband loses his

---

[8] The year 2020 has a symbolic importance in Malaysian politics and policy making. It being the date that former Prime Minister Mahathir Mohammed promised that Malaysia would attain developed country status by and the date continues to loom large in state development plans, documents and ministerial announcements.

job and the bills pile up (reflective of the rising concerns about levels of household indebtedness discussed in Rethel's chapter). Susan desperately clings to her perceived class status (flying on Malaysian Airlines to Hong Kong rather than on a budget airline), and yet as she reflects on her situation at the airport, she becomes acutely aware of how her status as a middle-class Malaysian woman had been dependent on the exploitation of domestic workers:

It was only three years ago that she had had her own live-in Indonesian maid in Bukit Damansara. She remembers how she had complained to her neighbour when her husband took the maid to Pantai Hospital for treatment when she collapsed suddenly.
    'No need to waste so much money, mah', she had told Mrs Khoo. 'She's only a servant, what?'
    She, suddenly, stops in her tracks. 'Oh my God; what if they beat me?' (Ram 2012)

These stories point to one of the many ways in which the production of modern, competitive Malaysia is contested via counternarratives in which the economic insecurities of the middle classes emerge in highly gendered terms. Nonetheless, more mainstream press coverage takes a somewhat different position, reassuring Malaysians by pointing to examples from Western states that *not* having domestic workers is in itself a form of modern living (while conveniently ignoring the inadequacies of the Malaysian welfare system in making this comparison). Not employing domestic workers is instead presented as 'the new middle class reality' (Lau and Koh 2012). The semi-official *New Straits Times* stated in a frontpage editorial that '[a]fter nearly three years of a supply cut of Indonesian domestic workers … one would have thought Malaysians would accept the reality by now: Indonesian maids are not coming anymore … Stop day dreaming, live in reality and find some other solutions' (cited in Kuppusamy 2012). Middle-class Malaysian households are thus encouraged to do their own housework and to use private childcare centres and to invest in labour-saving electronic devices such as dishwashers and robotic vacuum cleaners (Ahmad 2011; Unni 2014). Indeed, in early 2015, Malaysian and Indonesian press covered a story concerning how a Malaysian robotic vacuum cleaner was being marketed with the tagline 'Fire Your Indonesian Maid Now', leading to official complaints by the Indonesian government to the Malaysian foreign ministry (Jakarta Globe 2015).

    But even in the face of this 'new reality', what remains unchanged is that the market for migrant domestic work rests, fundamentally, on the state's non-recognition of domestic work (domestic workers are mere 'helpers' and have no access to formal labour rights under the terms of Malaysia's 1955 Employment Act) and thus not requiring the higher wages and benefits available in other jobs. Invariably then, efforts by the Malaysian women's ministry to create 'household manager' positions through training schemes met with little success. Despite the effort to rebrand and 'professionalize' domestic work, these initiatives are structurally constrained by both the official non-recognition of domestic work and the impact of state policies that have institutionalized a system of employment that ensures that this low-wage, low-status work is performed by non-citizen others. The possible collapse of this system in the face of the ongoing embargo has not as yet forced the Malaysian government to address some very thorny issues in relation to inadequacies in the provision of child and elderly care and in systems of maternity leave (Elias 2011), with the widespread assumption in place that arrivals of Indonesian domestic workers are immanent or can be easily replaced by other low-wage groups of workers from the region.

Everyday Actors and Return Migration Systems

In this final section, we return to examine how the everyday practices of the actors located within return migration systems serve to reproduce the structures of inequality and disadvantage in ways that limit, but at the same time do not completely obscure, the possibilities for resistance by migrant domestic workers themselves. We place particular significance on the role of recruitment agents and broker networks as central components of the everyday politics of migration. The limits of viewing migration as a simplistic state-to-state transfer of people regulated via some sort of bilateral arrangement or MOU is emphasized by Lindquist, Xiang and Yeoh (2011) who point to the significance of broker networks which operate not entirely externally to the state. The Cambodian case illustrates quite successfully the way in which the move to formalize the 'export' of women to the expanding regional labour market led to a rapid increase in the registered number of recruitment agencies from four in the early 2000s (Piper 2002) to thirty by 2011 with approximately sixty smaller firms operating under license (HRW 2011).

As Liang (2011) points out, recruitment agencies play a significant role in creating the image of the 'ideal maid' and, in the process, construct women as submissive, docile, non-citizen workers. Thus, such practices might best be conceptualized in relation to forms of (Foucauldian) governmentality that create both appropriate worker subjectivities and serve to reproduce national boundaries. For example, prior to the Cambodian ban, pictures appeared in the Malaysian media showing Cambodian women undergoing 'training' in order to take up employment as domestic workers in Malaysia (Hariati and Fong 2010). The pictures show a group of Cambodian women clad in matching yellow T-shirts cradling baby dolls and receiving cooking lessons in a domestic worker training facility (similar media images can also be found of Indonesian women prior to the Indonesian moratorium). Such images not only serve to justify the exorbitant 'training fees' charged by agencies, they also perpetuate ideas that the kind of women taking up employment as domestic workers lack any kind of marketizable skills *whatsoever* – even those skills that would be part of their everyday gendered household responsibilities – and thus construct certain groups of migrant women as deeply unskilled and not deserving higher rates of pay.

Thus, as Rodriguez and Schwenken (2013) argue, while regularized systems of return migration exist *because* of agreements between states, a state-centric (or regulatory) perspective is inadequate in understanding how and why ideal migrant subjects are produced and contested. Calling for a focus on 'wider societal practices', Rodriguez and Schwenken suggest:

> The production of migrant subjects is multidirectional and diffuse. Private business actors such as recruiters, employers or money lenders, state agencies, non-governmental organisations, and, last but not least, the migrants themselves engage in a wide array of disciplinary and regulatory techniques of forming ideal migrants for different ends. These subject positions are gendered, both in terms of masculinities as well as femininities, and racialized. They speak to local conditions as well as to global expectations about 'good migrants'. (2013: 376)

These local and global expectations concerning the 'good migrant' are evident in deeply commodified understanding of the foreign domestic worker that serves to deflect attention away from the unethical and oftentimes corrupt practices that agencies engage in. For example, in a Bank Indonesia survey of foreign migrant workers, the effective confinement of workers to training centres prior to departure was justified on the grounds that workers might run away and that 'this would be losses [sic] to the recruitment agency that have incurred costs in bringing them' (2008: 25). Human Rights Watch (2011) recount instances of Cambodian women having to pay large sums of money or hand over land titles to agents in order to leave training centres even for short periods. Furthermore, a central component of the efforts to regularize and manage return migration for domestic workers has been the reproduction of an anti-trafficking 'rescue' narrative whereby potential migrants are continually warned of the dangers of making the journey overseas in terms of the risk of being trafficked into sex work (Killias 2010). Especially in Cambodia, this is deeply problematic given the extremely legally and ethically dubious practices that have characterized the operations of recruitment agents (Hing et al. 2011). These 'rescue narratives' serve to further legitimize the activities of legal migration brokers and agencies – as those actors are best able to offer advice and protection to vulnerable groups of women.

Numerous studies of Southeast Asian domestic workers do, of course, point to the everyday acts of agency and resistance that workers engage in – a literature that counters the view that domestic workers are the voiceless victims of a patriarchal capitalist system (Yeoh and Huang 1998; Arnado 2010). As Rodriguez and Schwenken (2013: 376) suggest, these resistances (presented in Scott's (1990) terms as 'hidden transcripts') 'point to the ways that there is overall contestation of the rise in temporary labour migration programmes'. One of the most interesting studies, by Killias (2010), demonstrates that when domestic workers run away from an employer, in spite of the fact that they face certain insecurities that stem from their undocumented status, this can also be understood as a mode of resistance that enables workers to break free of state-sanctioned migration schemes and acquire better-paying, higher-status work. Unsurprisingly in the Cambodian context, there is considerable distrust of recruitment agencies that have themselves emerged as key perpetrators of abuses; (potential) recruits often cite a preference to join the illegal migration flows instead of pursuing government-sanctioned routes (Holliday 2011).[9] These accounts are important not simply in terms of how we think about the ways in which state control over the lives of migrant workers is reproduced and how this is resisted at the level of the everyday but also because they draw attention to the ways in which the distinctions between formal and informal migratory systems are frequently overemphasized. After all, both operate within the context of global inequalities that render the unskilled migrant particularly powerless. There is a very blurry line between documented and undocumented migration into Malaysia – a line that has blurred further as the Malaysian government and recruitment agencies have sought out ways to circumvent the impact of the freeze on new arrivals of domestic workers from Indonesia and Cambodia. Insecurities for migrant domestic workers are thus produced largely by state attempts to regularize the market for domestic work in order to meet development objectives. As an example, during the dispute between Malaysia and Indonesia, the Indonesian Embassy in Malaysia sought to push the Indonesian government to end the domestic worker ban on the grounds that domestic workers are even more vulnerable to abuse when they are employed through informal arrangements. However, this is a position that overlooks the multiple vulnerabilities that migrant domestic workers face within regularized systems of employment that function outside of national labour laws.

Conclusion

The twenty-four-year jail sentence handed down to a Malaysian couple for starving their maid to death sparked much of the initial uproar in Cambodia and

---

[9] In a personal interview (by Louth with a consultant at the International Organization for Migration Cambodia, Phnom Penh, 7 March 2014), it was suggested that almost all domestic worker migration to Malaysia had gone via informal/unofficial routes, a reflection both of the poor capacity of the state to actually regulate domestic worker flows as well as an overall lack of trust in state institutions.

perhaps illustrated a greater willingness by the Malaysian government to pros-
ecute crimes against domestic workers. Yet the judge's comments at sentencing
probably represent an uglier truth. The judge warned Malaysians not to create
a bad image for the country by abusing 'maids', before surmising that should
households face particular problems with a domestic worker, 'you can send
them back' (Kaur 2013). Domestic workers, thus, become something of a 'dis-
posable' commodity – a construction that also fits rather neatly with a broader
representation of handling risk and diversification when sourcing commodities.
Indeed, it is an issue that in the lead-up to the most recent Malaysian elections
became an issue of national importance. As part of a Malaysian delegation to
discuss deeper economic ties with Myanmar, Prime Minister Najib Razak stated
that domestic workers could be sourced from Myanmar, declaring that 'They
are an industrious and polite people. I think they could fit in culturally with the
Malaysian setting. I don't think there will be that great a difficulty' (*New Straits
Times* 2012). It would seem that sourcing domestic workers has become the
fare of trade delegations, while sourcing the right sort of domestic worker is
becoming an issue to be resolved by state-sanctioned market actors (recruitment
agents). Competing factors within the marketization of the demand for domestic
workers reside on tension between race, ethnicity, gender and cost. For instance,
the president of the Malaysian National Association of Employment Agencies
expressed the need to resolve the Cambodian situations so as to ease the dependence on Indonesian maids – as the cost of Indonesian domestic workers had
increased because of better conditions within the MOU (Aruna 2013).

In this chapter, we have drawn attention to the role that states – both host states
and sender states – play in reproducing deeply exploitative labour practices. Our
argument thus follows that of Rodriguez (2010) in suggesting that the labour
brokerage model is about states being able to continue to send low-cost workers
to particular states – without significantly challenging the exploitative terms on
which this takes place. It is a model that rests fundamentally on viewing workers
merely as economic commodities to be mobilized in the name of earning foreign
currency and alleviating poverty. Anti-trafficking approaches appear merely to
consolidate and shore up this migratory model, granting considerable power to
private actors (agents) in overseeing this process. The recognition that engaging
in practices of labour brokerage is a fundamental acknowledgement of the weakness of sender countries is perhaps best reflected in the desire by the Indonesian
state to move away from engagement in systems of short-term return migration
for unskilled work altogether. Such announcements do, however, overlook the
extent to which poor Indonesian households are often highly dependent on the
remittances sent home by unskilled migrants and are unlikely to stem the undocumented flows of Indonesians into Malaysia in search of work.

Migration for domestic work involves a spatial reorganizing of both work
and the household, and fundamental to understanding these transformations is

a focus on social reproduction. In particular, we would suggest that there is a need to consider the ways through which the emergence of regulatory migration regimes and disputes over migrant domestic work takes shape within the context of a transnationalization of social relations of reproduction. On the one hand, this is reflected in terms of the emergence of 'global households' – often poor households in which one or more members have migrated but continue to send money back (Douglass 2006; Safri and Graham 2010). But on the other hand, it is also a reflection of the ways through which states with large middle-class populations, such as Malaysia, seek to plug gaps in welfare state provisioning and provide the perceived domestic labour needs of an ever-growing and aspirational middle class. A focus on social reproduction then provides some important insights into the mechanisms through which the everyday is transformed and marketized – how arenas of social life such as the household previously viewed as marginal to the functioning of the global economy have come to be seen as new sites for the widening and deepening of the market economy. Indeed, the significance of the issue of labour migration for domestic work is reflected in the ways in which this issue has emerged as an important foreign policy concern between states in the Southeast Asian region.

References

Ahmed, A. (2011) 'Coping Well Without Maids', *The Star Online*, June 5, www.thestar .com.my/Story/?file=%2F2011%2F6%2F5%2Fnation%2F8747993.

Arat-Kroc, S. (2006) 'Whose social reproduction? Transnational mortherhood and challenges to feminist political economy', in K. Beznson and M. Luxton (eds.) *Social Reproduction: Feminist Political Economy Challenges Neo-Liberalism*. Montreal and Kingston: McGill-Queen's University Press, pp. 75–92.

Arnado, J. (2010) 'Performances across time and space: drama in the global households of Filipina transmigrant workers', *International Migration* 48(6): 132–154.

Aruna, P. (2013) 'More maid woes likely judging from report by Cambodia', *The Star Online*, February 2, http://thestar.com.my/news/story.asp?file=/2013/2/2/ nation/12660085&sec=nation.

AsiaOneNews (2011) 'Malaysia Needs Maids Urgently', *The Star/Asia News Network*, 11 January, http://news.asiaone.com/News/AsiaOne%2BNews/Malaysia/Story/ A1Story20110111-257475.html.

Bakker, I. (2007) 'Social reproduction and the constitution of a gendered political economy', *New Political Economy* 12(4): 541–556.

Bank Indonesia (2009) *Report on National Survey of Remittance Patterns of Indonesian Migrant Workers 2008*. Jakarta: Directorate of Economic and Monetary Statistics.

Bopha, P. and Lewis, S. (2012) 'Agreement to protect maids needs strengthening, gov't says', *Cambodia Daily*, April 21.

Boris, E. and Parreñas, R. (eds.) (2010) *Intimate Labours: Culture, Technologies and Politics of Care*. Stanford: Stanford University Press.

Briones, L. (2009) *Empowering Migrant Women: Why Agency and Rights are Not Enough*. Aldershot: Ashgate.

Carroll, T. and Jarvis, D. (eds.) (2014) *The Politics of Marketising Asia*. London: Palgrave MacMillan.

Chin, C. B. N. (1998) *In Service and Servitude: Foreign Female Domestic Workers and the Malaysian 'Modernity' Project*. New York: Columbia University Press.

Davies, M. (2006) 'Everyday life in the global political economy', in M. de Goede (ed.) *International Political Economy and Poststructural Politics*. Basingstoke: Palgrave MacMillan.

(2014) 'Production in everyday life: poetics and prosaics', Paper presented to the International Studies Convention, Toronto, March 26–29.

Douglass, M. (2006) 'Global householding in Pacific Asia', *International Development Planning Review* 28(4): 421–446.

Elias, J. (2008) 'Struggles over the rights of foreign domestic workers in Malaysia: the possibilities and limitations of "rights talk"', *Economy & Society* 10(4): 282–303.

(2011) 'The gender politics of economic competitiveness in Malaysia's transition to a knowledge-economy', *Pacific Review* 24(5): 529–552.

(2013) 'Foreign policy and the domestic worker: the Malaysia-Indonesia domestic worker dispute', *International Feminist Journal of Politics* 15(3): 391–410.

Elias, J. and Gunawardana, S. (2013) 'The global political economy of the household in Asia: an introduction', in J. Elias and S. Gunawardana (eds.) *The Global Political Economy of the Household in Asia*. London: Palgrave MacMillan, pp. 1–13.

Felski, R. (2000) 'The invention of everyday life', *New Formations* 39: 15–31.

Ford, M. and Piper, N. (2007) 'Southern sites of female agency: informal regimes and female migrant labour resistance in east and southeast Asia', in J. M. Hobson and L. Seabrooke (eds.) *Everyday Politics of the World Economy*. Cambridge: Cambridge University Press, pp. 63–79.

Fortunati, L. (1995 [1981]) *The Arcane of Reproduction: Housework, Prostitution, Labour and Capital*. New York: Autonomedia.

Gan, K. (2012) 'Malaysia in the year 2020: a maid exporter, bankrupt and a policy state?', https://hornbillunleashed.wordpress.com/2012/03/09/28209/

Gibson, K., Law, L. and McKay, D. (2001) 'Beyond heroes and victims: Filipina contract migrants, economic activism and class transformations', *International Feminist Journal of Politics* 3(3): 365–386.

Green, B. (2012) 'Complaints of everyday life: feminist periodical culture and correspondence columns in the woman worker, women folk and the freewoman', *Modernism/Modernity* 19(3): 461–485.

Hariati, A. and Fong, J. (2010) 'Filling the maid void', *The Star*, November 21, http://thestar.com.my/news/story.asp?file=/2010/11/21/nation/7471669&sec=nation.

Heder, S. (2012) 'Cambodia: capitalist transformation by neither liberal democracy nor dictatorship', *Southeast Asian Affairs* 103–115.

Hing, V., Pide, L. and Dalis, P. (2011) 'Irregular Migration From Cambodia: Characteristics, Challenges and Regulatory Approach Cambodia Development Resource Institute', *CDRI Working Paper Series*, No. 58, Phnom Penh, Cambodia.

Hobson, J. M. and Seabrooke, L. eds. (2007) *Everyday Politics of the World Economy*. Cambridge: Cambridge University Press.

(2007) 'Everyday IPE: revealing everyday forms of change in the world economy', in J. M. Hobson and L. Seabrooke (eds.) *Everyday Politics of the World Economy*. Cambridge: Cambridge University Press, pp. 1–24.

Holliday, J. (2011) *Cambodia's Labor Migration: Analysis of the Legal Framework.* Phnom Penh, Cambodia: The Asia Foundation.

(2012) 'Turning the table on the exploitative recruitment of migrant workers: the Cambodian experience', *Asian Journal of Social Science* 40: 464–485.

Human Rights Watch (2004) *Help Wanted: Abuses Against Female Migrant Domestic Workers in Indonesia and Malaysia.* New York: Human Rights Watch.

(2011) *"They Deceived Us at Every Step": Abuse of Cambodian Domestic Workers Migrating to Malaysia.* New York: Human Rights Watch.

Hugo, G. (2008) 'International migration in Indonesia and its impacts on regional development', in T. van Naerssen, E. Spaan and A. Zoomers (eds.) *Global Migration and Development.* New York and Abingdon: Routledge, pp. 43–65.

Ismail, S. (2006) *Political Life in Cairo's New Quarters: Encountering the Everyday State.* Minnesota: University of Minnesota Press.

Jakarta Globe (2015) 'Indonesia Files Complaint with Malaysia over Vacuum Cleaner Commercial', February 4, http://thejakartaglobe.beritasatu.com/news/indonesia-files-complaint-malaysia-vaccum-cleaner-commercial/.

Jayasuriya, K. (2005) 'Beyond institutional fetishism: from the developmental to the regulatory state', *New Political Economy* 10(3): 381–387.

Kaur, S. (2013) 'Couple jailed 24 years for starving Cambodian maid to death', *The Star Online*, May 17, http://thestar.com.my/news/story.asp?file=/2013/5/17/courts/13122049&sec=courts.

Kerkvliet, B. J. T. (2009) 'Everyday politics in peasant societies (and ours)', *The Journal of Peasant Studies* 36(1): 227–243.

Killias, O. (2010) ' "Illegal" migration as resistance: legality, morality and coercion in Indonesian domestic worker migration to Malaysia', *Asian Journal of Social Science* 38(6): 897–914.

Kingdom of Cambodia/ILO (2010) 'Policy on Labour Migration for Cambodia', Ministry of Labour and Vocational Training, General Department of Labour, Department of Employment and Manpower, www.ilo.org/wcmsp5/groups/public/---asia/---ro-bangkok/documents/publication/wcms_145704.pdf.

Kunz, R. (2008) 'Remittances are beautiful: gender implications of the new global remittances trend', *Third World Quarterly* 29(7): 1389–1409.

Kuppusamy, B. (2012) 'Malaysians Miss Indonesian Hired Help', *Inter Press Service News Agency*, www.ipsnews.net/2012/03/malaysians-miss-indonesian-hired-help.

Lau, J. and Koh, L. (2012) 'Maids and the New Middle-Class Reality', August 5, http://www.malaysianinsider.com.

LeBaron, G. (2010) 'The political economy of the household: neoliberal restructuring enclosures, and daily life', *Review of International Political Economy* 17(5): 889–912.

Lefebvre, H. (1995 [1962]) *Introduction to Modernity: Twelve Preludes September 1959–May 1961* (J. Moore, trans.). London: Verso.

(2004 [1992]) *Rhythmanalysis: Space, Time and Everydaylife.* London: Bloomsbury.

Lewis, D. (2011) *Bangladesh: Politics, Economy and Civil Society.* Cambridge: Cambridge University Press.

Liang, L.-F. (2011) 'The making of an "ideal" live-in migrant care worker: recruiting, training, matching and disciplining', *Ethnic and Racial Studies* 34(11): 1815–1834.

LICADHO (Cambodian League For the Promotion and Defense of Human Rights) (2011) 'New sub-decree on migrant labor fails dismally on workers rights', available at: www.licadho-cambodia.org/pressrelease.php?perm=257 (accessed 3 June 2013).

Lindquist, J., Xiang, B. and Yeoh, B. S. A. (2012) 'Opening the black box of migration: brokers, the organization of transnational mobility and the changing political economy in Asia', *Pacific Affairs* 85(1): 7–19.

New Straits Times (2012) 'Myanmar Maids Next?', 30 March.

Olson, L. (2011) 'Everyday life studies: a review', *Modernism/Modernity* 18(1): 175–180.

Parinduri, R. A. and Thangavelu, S. M. (2008) 'Remittance and Migrant Households', Consumption and Saving Patterns: Evidence from Indonesia', Nottingham University Business School Malaysia Campus Research Paper No. 08-02.

Parreñas, R. S. (2005) *Children of Global Migration: Transnational Families and Gendered Woes*. Stanford: Stanford University Press.

Piper, N. (2002) 'Gender and Migration Policies in Southeast Asia – Preliminary Observations from the Mekong Region', Paper for presentation the IUSSP Conference "Southeast Asia's Population in a Changing Asian Context"', Siam City Hotel, Bangkok, Thailand, 10–13.

(2008) 'Feminisation of migration and the social dimensions of development: the Asian case', *Third World Quarterly* 29(7): 1287–1303.

Ram, K. (2012) 'MH72', http://silverfishstories.blogspot.co.uk/search?updated-max =2013-08-01T11%3A56%3A00%2B08%3A00&max-results=4.

Rodriguez, R. M. (2010) *Migrants for Export: How the Philippine State Brokers Labor to the World*. Minnesota: University of Minnesota Press.

Rodriguez, R. M. and Schwenken, H. (2013) 'Becoming a migrant at home: subjectivation processes in migrant-sending countries prior to departure', *Population, Space and Place* 19(4): 375–388.

Safri and Graham (2010) 'The global household: towards a feminist postcapitalist politics', *Signs* 36(1): 99–125.

Scott, J. C. (1990) *Domination and the Arts of Resistance: Hidden Transcripts*. New Haven: Yale University Press.

Springer, S. (2009) 'Violence, democracy, and the neoliberal "order": the contestation of public space in posttransitional Cambodia', *Annals of the Association of American Geographers* 99(1): 138–162.

Steans, J. and Tepe, D. (2010) 'Introduction: social reproduction in international political economy: theoretical insights and international, transnational and local sitings', *Review of International Political Economy* 17(5): 807–815.

Teo, Y. (2013) 'Women hold up the anti-Welfare regime: how social policies produce social differentiation in Singapore', in J. Elias and S. J. Gunawardana (eds.) *The Global Political Economy of the Household in Asia*. Basingstoke: Palgrave MacMillan, pp. 15–27.

United Nations Development Fund for Women (UNIFEM) (2006) 'Cambodian Women Migrant Workers: Findings from a Migration Mapping Study', *Regional Program on Empowering Women Migrant Workers in Asia*, Phnom Penh, Cambodia.

Unni, B. (2014) 'Managing Life Without a Maid', *Malaysian Digest*, January 23, http://malaysiandigest.com/opinion/484995-managing-life-without-a-maid .html.

Voice of America (VOA) (2011) 'Despite Ban, Cambodian Maids Still Being Sent to Malaysia', October 16, www.voanews.com/content/despite-ban-cambodian-maids-still-being-sent-to-malaysia-131977668/168113.html.

World Bank (2009) 'Swimming Against the Tide: How Developing Countries are Coping With the Global Crisis Background Paper', Prepared by World Bank Staff for the G20 Finance Ministers and Central Bank Governors Meeting, Horsham, UK, March 13–14.

(2013) 'Migration & remittances data: annual remittances data', *Inflows*, http://econ.worldbank.org/WBSITE/EXTERNAL/EXTDEC/EXTDECPROSPECTS/0,,contentMDK:22759429~pagePK:64165401~piPK:64165026~theSitePK:476883,00.html#Remittances.

Yeoh, B. and Huang, S. (1998) 'Negotiating public space: strategies and styles of migrant female domestic workers in Singapore', *Urban Studies* 35(3): 583–602.

11 Enforcing Socioeconomic Rights: Everyday Agency, Resistance and Community Resources among Indonesian Migrant Domestic Workers in Hong Kong

Carol G. S. Tan

Introduction

There are currently over 320,000 full-time, live-in migrant domestic workers (MDWs) in Hong Kong, the vast majority of whom are from Southeast Asia. In recent years, women from the Philippines and Indonesia have constituted 48 per cent and 49 per cent, respectively, of the MDW population, with women from Thailand, Sri Lanka and Nepal making up most of the remainder (Immigration Department 2012). These women and previous generations of women from Southeast Asia account for a significant proportion of the intra-Asia migration of workers, being at the same time a part of the widely observed feminization of migration (see also Elias and Louth, this volume). In the social fabric of Hong Kong, their arrival in ever-increasing numbers, especially since the second half of the 1980s, also marked a sea change in which household chores, child and elder care were commoditized to the extent that in approximately one in eight Hong Kong households an MDW carries out or helps with these tasks.

The nature of domestic work, its private location and the dispersal of its workers, very often as single employees in a household, coalesce to produce a vulnerability that is, in many parts of Asia, worsened by live-in arrangements which may have an impact on access to unions or to help and advice. This vulnerability is why the International Labour Organization has identified women domestic workers as one of the three most vulnerable groups of migrant workers (ILO 2004) and why a Domestic Workers' Convention has now been adopted (ILO number 189). This convention and the longer-standing UN Convention on the Protection of the Rights of All Migrant Workers and Members of their Families (1990) have had some indirect impact in Hong Kong in terms of consciousness raising and lobbying. NGOs and migrant workers' unions, which in Hong Kong are permitted the political space in which to establish themselves and pursue their activities, have invoked both conventions in their ongoing campaigns and, arguably, drawn legitimacy from them in fighting two recent major issues: the exclusion of MDWs from the right of abode (akin to permanent residency) (*Vallejos and Domingo* v *Commissioner of Registration* 2011) and the exclusion of domestic work from the minimum wage regulations.

These types of high-profile campaigns have often resulted, in Hong Kong and elsewhere, in attention being drawn to the activities of NGOs, unions and human rights activists, with the effect of reinforcing the portrayal of MDWs, along with other female migrant workers, 'as having little or no agency in the world economy' (Ford and Piper 2007: 63). An obvious corrective to this is to examine MDW involvement in collective activism and struggles as Ford and Piper have done. At the level of the individual, ethnographic studies of MDWs have also sought to uncover MDW agency and to do so with fine-grained attention to how individual MDWs view, interpret, respond to and negotiate their subordinate status while often cleverly acting out 'boundary work' as part of the daily performance of their status (Lan 2006; Constable 2007).

A quite different enactment of everyday agency is explored in this chapter – namely the role of MDWs as individual litigants seeking compensation from their employer. The research is based upon a number of interviews with Indonesian MDW litigants in Hong Kong. The quite exceptional nature (at least within the context of Asia) of the Hong Kong dispute resolution regime for MDWs is a key factor in enabling migrant workers to sue their employers. However, the examination of these women's experiences points to the very dynamic everyday processes through which MDWs, as a marginalized and economically vulnerable group of actors, are able to access the courts in order to seek redress for a range of injustices. This focus on MDWs as individual litigants seeking justice for themselves (compared to class or representative action) should not be understood in Scott's conception of 'weapons of the weak' not least because, as Piper and Ford and others have pointed out, collective activism and protest is not lacking in Hong Kong (Constable 2010; Hsia 2010). Collective and individual struggles do not, of course, inhabit sealed-off areas that permit no interaction or seepage between the two. One objective of this chapter is also to show how individual MDWs, most likely because of an increase of rights consciousness resulting from collective efforts, are effective interveners in the journeys of other MDWs towards litigation.

It is notable that MDWs as litigants have also been neglected by the scholarship on social and economic rights – an oversight that reflects the general tendency of this literature to treat economic and social rights within the frame of 'citizenship' (specifically the role that constitutionally guaranteed rights can play in generating transformative social change – see also Rosser, this volume). In their work on courts, public policy litigation and economic and social rights, Gauri and Brinks (2008) ask whether courts have been able to effect social transformation by delivering judgements which increase the provision of social and economic goods along with the question of whether courts are the correct or better institutions for policy making (see also Gargarella and Domingo 2006). These studies necessarily put courts (especially Supreme Courts or constitutional courts) centre-stage; the litigant is placed somewhat in the wings.

Nonetheless, when Gauri and Brinks turn to mapping the triangle of relationships which connects the state, providers and recipients of socioeconomic rights, they are keen to highlight the sphere of private obligation that connects the providers and recipients of socioeconomic goods – a sphere which has, all too often, been neglected in analyses because of what they characterize as the 'difficult-to-shake background notion that social and economic rights must involve the state' (2008: 11). In this sphere, private enforcement or litigation by the recipient against the provider can, they argue, lead to improved provision of socioeconomic goods. It is perhaps here that we might place the focus of this chapter: MDWs who sue their employers. With some adaptation, their triangle can help us consider the case of MDWs as litigants. MDWs with claims against their employers are seeking labour rights that can be regarded as socioeconomic rights. These rights, in so far as they are embodied in the employment contract between the MDW and her employer, are derived most immediately from private obligations. While the legal framework in Hong Kong would permit state prosecution of employers for failure to provide at least some of those rights, the reality is that enforcement will, to a large extent, rest with the individual MDW as an employee.[1] Although the Gauri and Brinks triangle offers a place for locating MDWs who sue their employers, an important point of departure from the type of litigation foremost in their minds is that MDWs in Hong Kong who sue their employers are seeking corrective, not distributive, justice. Their aim is not to seek policy changes or novel extensions of existing rights or the recognition of new socioeconomic rights through judicial interpretation. Rather, they are seeking the enforcement of rights already possessed. The importance of studying litigation and other forms of dispute resolution lies in the persistent need to enforce rights by means of seeking corrective justice: it is only through such claims for justice that rights are turned into material compensation for the rights-holder. It is also worth noting that the importance of litigation will only increase with any future enlargement in the socioeconomic rights won by and for MDWs. There is thus no reason to see individual MDW litigation as 'small arms fire' in contrast to the organized 'revolution' of class or representative actions that seek distributive justice. It is appropriate, however, to treat litigation for corrective justice as 'small arms fire' and 'weapons of the weak' in that suing one's employer involves 'everyday' enactments of resistance that arise through processes involving the

---

[1] In this regard, there is little to differentiate a low-skilled employee from a skilled employee.

litigant's action or reaction and that of other MDWs acting as individuals, supported by available community and other resources.

Focusing on the contractual character of the relationship between the employer and the MDW can lead us to overlook the fact that these litigants are non-citizens[2]. Theirs is thus a case of non-citizens claiming socioeconomic rights. From the perspective of the general principles of private international law, in particular the question of jurisdiction, MDWs suing their employers is unexceptional because the rules on the jurisdiction of courts usually allow jurisdiction to follow the place of performance of the employment contract. The reality in many Asian MDW destinations, however, is that an MDW dispute with her employer is prohibited from the courts that would be used by non-migrants and instead channelled into a special – though not necessarily specialized – dispute resolution forum. If we take this into account, MDWs litigating in the courts of Hong Kong is exceptional. Moreover, the literature on rights-based approaches to socioeconomic rights presupposes the citizen–state relationship as the main axis for claiming socioeconomic rights (Joshi 2010). From this vantage point too, the fact that non-citizens such as MDWs can enforce their rights in a court is exceptional.

MDWs in Hong Kong have the best terms and conditions in Asia (and probably also in the Middle East). An MDW is legally entitled to a rest day of 24 hours' duration in every seven-day period, statutory holidays, progressive annual leave, adequate food or a food allowance, the cost of travel to her place of origin upon termination of the contract and limits on the deductions that can lawfully be made from her salary. In addition, there is a minimum wage, statutory limits on how much she may be charged for services rendered by the employment agency (EA), and her contract shields her from being asked to work in premises other than the employer's residence. Each contract is of two years' duration and without a probationary period. Both the employer and the MDW may terminate the contract by giving a month's notice. MDWs are also entitled to long-service payments, medical expenses and employment protection for pregnancy and childbirth. These minimum terms and conditions are secured in the three overlapping layers of the contract, employment legislation and labour or immigration department regulations. Moreover, MDWs are supported by aspects of the socio-legal environment in Hong Kong. First, there is a relative absence of extortion and abuse by the personnel of the authorities (police, immigration and labour departments as well as the relevant tribunals). Second, the dispute resolution mechanisms are relatively efficient and are also free to the parties. Third, an active civil society provides a bedrock of resources for the distressed or exploited MDW.

---

[2] See also the discussion in Elias and Louth (this volume) regarding the uncertain place of non-citizens in bilateral labour regimes designed to 'protect' migrant domestic workers.

Nevertheless, MDWs do not always receive their contractual dues. Surveys carried out by NGOs show the pattern and frequency of exploitation and abuse (Asian Migrant Centre 2005, 2007; Chiu and Asian Migrant Centre 2005). Moreover, despite reasonable access to justice, those who litigate represent only a small fraction of the MDWs who have experienced sub-contractual and unlawful terms and conditions. The MDW's status, daily experiences and choices are highly constrained, not least by the costs of migration, by the law itself (Tan 2014) and by the sharp practices of some employers (Tan 2000). Low wages, the risk of unemployment, the short two-week window in which they are permitted by the immigration authorities to secure a new employment contract, living in her employer's home and her prohibition against employment pending the conclusion of a claim against her employer constitute basic contours of the constraints against which a decision to sue her employer is taken. For Indonesian MDWs, these constraints are greatly worsened by the state-sanctioned labour migration practices which include high agency fees and long periods in what are officially termed 'training centres', a euphemism for 'labour camps' in which the agencies can 'warehouse labor stock' to meet the vicissitudes of demand for labour (Sim and Wee 2010: 155). These are also places in which the potential migrant worker suffers restrictions on her personal freedom and other forms of coercion. The aim of this chapter is to explore how it is that some MDWs, despite these structural constraints, do end up litigating. What circumstances, factors and conditions account for the MDW 'going to Labour'[3] and what can we learn about the impediments and challenges MDWs experience along the way which may have prevented others from suing their employers? When the enquiry is directed at the path along which each MDW journeyed or stumbled, the circumstances that triggered the journey, and the various twists and turns along the way, MDWs emerge as actors who draw upon resources available to them.

MDWs 'Going to Labour' in Hong Kong

In late 2010 and early 2011, interviews with eighteen Indonesian MDWs were carried out.[4] They were all women who were, at the time, living in one of the several shelters run by Islamic or Christian organizations. Almost all MDWs who spend more than a few days living in a shelter are those whose lives have become entangled in either civil or criminal proceedings. I was interested in how MDWs, in spite of the structural constraints, came to be litigants. The

---

[3] I use this phrase as an umbrella term to include the initial processes of dispute settlement in the Labour Department as well as the processes at the Labour Tribunal or Minor Employment Claims Adjudication Bureau.

[4] Only a few of the eighteen cases are discussed in this chapter. Interviewees will be referred to using pseudonyms. The interviews were conducted by a native Indonesian speaker.

main section of the interview asked the open-ended question of how the interviewee came to be in the shelter. The interview also included more closed questions about sources of information and advice that the MDW had received prior to arrival in Hong Kong as well as subsequently. All the women interviewed had a contractual claim pending and, because of this, they had already interacted, to a greater or lesser extent, with legal advisers and legal processes. Their stories thus bore the effects of some of the ordering demanded by legal processes. Most of the women were, for instance, very clear and fluent on the dates of particular events on which their claims were founded and sometimes also fluent in providing explanations for their action or inaction. Some of the women volunteered to be interviewed because it was a chance to practise telling their side of the story. Telling their story without breaking down emotionally, especially if they had been through a harrowing experience, was part of their strategy for seeing their claim to fruition. Despite this filtration process, the women's stories reveal much about MDWs as everyday actors.

In the majority of cases, the women were claiming pay in lieu of the required one month's notice of termination of their contracts; for unpaid wages between termination and their last wage packet; and for the cost of an air ticket and travel expenses from Hong Kong to their place of origin. I refer to these collectively as 'end' rights (i.e., after termination of employment) and contrast them with 'term' rights (i.e., during employment), common elements of which are unpaid wages up to the time when the last monthly wage was paid or ought to have been paid, rest days uncompensated in wages or unlawful wage deductions occurring during employment. MDW claims sometimes include term and end rights although end rights–only cases occur more frequently and there appears to be a correlation between cases including a combination of term and end rights with litigants who can be said to have been prime agents in their own journey towards litigation. Litigants whose claims comprised only end rights, on the other hand, became litigants as a result of the experience of (oftentimes extreme and violent) abuse. This correlation is discussed in the rest of this chapter, in the course of which I also examine the triggers and processes through which MDWs become litigants, emphasizing the everyday processes and networks that are key enabling factors.

The Litigant as a Prime Agent

A case exemplifying prime agency on the part of the MDW is that of Ina. On a rest day, through a conversation with another MDW 'active in an organization', Ina discovered that her salary was unlawful. She then confronted her employer about her terms and conditions, recording the conversation as had been advised by her fellow MDW. Her employer implied that information on the terms and conditions of employment should have been conveyed by the EA before the start of her employment. She then added that the full salary was only for able/ skilled (*'pintar'*) helpers who had four years of previous experience. Ina was still in her first contract in Hong Kong and had, before this contract, never worked as an MDW. She requested a day off some time later, and on that day, accompanied by a friend, she went to Christian Action (one of a small number of legal advice centres) and from there to a shelter. Her claim was for unpaid wages, wages in lieu of rest days and public holidays, as well as wages in lieu of a month's notice, her repatriation costs and salary for the days worked since her last pay packet. Cases such as Ina's, in which the MDW is the prime agent, will often involve term rights as well as end rights. Several aspects of Ina's case are worth noting because they are recurring motifs in the everyday experiences of other MDW litigants.

First, Ina's EA posed a significant obstacle. When Ina went to the EA to retrieve her passport and contract, they refused and only produced the documents when she threatened to call the police. As we shall see, the EA – its proprietor and staff – emerge as a key determinant in whether the MDW becomes a litigant. Second, as we have just seen, Ina invoked the threat of the police. In fact, an MDW who terminates her employment is invariably advised to return to her employer to collect her belongings accompanied by the police (largely to lessen the likelihood of an accusation of theft by the employer). Third, Ina's knowledge and subsequent action were probably delayed because she had been denied rest days until she had worked for several months. Only when she was able to have a rest day was she free to go to Tin Hau (an area frequented by many Indonesian MDWs on their rest days) where she had the critical encounter with an MDW on whose advice she later relied. Rest days create opportunities for extended conversations with other, more experienced MDWs, to pick up a copy of a newspaper, to seek advice before deciding what to do and so forth. Fourth, the likelihood of Ina's claim against her employer succeeding was considerably weakened by the fact that she had signed receipts acknowledging the full salary and rest days. Ina insisted that when she signed the receipts she was told by her employer that these were merely sample documents.

Timing One's Departure from an Employer

Ina's case is fairly straightforward in the sense that once she was clear that her employer was acting unlawfully, she took action to escape that situation. Her own resolve, combined with the conversation with the more experienced MDW and strengthened by the advice she received at the legal advice centre, led her to become a litigant. Other respondents waited a while before taking action. Nuri explained that she first knew that her salary was an underpayment in her fourth month of work. She had the telephone number of Christian Action because she had been given a newspaper by an acquaintance when she went to pick up her employer's child one day. However, she did not dare take action ('*tidak berani*') because her salary was still subject to a deduction ('*masih potongan*') of HKD 2,000 per month. In her seventh month of work, she did go to Christian Action where she was advised to collect relevant evidence of her underpayment. Nuri recorded a conversation in which her employer showed her a note signed by Nuri, agreeing to a monthly salary of HKD 2,200 without rest days. The employer reacted angrily at Nuri's queries and threatened to return her to the EA. This threat was in fact carried out but was thwarted by Nuri because en route, with only her mobile telephone and the clothes on her back, she escaped to a shelter, having already been informed about shelters by Christian Action. Nuri's decision to wait until she had repaid her loans is probably not uncommon. Whatever other uncertainties, she had the comfort of knowing that she has no outstanding loans.

The pressure to sit out the period of deductions from her wages to repay loans can be strong enough to persuade an MDW that she should endure several months of very poor conditions such as insufficient sleep, being assaulted by her employer and even being bitten by the employer's dog. Elena recounted how, when she was walking the dog, a friend lent her a newspaper from which she noted the telephone numbers of Christian Action, the Indonesian consulate and the police. Despite this, only in her sixth month did she, on her rest day, find out more from a fellow MDW 'active in an organization' that she should report her conditions to the consulate. Like Nuri, she said that she was too afraid to act before her loans had been repaid.

Some respondents preferred to take action only when they were approaching the end of their contracts. Litigation is risky even when one's case is strong. For many employees including MDWs, litigating is also likely to mean unemployment. On the other hand, if there are term rights involved, the longer an MDW continues to work, the larger the deficit in entitlements will be. Yet, working for longer means having the chance to save up more money which can provide an economic buffer against having no salary while her claim is pending. Furthermore, for the MDWs who take action only towards the end of their two-year contract, the time for looking for a new employer is close at hand and they have probably made up their mind not to seek a further contract with the same employer. The extent to which an MDW feels empowered to finding a new employer is, therefore, important.

In the examples discussed above, the MDW has knowledge that she was being denied a contractual entitlement. She then either leaves her employer, or her employer terminates her employment. The experiences of this group of MDWs suggest that, even where the MDW has been the prime agent in her leap from exploitation to litigation, chance conversations with other MDWs are critical because of the capacity of these contacts to give basic advice on the law and where to find legal advice or refuge. Newspapers, too, are important vectors carrying, as they do, telephone numbers that will connect the MDW with the advice centres. The pivotal role played by legal advice centres and shelters is also clear. It is important to note that the MDW is not always in control of the situation, although planning the sequence of her actions with some care may help her to retain control.

End Rights–Only Claims

An MDW with an end rights–only claim is in a peculiar category because, by definition, she will have no grounds for a claim against her employer until after her employment ended. Her claim is generated by the termination of the contract and the circumstances surrounding it. An MDW running away is not likely to have confronted her employer for her termination benefits and, if dismissed suddenly, is likely to have been evicted without the opportunity to discuss her termination rights.

Two cases will be mentioned briefly. Yuli had suffered assaults by the grandmother in the household soon after she started her contract. She had learnt from the neighbours that her predecessors had experienced the same treatment. She tried to be patient, and when she felt she needed to do something about it, she reported it first to the grandmother's daughter-in-law and later to the grandmother's son. However, the assaults continued and her injuries became unbearable, not least because she was not allowed to seek medical attention. When she could no longer endure the abuse, Yuli sought to terminate the contract, but her employer refused. She then called the police with the result that she was taken to a hospital and eventually to a shelter. Yuli had initiated the termination of the contract but had left without being properly compensated. Having arrived at a shelter with the help of the police, she was only a step away from a legal advice centre where she could be advised on her end-of-contract entitlements. Yuli's case is probably rare in that many MDWs who are physically abused are also those not in receipt of their contractual entitlements, that is, most MDWs who suffer assaults will also have been denied their rights under their contracts. The second case is that of Sari, who reported to the police that she had been repeatedly raped by her employer's husband. She was put in a government-run crisis centre, and her employment was only subsequently terminated. It was this termination that led to Sari bringing a claim for her end-of-contract entitlements.

Far from being of limited value, the end rights–only claims offer significant insights. First, it is precisely because, in most of these end rights–only claims, the MDW flees or is evicted, and, paradoxically, the fact of running away or having been evicted that increases her chances of arriving at a shelter or a legal advice centre. The very acuteness of a woman's situation (as we have seen, this includes the cases of physical harm) makes her more likely to be helped at a shelter or advice centre. Second, the circumstances surrounding end rights–only claims suggest that those who have term claims but who are not dismissed suddenly or who do not run away from their employers are less likely to become litigants. Indeed, the majority of women interviewed had end rights–only claims. The overrepresentation of such claims in the face of widespread underpayment of wages and other common breaches of the law suggests that MDWs with term claims are significantly less likely to sue their employers.

Physical Harm as the Trigger for Flight

Having seen the incidence of assault and rape in Yuli and Sari's experiences in the context of a discussion of the overrepresentation of end rights–only claims, this section looks at two other cases of physical harm that resulted in claims which included term rights. It appears that in these cases the claim came to be made because physical harm caused the MDW to flee. Indeed, most of those interviewed had come to sue their employer because of the experience of physical abuse forcing them to flee – it was only at this critical juncture that they became aware of their legal rights. Both the cases examined next – Maya and Tuti – suggest that were it not for the physical abuse their claims may not have been brought.

Maya's experiences were among the most harrowing of the experiences of those interviewed. She was starved of food and suffered severe mental abuse. She recounted how she had been driven to attempt suicide, but as she was preparing to jump out of the window, her purse fell, scattering photographs of her children. She explained that she was a widow with two sons and a daughter. Her daughter was born only a month after her husband had died. She had decided not to put her daughter up for adoption, resolving to struggle on by herself to educate her children. She recalled her great sadness at that moment when she saw their photographs and realized that she had not been able to send them money. She suggested that she might have persevered if she had been given adequate food. 'How can one work without eating?' she asked. In two months, her weight had decreased from fifty-eight kilograms to fifty-three kilograms. She resolved to run away on her next rest day. She went to Causeway Bay, an area with a high concentration of Indonesian MDWs and which is also the location of the Indonesian Migrant Workers Union (IMWU). Other MDWs, seeing her looking confused, enquired about her circumstances. She did in fact go to IMWU, then to a shelter and then to Christian Action. When she ran away, she had no idea where she should go, let alone have any plan to pursue a claim. She was fleeing the mental abuse, hunger and chronic tiredness.

Tuti had a claim pending against her employer for unpaid wages, wages in lieu of rest days as well as for her end-of-contract benefits. Similar to Maya, she ran away because of ongoing assaults at her employer's hands and not because she wished to sue her employer. Tuti's employer had told her not to inform the police of the assaults because they would imprison and torture her. She had learnt from the neighbours that the employer had had eleven MDWs from a variety of countries, none of whom had finished their contracts. She remembered the EA's advice to be patient and she did indeed remain with her employer for five months (from May till September) until her employer threatened her with termination without repatriation expenses. While having lunch outside the employer's home the next day, she was asked by an Indonesian MDW why she was so pale. She confided in this fellow MDW, who then offered to take her to a shelter. She left immediately for the shelter and that act brought her employment to an end.

Here again, as we noted with the prime agency cases, the role played by individual MDWs in assisting fellow MDWs cannot be overstated. Some MDWs made enquiries of fellow MDWs when they sensed that something was wrong. More experienced MDWs advised other MDWs on strategy, for example, recording conversations with the employer, and they directed MDWs to shelters or legal advice centres. In other cases, the advice emerged through conversations about salary levels and rest days, including advice to convince the less-experienced MDW that underpayment and the lack of rest days is unlawful. In yet another instance, an MDW gave a fellow MDW the confidence to leave when she explained that her needs would be met at the shelter and that she should not return to her employer. In these ways, the advising MDW acted as a preliminary source of legal advice before the MDW reached a legal advice centre. MDWs also passed round local Indonesian newspapers that publish important telephone numbers and publicize cases of MDWs taking action against their employers. MDWs may also offer assistance in the form of providing temporary shelter, seizing opportunities such as the absence on an overseas trip of an employer (see the case of Dewi, below, and Tan 2014).

The help extended by MDWs also shows how important rest days are for the transmission of advice and comparing notes. Apart from offering respite from the daily grind of menial tasks, rest days are also important because it is then that MDWs with activist or political interests can become involved in NGOs and unions (Nehrling 2010) and, thereby, accumulate the knowledge that enables them to give advice to MDWs facing sub-contractual working conditions. As discussed, quite a few claimant MDWs reported relying on advice from an MDW 'active' in one of the NGOs. On the other hand, so long as an MDW has some opportunity to meet with other MDWs – even fleeting encounters when walking the dog, doing the shopping or collecting the employer's children from school – the MDW may still have the opportunity to speak with other MDWs.

Shelters and Legal Advice Centres

It is very clear from the experiences of the respondents that, if they managed to reach a shelter, the shelter would direct them to the legal advice centre where they would then take steps towards litigation. Because few MDWs in distress go straight to a legal advice centre, shelters act as the most important conduit between the MDW and the legal advice centre. Their importance also lies in the provision of accommodation, food and social activities, all of which help to make suing an employer practicable, given that, in most cases, the litigant is prohibited from taking up other employment. Migrant workers in Hong Kong are comparatively fortunate in having several NGO-run shelters, including some that are run by the organizations that provide active legal advice centres. This means that migrant workers are not solely dependent on their diplomatic missions for safety and refuge or, for that matter, advice and assistance. Given the rise in the view among Indonesian migrant workers that their own government is exploitative rather than ready to assist, the possibility of side-stepping the Indonesian consulate no doubt encourages MDWs to seek redress elsewhere.

As much as shelters efficiently conduct domestic helpers to the legal advice centres, it is the amassed capacity of the legal advice centres that helps the MDWs to navigate the procedures involved in making a claim against her employer. Here the MDW's experience is given its fullest legal potential as her experience is transformed into the paragraphs of her petition. The MDW is given advice on the amount of her claim, the likelihood of success and how long it might take. Paralegal advice centres may also advise the MDW on how to collect evidence before leaving her employer and how to avoid an accusation of theft. It is also the legal advice centres that carry out the role of petition writers by drafting vital letters that the MDW takes to the police, the immigration department, the labour department and to her employer. She is then able to collect her belongings, extend her visa and inform her employer of the action she is taking.

It needs to be stressed that it is often through legal advice centres that the MDW's term claims are conceived. As we have already seen, in a number of cases, the MDW ends up bringing a claim for, say, underpayment over the course of her employment or for wages in lieu of rest days. In some of these cases, it has never really crossed her mind that she could sue her employer for this. In other cases, she may even have known that she was not receiving the contractual wage she had seen in her contract but had not reached the stage of articulating her complaint to her employer or seeking advice. In both these scenarios, if not for her arrival at a shelter or legal advice centre, the MDW would probably not have made these term claims.

Employment Agencies

In contrast to shelters, NGOs and unions, there is almost nothing to suggest that EAs will direct an MDW to the police or to the legal advice centre. EAs have usually colluded in or are aware of the fact that the employer has made unlawful deductions from the MDW's salary or that the MDW has not been paid the minimum wage. The business model of the EA simply does not incentivize them to advise the MDW to sue her employer or to seek help so to do. Instead, it is in their business interest to redeploy an MDW as quickly as possible. Trite as these remarks are, particularly in the current climate in Hong Kong in which EAs have been the target of criticism and campaigns over the high fees they charge MDWs, EAs and their relationships with the MDW and the employer still require some consideration. These relationships are complex and are a feature of the employment of migrant, low-skilled labour and, more specifically, of domestic workers, which is absent in the case of skilled or professional workers.

The relationship between the EA and the MDW is one of some complexity – they may be tied by bonds that are financial, involving loans repayable to the EA or its sister company. Other bonds of dependency and trust may arise from the EA being the first port of call for newly arrived MDWs. Many MDWs spend at least a few days at the EA on arrival. This early period at the EA is also where MDWs meet other newly arrived MDWs and have experiences that may shape their expectations in respect of their employment. Ina, for instance, said that she learned from other newly arrived MDWs that they were all expecting a salary of HKD 2,000. She reported that the EA had said little about rest days and salary. Furthermore, the MDW may be able to find temporary accommodation at the agency. EAs may also have staff who are able to speak in Indonesian and who may have kept an eye on new MDWs in the first few days or weeks of their employment, acting as a go-between for the employer and the MDW.

Ina's employer, who is probably not alone among employers to do this, sent her to the premises of the EA on her day off, permitting Ina to spend her rest day only under the supervision of the EA and its staff. Thus, an MDW's relationship with the employer can extend well into the period of the contract of employment. Against this backdrop, it is no surprise that some MDWs should feel that the EA is where they can find shelter as well as, depending on the situation, someone who can intervene in a dispute with the employer. Depending on her work conditions but also on the individual MDW's own social capital, she may have few friends or family to turn to in Hong Kong, though this situation would, for most MDWs, improve with time. There is also the fact that agents commonly hold the MDW's passport and other documents. Most of the women interviewed reported that they had to go to the EA to retrieve their passports and contracts after leaving their employers. MDWs such as Dewi also report that they are advised by government authorities to contact the EA if they encounter problems.

First-time MDWs are likely to be more dependent on the EA than more experienced MDWs, and an MDW who is still indebted to an EA will not find it so easy to end her dependency. For some interviewees, the employment agent is where, of their own accord, they turned for help. Dewi, who had suffered repeated minor assaults perpetrated by her employer, contacted her EA when she first ran away from her employer. The EA talked her into returning to her employer. She ran away again seven months later. This time a fellow MDW took Dewi to another EA. She might have stayed there until an employer was found were it not for making three acquaintances there, one of whom had been in Hong Kong for six years and who gave her the telephone number of one of the NGOs. Dewi was soon in the shelter and at a legal advice centre.

For some MDWs, the EA provides them with useful services – for example, a contract with a new employer, the necessary paperwork and repatriation entitlements from the previous employer. Tini, for example, had, through the EAs, completed three contracts. Her fourth contract was terminated early, but she received, through the EA, all that was due to her. That EA had then found her a fifth employer, but this contract was terminated shortly, resulting in Tini being returned to the EA. If not for a conversation with an MDW, who gave her advice to go to a shelter, she might have started a new contract without suing her fifth employer for her end rights. In her case, it was quite natural, given what she had earlier experienced of the EA's services, to trust the EA.

Among other respondents, some either took evasive action to avoid being sent back to the EA or, after being returned to the EA, found a way of escaping. It would appear that, when the trust between the EA and the MDW has broken down, even if the rupture is caused by something trivial, it is more likely that the MDW will end up suing her employer. This is what the experience of Yanti suggests. She had been returned to the EA when her employer became bankrupt. Before sending her to the EA, the employer had provided her with her end benefits. Not many days later the agency found her a new employer with whom she signed a contract. However, before her employment could start, she fell out with the agent over a borrowed umbrella and was ejected from the EA's hostel. Being suddenly homeless, she sought help from a friend and before long found herself successively in the offices of the IMWU, the premises of a Muslim organization, a shelter and then Christian Action. Her subsequent claim against her employer was for wages in lieu of rest days, a matter about which she had never previously confronted her employer. Her experience suggests that had the EA not made her homeless, she might have started her new contract without looking back.

Wati is another MDW who may well not have made a claim. She had previously worked for an employer for ten months without her full salary, for very long hours and without all her rest days. At the termination of this contract, she went back to the EA and some weeks later started a new contract. This new contract was fine until, after six months had passed, she was accused of using her male employer's toothbrush. She was then summoned back to the EA, but her female employer explained that this was so that Wati could have a period of 'introspection' rather than because her contract was being terminated. Thereafter, the EA moved her from one place to another and asked her to work for them. Unhappy about this, she ran away to Dompet Dhuafa, an Islamic charity that runs a shelter. In Wati's case, during her six-week stay in Macau to await her visa before taking up her second contract,[5] she met with an MDW who advised her about her rights and who informed her about Dompet Dhuafa.

The employer's relationship with the EA is also complex. Although, in law, once the employment of the MDW commences, any dispute regarding the employment contract should be a matter between the employer and the MDW, it is common for employers to turn to the EA and, should they wish to terminate an MDW's contract, to 'return' the MDW to the agent. The employer may rely on the EA to take care of the repatriation arrangements and to help them issue written termination agreements for the parties to sign, inform the relevant authorities and so forth. Employers unhappy with the MDW they have been sent and seeking a 'replacement' are very likely to return the MDW to the EA and negotiate a reduced fee for a new MDW. This is a practice that is reinforced by the contract between the employer and the EA. The agency, on the other hand, has an interest in placing the returned MDW with another employer as quickly as possible.

Conclusion

Some MDWs, despite the multiple structural disadvantages, manage to sue their employers for breaches of their employment contract. The relatively small number of interviews with Indonesian MDWs suggests two main observations regarding who, and in what circumstances and processes, manages to sue. First, few MDWs sue their employers without the aggravating experience of physical violence. It may be inferred that many of those suffering the commonest breaches of contract, such as a lack of rest days or underpayment of

---

[5] For an explanation of why neighbouring Macau has become an 'overflow' area for MDWs out of work in Hong Kong see Sim and Wee (2010).

wages, do not sue their employers. Second, among those who became litigants, few were prime agents in the sense described earlier. If they took the decision to run away, it was to escape physical abuse and not due to any intention, however vague, to seek redress for breaches of their employment contracts.

The women who end up as litigants constitute a minority. Yet, rather than dismissing their experiences on the basis that they have nothing to tell us about the women who do not litigate, their experiences in fact shed much light. They illuminate the interplay between the MDW's personal capital and resolve, events beyond her control, lesser and more significant interventions by others and available resources for help and advice that facilitate litigation. They show that 'labour' is often an unplanned destination; the journey towards litigation is triggered by a dramatic event or an experience of acute stress that ruptures the relationship with her employer. We can infer from this that, in the absence of such an event, MDWs may continue in their contracts without seeking redress, perhaps weighing in the balance also the extent to which they find their employment conditions tolerable, or even satisfactory.

The women's stories also allow us to order by impact several factors. When a dramatic event has occurred, MDWs manage to litigate because of the legal advice centres and shelters that exist in Hong Kong. The experiences of the respondents suggest that few initiate their journey towards litigation without the intervention of others, particularly fellow MDWs. The capacity of Indonesian MDWs to advise and assist one another is clear. It is very likely to be a result of the political and social space which has allowed NGOs attentive to migrant workers to operate, spread their message and help with that capacity building. MDWs as sources of advice are much needed given that a number of MDWs reported that the advice given to them before departing Indonesia was confined to matters more connected with morals, sexual relationships and directed at preparing MDWs to be disciplined workers.

After arrival, there is the role of the free newspapers that circulate among MDWs and which appear to be more effective than the guide books prepared for MDWs by the Hong Kong government agencies or the Indonesian consulate. A number of women reported that their copy of the guide book was confiscated by either the EA or their employer. Some MDWs may be able to conceal the guide book or to persuade her employer that it was 'nothing'. As one MDW commented, a piece of paper with the relevant telephone numbers or addresses is easier to conceal. MDWs are able to sue their employers also because they have been able to count on police assistance at the key moment when they wish to leave their employer's home. Without the police, an MDW would have to rely on the EA and the MDW's respective consular services unless she was able to make contact with a union representative. As discussed above, EAs are inhibitors because it is not in their interests to advise the MDW on her rights against her employer or to point her towards the legal advice centres. Their aim is to recycle the MDW into another contract as soon as possible. Only if there is a destabilization of her relationship with the EA will an MDW's chances of becoming a litigant increase. The Indonesian consulate has few defenders when it comes to their record of serving the interests of Indonesian MDWs. In thinking of what action to take, resources we have not examined here include the MDW's experience of work and life and her personal financial situation. Her personal capital no doubt influences the extent to which she is able to exercise agency – be that to act, to resist or to assist an MDW in distress. As a matter of policy, the continued funding of legal advice centres, shelters and proper training of the police (so that they do not send MDWs back to EAs, for example) is vital.

Over and above these particular observations, the stories of the MDWs who litigate destabilize the still dominant portrayal of MDWs in which the language of 'protection' and 'structural constraints' denies them their agency. They also redress the imbalance caused when attention is inevitably drawn to the high-profile campaigns for the improvement of the rights of MDWs in which collective action for or by MDWs is featured. In litigation, we see how some MDWs use the narrowest of opportunities to seek advice or to collect vital evidence with which to overcome earlier detrimental acts such as signing receipts for full wages and rest days. An MDW may initiate a dispute by voicing her complaint to her employer; she may, with the help of other MDWs, calculate when she should run away from her employer; she may have to either resist being sent to the EA or engineer her escape from the EA. In possession of professional advice, she chooses whether or not to proceed with a claim and she finds the courage to attend labour department meetings or tribunal hearings without representation in which her employer will be present. She determines, usually without professional advice, if she should accept an offer to settle. Initiating action or reacting to their circumstances as litigants, we see MDWs as everyday actors who can change the course of their own paths and who can negotiate hurdles and overcome challenges in order to improve their fortunes or avoid further harm.

References

Asian Migrant Centre (2005) Underpayment: Systematic Extortion of Indonesian Migrant Workers in Hong Kong. www.asian-migrants.org/index.php?option=com_content&task=view&id=4&Itemid=29.

(2007) Underpayment 2: The Continuing Systematic Extortion of Indonesian Migrant Workers in Hong Kong. www.ilo.org/jakarta/whatwedo/publications/WCMS_116888/lang--en/index.htm.

Chiu, S. W. K. and Asian Migrant Centre (2005) *A Stranger in the House: Foreign Domestic Helpers in Hong Kong*. Hong Kong: Hong Kong Institute of Asia-Pacific Studies.

Constable, N. (2007) *Maid to Order in Hong Kong: Stories of Migrant Workers*, 2nd edition. Ithaca: Cornell University.

   (2010) 'Migrant workers and the many states of protest in Hong Kong', in N. Constable (ed.) *Migrant Workers in Asia: Distant Divides, Intimate Connections*. Abingdon: Routledge, pp. 127–144.

Ford, M. and Piper, M. (2007) 'Southern Sites of Female Agency: Informal Regimes and Female Migrant Labour Resistance in East and Southeast Asia', in Hobson, J. M. and Seabrooke, L. (eds.) *Everyday Politics of the World Economy*. Cambridge: Cambridge University Press, pp. 63–80.

Gargarella, R. and Domingo, P. (2006) *Courts and Social Transformation in New Democracies*. Aldershot: Ashgate.

Gauri, V. and Brinks, D. M. (2008) 'Introduction: the elements of legalization and the triangular shape of social and economic rights', in V. Gauri and D. M. Brinks (eds.) *Courting Social Justice: Judicial Enforcement of Social and Economic Rights in the Developing World*. Cambridge: Cambridge University Press, pp. 1–37.

Hsia, H.-C. (2010) 'The making of a transnational grassroots migrant movement: a case study of Hong Kong's Asian migrants' coordinating body', in N. Constable (ed.) *Migrant Workers in Asia: Distant Divides, Intimate Connections*. Abingdon: Routledge, pp. 105–126.

Immigration Department (2012) Annual Report 2011. www.immd.gov.hk/publications/a_report_2011/en/foreword/vision.html.

ILO (2004) *Towards a Fair Deal for Migrant Workers in the Global Economy*. Geneva: International Labour Organization.

Joshi, A. (2010) 'Do rights work? Law, activism and the employment guarantee scheme', *World Development* 38(4): 620–630.

Lan, P.-C. (2006) *Global Cinderellas: Migrant Domestics and Newly Rich Employers in Taiwan*. Durham: Duke University Press.

Nehrling, E. (2010) 'Beyond the Right to Rest: An Evaluation of the Social and Legal Structures Shaping the Agency of Foreign Domestic Workers in Singapore', *SEARC Working Paper Series*, No. 107, City University of Hong Kong.

Sim, A. and Wee, V. (2010) 'Undocumented Indonesian workers in Macau: the human outcome of colluding interests', in N. Constable (ed.) *Migrant Workers in Asia: Distant Divides, Intimate Connections*. Abingdon: Routledge, pp. 145–163.

Tan, C. G. S. (2000) 'Why rights are not enjoyed: the case of foreign domestic helpers in Hong Kong', *Hong Kong Law Journal* 30(3): 354–360.

   (2014) 'How Dewi Became a Litigant: Migrant Domestic Workers as Litigants in Hong Kong', *SEARC Working Paper Series*, No 151, City University of Hong Kong.

Vallejos Evangeline B v Commissioner of Registration, HCAL 124/2010 (30 September 2011).

Part V

Conclusion

12 Everyday International Political Economy Meets the Everyday Political Economy of Southeast Asia

Juanita Elias, John M. Hobson, Lena Rethel and Leonard Seabrooke

At its core, this volume has focused on everyday practices of economic engagement that have transformed – and are being transformed by – the Southeast Asian region's embrace of market-led developmentalism. To this end, the chapters in this volume have sought to illustrate the many and varied ways in which everyday actors and their practices of everyday life both constitute and operate within Southeast Asian political economies. Our contributors have considered the production of Southeast Asia's Everyday Political Economy (EPE) within distinct country contexts, drawing together different disciplinary perspectives and engaging a range of methodological and theoretical tools. Concluding a volume of this nature is no easy task. In this endeavour, the editors Elias and Rethel have been joined by John Hobson and Leonard Seabrooke, the authors of the influential 2007 book *Everyday Politics of the World Economy*, which, in setting out their Everyday International Political Economy (EIPE) approach, provided an important intellectual precursor to this volume. We use this as an opportunity to reflect about how this book project has sought to push the notion of *everyday* political economy in some quite distinctive directions to that originally put forward by Hobson and Seabrooke. Thus, in these concluding comments, we highlight the points of commonality and differences between the EIPE and EPE projects.

The argument in this chapter unfolds in two steps. We first sketch IPE's journey from a focus on what Hobson and Seabrooke (2007b) called 'regulatory' IPE (or RIPE) to a greater concern with the everyday. We then consider the chapters of this book against this background. One final point of note here is that the starting point of analysis of this book is distinct to that advanced in Hobson and Seabrooke's volume. There the authors were centrally interested in the relationship between everyday actor agency and its effect on the *global* political economy. The current book, however, tends to focus more on developments *within* particular national economies situated in the Southeast Asian region. This is not to say that the global political economy is ignored; but to the extent that it is discussed, it is mainly in the context of how international influences and pressures are negotiated, mediated and, in some cases, significantly transformed at the national/local level and the role that everyday actors (can) play in acquiescing, contesting or resisting them. This means that this book is located more within what was termed in the introduction an EPE – rather than an EIPE – perspective. In other words, it is a book that can be located much more straightforwardly within a body of scholarship on everyday politics, everyday life and everyday resistance. Accordingly, the focus is different to that deployed in the Hobson and Seabrooke volume, which sought to address a persistent problem found within studies of the *International* Political Economy – that is, the reification of the actions of global regulatory elites in developing an understanding of ongoing processes of change and transformation in the global economy. We hasten to add that the focus on Southeast Asian national economies returns EPE to its origins, to works by James C. Scott (1976, 1985, 1990) and Benedict J. Tria Kerkvliet (1990, 2005) that inspired the Hobson and Seabrooke volume.

Locating the Everyday in IPE

In this section, we first briefly outline the problematique of what Hobson and Seabrooke referred to as 'regulatory' IPE (or RIPE). We then move to identifying two points of departure for approaching EPE – an everyday life perspective and an everyday politics perspective. However, as we shall argue, it is perfectly possible to straddle, or draw from, both strands when crafting an EPE approach. From there, in the second section, we consider how the different chapters of this volume map across these two approaches and how the book as a whole advances the cause of EPE, not just in the discipline of IPE but also specifically in the study of the Southeast Asian region.

The Problematique of RIPE

Hobson and Seabrooke's (2007a) volume highlights the dominance of top-down understandings of the global political economy. This is seen as reflecting in part the intellectual shadow that studies of International Relations have cast over the field of IPE. Students of IPE have, for example, long been taught in terms of competing theoretical agendas such as neorealism, neoliberal institutionalism and constructivism derived largely from the academic study of International Relations. While Marxism is also recognized as bringing important alternative political agendas to the study of the global political economy (and was much more clearly and obviously rooted in a broader tradition of political economy scholarship), much Marxist scholarship *in IPE* proceeds to deal with essentially regulatory questions and issues – favouring a focus on the role of transnational business and regulatory elites in research agendas that frequently ignored the role of bottom-up class agency.

RIPE's central organizing question in effect asks 'who governs and how is international order regulated'. Such a question immediately directs our analytical focus or gaze onto the key structures, international institutions and particular elites within the global economy, all of which are rendered as the prime objects of study. For neorealism and neoliberal institutionalism in particular, the prime mandate is to find ways of restoring and maintaining world order as well as maximizing global economic growth (cf. Keohane 1984; Gilpin 1987). Certain liberal systemic constructivists have also bought into this generic approach, arguing that interstate cooperation and world order is promoted through states' deep socialization of 'progressive' norms of behaviour (e.g., Finnemore 1996; Wendt 1999). Indeed, systemic constructivists are interested primarily in revealing the positive ways in which states are 'civilized' and socialized into deep cooperation within an increasingly tight international society, thereby providing a kind of thicker version of neoliberal institutionalism (Avant et al. 2010). Even in the constructivist work that pays attention to domestic sensitivities, special emphasis is placed on elite actors or norm entrepreneurs who come to prominence in times of uncertainty or crisis and who promulgate new ways of ordering economies – for example, Keynes at the end of the Great Depression (Blyth 2002). As Colin Hay aptly points out, constructivists point to prominent elite actors to provide an 'ideational focus for the reconstruction of the perceived self-interest of the population at large' (2004: 210). And while the social constructivist field has developed at a quick pace to include more non-elite actors, it often tends towards a top-down focus (cf. Seabrooke 2007; Widmaier et al. 2007).

In short, these approaches reify or fetishize top-down processes connected to international institutions and states, hegemons, elite actors and global 'civilized' norms (most of which, it turns out, reflect the normative agenda of Western civilization). If we add in the point that these theories embody Eurocentric metanarratives (see Hobson 2012, 2013a, 2013b), then we end up with a highly skewed, one-eyed generic approach which reifies Western civilization whose developmental practices are to be emulated as the highest referent in the global economy, on the one hand, while focusing only on elite actors and structures of power as the key agents/directors of the global economy, on the other.

At this point, we can introduce Marxism into our discussion – or more specifically, that tradition of scholarship in IPE which seeks to critique Western structures of capitalist power as embodied principally in a transnational capitalist class. We, of course, note that many Marxist scholars do make vital contributions to the study of everyday life (see the work of Lefebvre 1971, 1991, in particular) and we acknowledge, too, that Marxist IPE scholarship has a critical aspect that differentiates it clearly from the other IPE approaches mentioned above. As such, it is uninterested in finding ways to restore global order and maximize global economic growth, rejecting such normative claims as typifying 'problem-solving' theory (Cox 1986) and, ideally at least, searching for ways in which the global capitalist order might be transcended and transformed. Moreover, this critical mandate finds resonance in EPE; as does Karl Marx's original emphasis on bottom-up class resistance – all of which means that Marxism potentially resides within an everyday approach and outside of RIPE.

However, there are a number of problems which amount to the proposition that much of Marxism fails to move beyond RIPE. First, between the 1970s and the early 1990s world systems theory comprised the key Marxist approach in IPE (e.g., Wallerstein 1974) – an approach that reified the structure of the capitalist world economy such that all notions of agency, especially in the 'periphery', are in effect dismissed. This also reflects the inherent Eurocentrism of the approach (Hobson 2012: ch. 10). Second, despite the rejection of 'problem-solving' approaches in the writings of Cox and others, the rise of Neo-Gramscian perspectives in IPE from the 1990s onwards replicated a persistent focus on elites found in much mainstream scholarship.[1] Indeed, not infrequently, it seems that much of contemporary Marxist IPE theory seems much more at home in discussing the power of the powerful rather than the 'power of the powerless' (cf. Overbeek 1990; Rupert 2000). Of course, there are some important and notable exceptions that focus much more on forms of resistance politics from below (e.g., Bieler 2006; Morton 2007) as well as on the micro-level interventions into the everyday lives of the poor that sustain capital accumulation (see Weber 2010). This is also in stark contrast to the social conflict (Murdoch School) approach taken in a significant body of literature on the political economy of the Southeast Asian region as discussed in the introductory chapter.

Hobson and Seabrooke's (2007b) central claim is that while we certainly need to consider elite actors in the world economy this should not be done at the cost of rejecting the everyday (with the 'everyday' constituting both non-elite actors and non-elite sites of agency as well as the study of everyday life itself, as we have argued in the introductory chapter and discuss further below). Not surprisingly, the elite suppliers of order – viewed as power-makers – constitute only a very small minority of the world's population. Indeed, one may be forgiven for thinking that RIPE provides the impression that the study of the world economy can be gleaned by examining only the actions of elites, especially within rich industrialized states or those within international organizations (both public and private), while the remainder are but power-takers whose actions are inconsequential for the making of the world economy (cf.

---

[1] See also Worth (2008) on the limits of the reliance on Cox's development of Gramscian thought in IPE.

Table 12.1 *EPE: analytical traditions and key components*

Analytical tradition	Everyday politics	Everyday life
Key components		
Understanding of Social Life	Logic of action	Logic of discipline
Focus of Analysis	Actor-centric	Agency-centric
Practices of Engagement	Non-elite actors' acquiescence, contestation and resistance to economic transformation	Routines of daily life that shape and are shaped by economic transformation
Political Economy Precursors	Structurationist approaches Social conflict approaches	Cultural political economy Feminist political economy

Tétreault and Lipschutz 2005: 167). However, elites do not operate within a social vacuum but find that their power and policies are mediated and refracted to a not insignificant extent through the actions of everyday agents in all manner of ways.

A range of scholars have been developing various approaches which rethink IPE so as to move beyond a conventional top-down view (Amoore 2002; Davies and Neimann 2002; Tickner 2003; Davies 2005; Franklin 2005; Tétreault and Lipschutz 2005; Watson 2005, 2013; Antoniades 2007; Langley 2008). Furthermore, more attention is now being paid to challenging conventional understandings of political and economic change through work that seeks to understand IPE from the perspective of non-core economies (Dunn and Shaw 2001; Tickner 2003; Hobson 2004, 2013b; Phillips 2005). Against this background, it seems to us that two main approaches have emerged in how political economists bring the 'everyday' into their analyses. The first approach focuses on the ways in which non-elite actors acquiesce to and resist the processes of economic change. In so doing, it centres on the 'logic of action' within *Everyday Politics*. The second approach can be characterized as an *Everyday Life* perspective in which the everyday is characterized either (a) as a realm governed and ordered by particular 'logics of discipline' or (b) as a site in which the mundane/ordinary comes to be valued on its own terms in order to subvert and challenge the traditional focus of much IPE scholarship. Table 12.1 summarizes key components of these two analytical traditions which will be elaborated upon in the remainder of this section. It is important to note here that these two analytical traditions serve as entry points of analysis and that the lines between these two approaches are purposely blurred, for the book demonstrates that the actions of 'everyday politics' and the routines of 'everyday life' intersect in many and variegated ways.

IPE as Everyday Politics

The everyday politics approach seeks to reveal how social actors exercise agency whether they are resisting power and power structures, or whether they are simply going about their everyday life even if this reinforces structures of power. Moreover, this approach envisages a variety of forms of non-elite actor agency ranging from subtle expressions of resistance to more dramatic exercises of defiance, on the one hand, as well as subtle expressions of everyday actions that when aggregated can promote change even if this was never the original intention of the individuals concerned. The approach is also particularly interested in how the actions of powerful actors are reacted to, mediated and even shaped through the actions of ordinary people whether this subverts or reinforces the powerful. In adopting '*who acts* and how do their actions enable change?' as central organizing question, this approach is inherently actor-centric while at the same time paying attention to a much broader range of actors than mainstream RIPE tends to do (Hobson and Seabrooke 2007b: 6; emphasis added).

This emphasis on everyday actor action/agency should by no means be taken to imply a belief on our part that everyday actors can behave entirely as they please or that they always succeed in getting what they want. As much as we reject overly voluntarist and liberal conceptions of agency, so do we not wish structures of power and repression out of existence. By definition, agents who are non-elites act within structurally repressive 'confines'. And yet, no agent is either entirely powerless or purely 'confined' within a logic of discipline for there is always a space, however small, for the expression of agency. Thus, a central purpose of EPE is neither to marginalize the importance of the dominant nor to reify the agency of the weak. Rather, it is to analyze the interactive relationship between the two. It deserves emphasizing that the space given over to agency does not mean that we ignore the important role of structure. But it is precisely because so much of IPE focuses on top-down processes – that is, dominant actors and structures – that EIPE feels it necessary to focus full-square upon agency from the bottom-up.

Hobson and Seabrooke's work draws from frameworks articulated earlier by Scott (1985) and Kerkvliet (2005), including a conception of non-elite actor agency that *contests* but *does not necessarily undermine* the power of elites. This occurs as subordinate actors challenge the legitimacy of elites and, in so doing, can pressurize them to change their policies. In the everyday politics literature, agency is generally expressed through subtle forms of defiance, which is conducted at the local level and is effected by everyday people in the form of verbal taunts, subversive stories, rumour, 'sly civility' and so on. As Kerkvliet's work demonstrates, everyday politics is more subtle and more common than the more grandiose and dramatic forms of overt resistance that we often associate subordinate agency with. For example, in his study of collectivized agriculture in Vietnam, Kerkvliet (2005) illustrates how everyday acts such as cheating on rice stocks, local stories and ignoring national government policies developed in small incremental ways. But crucially, these aggregated into affecting national policy change with regard to collective agriculture, not because of a national ideological change but because the system had become so compromised that it could no longer be legitimately sustained. Thus, while there were no overt protests or riots, economic policy was transformed nonetheless (Kerkvliet 2005). Moreover, as chapters in this volume show, the ongoing political economic transformation of the region has opened up new, more formalized pathways for non-elite actors to exercize their agency – be it, for example, in the form of establishing legally recognized trade unions in Myanmar (discussed by Henry) or the possibility for non-elite actors challenging education reforms in court in post–Suharto Indonesia (discussed by Rosser).

The work on everyday politics also reminds us that one key reason why an actor may want to reject a claim to legitimacy by those who seek to govern is that it conflicts with her or his identity. Much of RIPE places little importance on identity and tends to view actors' preferences as aligned with their material self-interest. Indeed an everyday politics approach requires a strong conception of identity that draws from everyday actors and everyday experience. Two themes are important here: (a) viewing identity as contestation – since social norms tend to 'bind people to each other and at the same time turn people so bound against others' (Elias 1996: 159–60) and (b) the importance of recognizing the potential for agency in everyday acts from peoples who have been marginalized, such as those who are repressed by discourses of Western dominance (Hobson 2004, 2007a, 2007b, 2013b). At this point, everyday politics theorists place strong emphasis on structures of exploitation and, above all, seek to reveal how they manifest but are also constituted by, and sometimes challenged at, the everyday level of ordinary people.

However, what is important here is to recognize not only the importance of complex and increasingly complicated identities in influencing how people relate to each other and engage in everyday economic processes of migration, work, consumption and finance among others, but how it is these processes themselves that constitute outlets for their agency – and are constituted precisely through this agency. Indeed, it is one of the most important contributions of the literature on everyday politics that it emphatically demonstrates that marginalized people have agency not because of, or despite of, being marginalized but because they are ordinary and yet extraordinary people living their ordinary and yet extraordinary lives. It is in this *agency of the mundane* that everyday life meets everyday politics.

IPE as Everyday Life

One particular body of work associated with everyday life within IPE draws inspiration from a range of European social theorists, philosophers and sociologists. Key among these thinkers are Henri Lefebvre (1971, 1991) for his work on 'everyday life' (see also de Certeau 1984) and Michel Foucault (1980) for his ideas about 'governmentality' and 'technologies of the self' that ordinary actors replicate in their own lives. An important aspect of the 'everyday life' approach is the point that in order to understand how our world is constructed, who holds power and who transforms political and economic environments, common assumptions must be challenged and denaturalized (Bratsis 2006). In such a way, the naturalized picture of order in the world that is bequeathed to us by the analytical approaches associated with RIPE becomes subjected to critique. In particular, it is important to reveal the logic of discipline that runs through, informs and replicates the everyday experiences and daily routines of ordinary actors (Langley 2007), as well as to consider how they internalize risks (Beck 1992). That is, order is not natural but is constructed through the inculcation of a logic of discipline before this is subsequently naturalized. To reveal the way in which this is transmitted, much emphasis is accorded to relationships of production and marketing which, in turn, focus on the social reproduction of everyday spaces and households, the marketing of lifestyles to be administered and the introduction and normalization of processes associated with the acceleration of modern capitalism (Lefebvre 1971: 23; cf. Peterson 2003). These processes provide what we understand as a new 'logic of discipline' that actors translate into their everyday lives. In so doing, daily routines and economic practices emerge as important sites of agency; paying attention to them makes this a very agency-centric approach.

Structures of power receive considerable emphasis and the analysis ultimately invokes a structurationism, insisting that structures and agency entwine in complex ways. In this way, elite power and non-elite agency are treated holistically. An example of this can be found in Matthew Paterson's work, which examines the role of cars in daily life and the global political economy. Paterson seeks to challenge what he refers to as the notion of 'automobility' – 'the conjoining of "autonomy" and "mobility" in such a way as to legitimize the imperatives for movement that underpin modernity in general and globalization in particular' (2007: 7) – of which the car is the principal artefact. Paterson traces how cars contribute to environmental degradation, the replication of late capitalism and global injustice, are a symbol of autonomy and modernization and undermine the potential for a more sustainable future through their enmeshment with everyday life (Paterson 2007: 28). Paterson's work is indicative here of the normative agenda integral to work on everyday life, the view that everyday life is being homogenized or colonized by changes in modern capitalism.

Similarly, Langley's (2007, 2008) work on the pension fund saving schemes and mortgage loan systems in the UK and the US examines how practices of saving and borrowing have been transformed at the macro-level to then turn to how such changes introduce new attitudes, routines and practices within people's everyday life. The key finding here is the introduction of greater uncertainties into people's everyday lives, exposing many to greater social and financial uncertainties. New logics of discipline are encouraged by governments and elites and produce a scenario where 'neoliberal governmental programmes demand a similarly entrepreneurial engagement with financial market risks [from workers] in order to provide for retirement ... [through] new forms of financial self-discipline that include investment as a technology of risk' (Langley 2008: 92). Langley's work also places a premium on identity politics within everyday life. In his work on mortgage finance, Langley is interested in how '[i]ncome and class are likely to be far from the only determinants in everyday experiences of financial inequality and, especially in terms of borrowing, representations of an increasingly "included" middle-class and an "excluded" poor and low-income other may well be highly problematic' (2008: 13).

A second strand of the literature on everyday life looks to how this everyday common sense can be revealed to have particularly gendered, racialized and heteronormative logics. This scholarship also has a strongly normative aspect – what Enloe (2013: 40) refers to as 'a feminist call – to investigate the personal as if it were political' which serves to show how power is 'deeply at work where it was least apparent'. Hence a focus on the mundane practices of everyday life was, and continues to be, central to the work of scholars engaged in feminist political economy research in large part because it provides an alternative lens for understanding the 'hard questions' of the 'globalizing political economy' (Enloe 2013: 48). Looking at the practices and routines of daily life in order to raise big-picture questions about foreign direct investment, development, globalization, the transformation of the state or the nature of work has indeed been a key contribution of feminist analyses. We would point to McCracken's (2014) study of the Mexican beauty economy, Elias's (2004) work on recruitment practices in multinational firms, Smith's (2012) and Chin's (2013) study of working lives in the commercial sex trade, Chin's (1998) study of the lives of domestic workers and their employers in Malaysia and, not least, Bedford's (2011) work on the gendered everyday forms of risk and speculative consumption that characterize the bingo industry as just some of the many examples of feminist scholarship that focuses on how the 'mundane matters'.

Although in this conclusion we contrast an everyday life approach with an everyday politics approach, we do not wish to suggest that overt *political* agency is absent in this scholarship. An emphasis on agency and sites and practices of both acquiescence and resistance remains a central theme in feminist political economy scholarship. Similarly, Paterson points to the 'alternative daily practices which might recognize and reinvigorate the sense of self which recognize obligations to others, communality, and so on' (2007: 18). So too, in detailing agency from the bottom-up, Langley's work traces forms of dissent to the common sense of the contemporary neoliberal order (be it in the form of artwork or alternative financial arrangements) (2008: 218, 228). In other words, while everyday economic subjects are deeply compromised by logics of discipline (much of which they self-impose through their own everyday actions such as saving, borrowing, consuming, etc.), there is also agency to resist. And this agency to resist can be emboldened through a critique of everyday life in order to clarify the normative agenda. We will now turn to situating the contributions to this volume in the context of these everyday approaches – not least because a major aim of the project has been to ensure that the many and varied ways of 'doing' EPE are sufficiently represented.

Locating the Everyday in the Political Economy of Southeast Asia

We will now consider the contributions of this volume through the prism or lens set up in the previous section. One of the first things to note is that the constituent chapters resist advancing a voluntaristic, quasi-liberal conception of EPE that accords a pure, unbounded notion of everyday actor agency, on the one hand, while, on the other, they acknowledge and indeed analyze how elites play a very important role in shaping national economic development and competitiveness agendas within the various countries of the Southeast Asian region. This reminds us of the important point that EPE, while seeking to bring a sharper focus on the role of everyday actor agency and experiences into the study of political economy, does not entail throwing the 'elite baby' out with the everyday agential bathwater. But while they indeed avoid the trap of everyday agent-monism, so too do they escape the trap of elite-centrism.

Navigating between the Scylla of elite-monism and the Charybdis of everyday actor-monism is the journey that this book undertakes as it plies the intellectual waterways of Southeast Asia. So, for example, Andrew Rosser, in his chapter on Indonesia, accepts that hard-fought gains that have been won by various groups of everyday actors in their resistance and contestation of the marketization of education need to be set against a background in which political elites exercise and retain considerable influence and the power to advance their desired goals. Lena Rethel perhaps goes further than any of the other authors in this regard, arguing that the development of Islamic finance in Malaysia has been fostered and promoted by the state as it has undertaken the programme of modernization, but that this in itself has thrown open new pathways to contest if not resist the increasing financialization of the Malaysian political economy. While it would be unfair to argue that the volume can be reduced to those who favour an everyday politics approach and those who advance an everyday life perspective, what we propose to do here is to discuss the various chapters and consider them in the light of these two analytical traditions, but also to highlight their interstitiality.

Drawing on an Everyday Politics Approach

The chapters that, in various ways, speak more directly to an everyday politics perspective are those by Rosser, Nem Singh and Camba, Henry and Tan. Thus, the chapters by Rosser, and Nem Singh and Camba explore how emerging coalitions of non-elite actors, ranging from local communities and civil society groupings to national advocacy organizations and intellectuals, contest statist developmental projects (and thus state power), be it the marketization of the Indonesian education system in the case of Rosser or the expansion of a foreign investment-led mining regime in the Philippines in the case of Nem Singh and Camba. By contrast, Henry and Tan focus more squarely on how non-elite actors draw on international and domestic norms and regimes – specifically for the protection of labour – to expand their agential capacity. This is done, for example, via the localization of ILO norms in the case of Myanmar studied by Henry or by domestic migrant workers pursuing legal means to enforce their contractual rights in the case of Hong Kong as explored by Tan. We will discuss these chapters in turn.

Andrew Rosser's chapter discusses the marketization of education along neoliberal lines in post–New Order/post–Suharto Indonesia and produces a deft balance between the politics of elite power and that of everyday non-elite resistance and agency. Undoubtedly, Indonesia is a powerful case to examine because under the New Order regime civil society had been deliberately disorganized as a result of government policy, to such an extent that it had effectively paralyzed the capacity for self-organization among groups such as the working class and the urban middle class. Thus, an analysis of the post–New Order situation is one that provides a hard test-case for revealing sites of everyday actor agency, particularly given the wealth of the extant literature that downplays such agency. Rosser begins his analysis by arguing that the democratization process that has occurred since the end of the New Order regime has opened up new opportunities for everyday actors to influence policy making. Rosser seeks to neither overplay the success of such democratization processes nor overestimate the success of everyday agency. He, nevertheless, insists that everyday acts of agency have made a difference in the case study that he deploys, specifically in resisting the excesses of the neoliberalization of education, even if such resistance has been more successful in watering down reforms rather than halting them altogether. The key means by which resistance has been conducted is through challenging state educational reforms through the Constitutional Court. Rosser singles out three key areas in which resistance has enjoyed some success. First, everyday actors have challenged the attempts to make educational institutions more autonomous of government in line with neoliberal principles. Second, they resisted government initiatives to create 'international standard schools', which would entail the privatization of the country's best schools so as to redirect state subsidies to schools that are located lower down the educational hierarchy. And third, the notion of a national exam was also successfully contested.

Jewellord Nem Singh and Alvin Camba explore the anti-mining movement in the Philippines. They show that this movement is 'far from uniform and homogeneous'. Indeed, two national coalitions have emerged, Alyansa Tigil Mina (Alliance against Mining) and Kalikasan (Nature). They differ not only in the methods they pursue but also in their visions on mining and social development, with Kalikasan pushing for small-scale mining as a national development strategy. Protest against the state-supported foreign investment-led mining regime takes both the form of more ad hoc resistance strategies such as rallies and human barricades and more formal legalized and institutionalized methods such as campaigns for mining moratoriums and countermapping. Nevertheless, as Nem Singh and Camba argue, social mobilization against mining projects is very much 'grounded in the concrete experience of marginalization by local communities and indigenous people that serve as the starting point for organized political resistance against large-scale mining'. Critically, everyday and localized practices of resistance create synergies with the national coalitions, which allow the latter to align 'specific local claims with the broader national framing of "anti-mining"' in terms of broader debates around social and economic justice.

Nicholas Henry considers the case of trade unions as agents of change in the context of the still highly repressive Myanmar regime. He rightly notes that the international norms propagated by the ILO lead many to assume that this would promote policy convergence among states. Nevertheless, he argues, they 'do not dictate the processes by which states and local actors achieve compliance, or the institutional form that compliance takes'. To understand how international norms play out in various national contexts requires a recognition of the relative autonomy of the local context in general and the role of local everyday actor agency in particular. In so doing, he insists, 'foregrounding the role of everyday actors in norm localization provides an alternative view to structuralist approaches that elide everyday agency'. Interestingly, he implicitly reiterates our point made earlier in this chapter regarding the limitations of Robert Cox's approach to IPE, pointing out that Cox views the ILO as a hegemonic institution that subverts trade unions into the capitalist-imperial project. Here Henry seeks to reveal the other side of hegemony or hegemonic governmentality, which reveals it as 'a site of social struggle and compromise through which everyday actors define the terms of their compliance with the authority of states and international organizations'. The key claim boils down to the assertion that the ILO empowers everyday actors to recognize their own agential capacity 'as active participants in global politics' rather than as 'passive recipients of rights bestowed from above by powerful international organizations'. For within the highly repressive political environment of Myanmar the emergence of trade unions and everyday actor resistance is a significant achievement.

From these three chapters, it should already be apparent that standard models of power which presume a binary relationship of winners and losers – conceived of as in effect clashing billiard ball-like entities – are insufficiently nuanced to be able to pick up some of the more interstitial forms of everyday actor agency that have been revealed thus far. But if we dispense with the pure billiard ball model of winners versus losers, we can begin to see how everyday actor agency works in more subtle ways within the interstices of this 'clash'. Indeed, behind the sometimes overly dramatic rhetoric of 'class struggle' or 'ethnic conflict' lies a far less dramatic, more mundane world of everyday contests and negotiations. Moreover, what is interesting – especially if we read these chapters against the 'everyday politics' approach pioneered by Scott and Kerkvliet – is that as the region has undergone rapid economic, political and social change, new and increasingly institutionalized pathways have emerged for everyday actors to contest top-down developmental projects (but see Jayasuriya and Rodan 2007). These range from the legalization of trade unions in Myanmar to the opening up of the court system to non-elite actors in Indonesia. And yet, it is these actors' lived experience that determines if and how they take action.

This point is further pursued in Carol Tan's chapter. Tan is a legal scholar and designed her study to look at how and why migrant domestic workers (MDWs) do or do not decide to sue their employers. The context here is a legal system that offers some protections to domestic workers, and yet such provisions do little to prevent consistent forms of labour abuse that are often seen as part of the ordinary and everyday experience of migrant workers. There is, in effect, deemed to be little point in 'making a fuss' since everyday forms of labour rights violations (e.g., holding on to passports or mobile phones, being denied rest days, subjected to CCTV surveillance by employers) are perceived as normal working practices. Individual acts of litigation are shown to take place only when workers face extreme forms of, usually violent, abuse. While Tan acknowledges that these are the 'extreme cases', the way in which domestic workers are made vulnerable to violent abuse stems from their positioning as non-citizens employed within the private sphere of the household. The view that 'what happens behind closed doors is a private matter' was seen most starkly in the case of Yuli when she recounts how neighbours had mentioned that other domestic workers had left her employer in the face of ongoing domestic abuse. Thus, while we are seeing the reconfiguration of Asian households as sites of the global political economy (i.e., sites of paid employment and immigration), these shifting household relations are maintained via forms of violence (True 2012). Nonetheless, Tan argues that

the stories of the MDWs who litigate destabilize the still dominant portrayal of MDWs in which the language of 'protection' and 'structural constraints' denies them their agency. They also redress the imbalance caused when attention is inevitably drawn to the high profile campaigns for the improvement of the rights of MDWs in which collective action for or by MDWs is featured. In litigation, we see how some MDWs use the narrowest of opportunities to seek advice or to collect vital evidence with which to overcome earlier detrimental acts such as signing receipts for full wages and rest days.

Happenstance plays a role in the workers becoming aware of their contractual rights – details of a shelter printed in a free newspaper or a leaflet passed to the worker on her day off. These are portrayed as events that serve as turning points in explaining these *formal* acts of resistance (though Tan is keen to point out that she is not discussing everyday strategies of resistance in the sense of Scott's 'weapons of the weak'). But this is not a straightforward story charting the emancipatory outcomes that access to socioeconomic rights grants to the oppressed. The chapter also provides accounts of things like the collusion of recruitment agencies in the abuses suffered by MDWs such as encouraging women not to report crimes, thereby allowing abusive employers to continue to employ domestic workers. And, ultimately, while Tan presents an important account of how migrant workers seek to resist an unjust economic system, the fact that women only sue their employers in the worst possible scenarios demonstrates how resistance takes shape within larger logics of discipline – namely the role of the law in upholding a neoliberal economic system that rests upon the exploitation of low-wage racialized groups of non-citizen others.

Drawing on an Everyday Life Approach

The chapters that we feel speak more directly to an everyday life perspective are those by Tyson, Franck, Elias and Louth, Fischer and Rethel. For Tyson, Franck, and Elias and Louth, the understanding of everyday life fits more within studies that have emphasized how, as Enloe states, 'the mundane matters', while for Fischer and Rethel, emphasis is placed much more firmly on the broader cultural reconfigurations and logics of discipline that lead to the production of everyday life. We will discuss these chapters in turn.

Adam Tyson examines the Malaysian government's attempt to stop the brain drain as part of its thrust to promote a knowledge-based economy, revealing a largely ignored site of agency – the migratory practices of professionals. The argument focuses on everyday ethnic struggles that in turn block the feasibility or success of top-down imposed policies focused on simultaneously promoting a politics of ethnic privilege while also seeking to attract top 'talent' back to Malaysia. Such policies are shown not only to contain inherent contradictions, but what we see in Tyson's account is how these contradictions are experienced by everyday actors. Hence, for example, Malaysian-Chinese doctors working in the UK are both targeted as a source of 'talent', wooed at talent fairs and other events, but express concern about the extent to which their working lives and opportunities for their children would be constrained by other government policies. Access to education – and the types of education – emerges as a key flash point in these discussions. An interesting comparison can be drawn then with Rosser's chapter on Indonesia in which a (more) neoliberal education policy was resisted at the grassroots by the poor. By contrast, in Malaysia, we see how the endurance of state education policies that channel resources towards one ethnic group (the Malays) impacts the lives of non-Malay social elites who have managed to maintain their privileged status through access to private education and employment overseas. Tyson's chapter thus provides an account of how forms of everyday resistance (albeit resistances that are *not* being undertaken by subaltern groups but by privileged outsiders who are increasingly recognized by the state as a vital economic resource) could play a role in shaping state policy.

The subtleties of an everyday life approach are, once again, on full display in Anja Franck's chapter that examines female employment participation rates in Malaysia. She asks why participation rates appear to significantly drop for women once they have married and had children. According to the official data, women exit formal employment when taking maternity leave but then fail to reenter it thereafter. But it turns out that women only leave employment in the formal economy choosing instead to enter informal employment once they return to work. Binary models read this as a function of women experiencing poverty and oppression or as 'the product of involuntary exclusion'. But her argument can be situated within an everyday life approach as she, in effect, seeks to restore female everyday agency to the centre of the story. Thus she insists that women choose to enter informal work as a result of a multitude of factors which include the desire for increased autonomy; more flexible working hours and the desire to create a more harmonious work–life balance; closer proximity between home and the workplace; greater satisfaction vis-à-vis working conditions. Thus, married women have moved out of formal employment in factories and services and have moved into informal employment either as employees or as employers, often working their own stalls in market places or working as unpaid family members in a domestic family business. Importantly, though, by moving into such informal workplaces, these women are not accounted for in the official data on employment and accordingly they 'go statistically missing'. But beneath the official data lies a very different story of what might be termed 'relative' female agency.

Like Tyson, Juanita Elias and Jonathon Louth also focus on migration, but migration at the bottom of the social pyramid. The authors suggest that an everyday life perspective (or, as they term it, a feminist EPE approach) can be helpful in order to understand wider political and economic shifts in the region. Starting with disputes that emerged over the sending of MDWs from Indonesia and Cambodia to Malaysia, the authors stress that in order to understand these disputes it is essential to situate them within the context of the transnationalization of systems of social reproduction that underpin the region's trade in domestic labour. In this respect, the authors attempt to bring together two bodies of literature: a feminist literature on social reproduction and writings on everyday life. The aim then is to explore the ways in which this 'site' of state politics (the regulation of flows of domestic workers) cannot be understood without an appreciation of what goes on within households – in many ways the ultimate site of everyday life, not least because of the ways in which households have been left out of much political economy scholarship. Asserting the significance of transnational households in understanding everyday life in Southeast Asia does not, however, mean that the authors completely reject the everyday politics approach – and the final section of the chapter points more towards the individual acts of agency that constitute everyday forms of resistance to the webs of state-sanctioned exploitation that characterize this employment sector. It remains to be seen whether or not these individual acts of agency serve to subvert or maintain broader logics of discipline.

Whereas the chapters by Tyson, Franck, and Elias and Louth focus on racialized and gendered practices of work and migration, Fischer and Rethel focus more squarely on the emergent logics of discipline that have accompanied the region's ongoing economic transformation. These two chapters in many ways cover similar issues – the ways in which the growing attention being directed towards personal piety in Islamic Southeast Asia has been harnessed as commercial opportunity by government and commercial elites. Looking at the rapidly expanding markets in halal goods (or even the market in halal certification) and Islamic finance, respectively, the authors seek to tease out how routines of daily life are shaping and being shaped by the expansion of these global and yet very local industries. Johan Fischer's work is situated within an approach to social anthropology in which ever greater attention is being placed on the rise of global markets and global pressures for change. This approach recognizes 'how anthropological subjects in everyday life' are positioned at the intersection of both the global and the local. The chapter thus provides an overview of the emergence of Singapore as a key player in the global halal market (an interesting development given the suspicion with which many in this ethnically Chinese-dominated state regard Malay Muslim citizens), before turning to explore the case of the FairPrice supermarket chain. We are thus provided with a picture of how ordinary Singaporeans experience the expanding market for halal, be they FairPrice employees or Malay Muslim shoppers. The key issue here is the role that certification schemes (deemed necessary in order for Singapore to engage in the global halal market) play in the increased standardization of products and religious practice that has accompanied the marketization of everyday life. Indeed, everyday life in this case is situated within the broader disciplinary logic of an 'audit culture' that contributes to 'the production of people and places in Singapore'.

Lena Rethel's chapter explores the rise of Islamic finance in Malaysia. While at first glance the expansion of Islamic finance in Malaysia appears to have been largely captured by elites, the further marketization of Islamic finance is fraught with tensions that we can start to unpack by taking an EPE perspective. Everyday routines of saving and borrowing contribute to the very processes of market widening and deepening that are being explored in the third section of the book. Cumulatively, they have resulted in the growing indebtedness of households in Malaysia and their increasingly direct exposure to financial uncertainty. Yet, this also opens new possibilities for resistance. Thus, whereas Rosser's chapter in the same section explores the impacts of this widening and deepening on the poor and the possibilities for resistance, Rethel, by contrast, looks at the centrality of the Islamicizing middle classes to the constitution of Islamic finance (and indeed the Malaysian modernity project more generally) while still pointing to the potentials for at least contestation that emerge out of this politicization and financialization of religion.

EPE at the Interstices of Everyday Politics and Everyday Life

Of the chapters in this book, the interstitiality of the EPE is perhaps most explicitly articulated by Jonathan Rigg, who examines how everyday actors negotiate the process of modernization. He argues that there is not so much resistance to modernization itself but to the *project* of modernization that is imposed by governments within Thailand and Vietnam, the two countries on which he focuses. The prism through which Rigg analyzes this comprises the manifold ways in which everyday actors negotiate rural–urban dynamics and the formal and informal systems that govern internal migrants within these two countries. In so doing, Rigg seeks to 'illuminate the explanatory and experiential gap between the instrumentalities of governments, reflected in the policies that are enacted, and the actions and activities of ordinary people'.

In Vietnam the household registration system was designed to block mobility and to permanently resettle people in one particular place (urban or rural but not both). The puzzle that needs unravelling is that while objectively there is much to be gained by individuals in signing up to full registration in a particular area (where they would be treated as full citizens), nevertheless, many prefer to remain 'floating' and to sign up to 'temporary' rather than 'full' residence in a particular area. But everyday actors have often chosen to reside in cities while retaining their links to the rural areas, partly for economic security reasons but also in good measure because of identity reasons. The latter comprises cultural notions derived from being connected to the land (i.e., 'home' or the 'home-land'). Thus, government-imposed conceptions of modernization are frustrated by choices made by everyday actors that prioritize not just their own economic but also identity-based interests. In his second case study, Rigg shows that even where tradition has become incorporated within the statist modernization project, such as perhaps most explicitly in the Thai concept of the 'sufficiency economy', statist ambitions are disjunct from how they are experienced on the ground – in this case by rural dwellers in Thailand's northeast region. In so doing, Rigg highlights the changing modalities of village life and livelihoods. In his words, alongside 'the village as resilient, where traditions remain important, is another village that has become reliant on migrant work, where consumer goods define success, and where the great majority of households are in significant debt'; this is where everyday politics meets everyday life.

In sum, then, the standard billiard ball conception of power is simply too bald and monolithic to be able to tease out these more subtle processes which reside within the interstices of power – in this case between everyday actors and government-imposed modernization programs – and the practices of daily life. Thus, if we shift our gaze to the ways in which modernization programs are imposed, received and negotiated by everyday actors on the ground so-to-speak, then new sites of everyday agency come to the fore. Indeed, as Rigg notes, 'it is at the margins – at the points of contact – where much of interest lies'. Thus, EPE is not simply a matter of giving 'voice' to non-elite actors but also about understanding how the conditions of everyday life are themselves produced.

Conclusion

We have argued here that regulatory approaches such as specifically what Hobson and Seabrooke (2007b) termed RIPE cannot provide us with all the information we need to understand practices of economic engagement in the world economy. This is so especially since it obscures how non-elites can transform national political economies and the world economy more broadly, be it through defiance, mimicry or habit-informed behaviour. In adopting, in various ways, an 'everyday lens', the chapters in this volume have sought to move beyond elite-centric accounts to allow for a theoretical and empirical engagement with both the significance of everyday actors to Southeast Asian political economy as well as the ways in which processes of economic transformation take shape as a form of everyday lived experience.

Some of the chapters have drawn on what can be broadly termed an 'everyday politics' analytical tradition to draw out the agency of non-elite actors within various national political economy settings in Southeast Asia. Importantly, this has allowed not only for analyses of how (coalitions of) non-elite actors have acquiesced to and resisted state policies and economic change, but how they develop their own agential capacity. Other chapters adopt a more 'everyday life' lens in that they focus on how the region's economic transformation is experienced on the ground and lived through daily routines. Yet, this also provides new avenues for a critique of our daily actions so that we may seek to change them. While some of the chapters have pointed to the role of everyday actors as (more or less) effective agents of change, others point to the gendered and racialized forms of inequality and destitution that characterize 'the violence of everyday life' (Scheper-Hughes 1993). To this end, as Rigg puts it in this volume, EPE offers not 'an alternative view of transformation, but [one] that … permits us to connect individual capabilities and volitions, national policies and socio-economic processes, and societal structures'.

In such ways, EPE opens up new vistas and new ways of studying Southeast Asian political economies – and the world economy more broadly – beyond the limited parsimonious framework of mainstream regulatory approaches. Of course, the recent emergence of EIPE – and the move from EIPE to EPE that we have made in this volume – is only in its formative stage. Much work remains to be done in terms of theoretical and empirical development. But we believe that these new approaches offer up exciting new pathways into the study of (not just) the Southeast Asian region and hope that others will be drawn into joining the project in order to drive it further.

References

Amoore, L. (2002) *Globalization Contested*. Manchester: Manchester University Press.
    (2004) 'Risk, reward and discipline at work', *Economy and Society* 33(2): 174–196.
Antoniades, A. (2008) 'Cave! Hic everyday life: repetition, hegemony and the social',
    British Journal of Politics and International Relations 10(3): 412–428.
Avant, D. D., Finnemore, M. and Sell, S. K. (eds.) (2010) *Who Governs the Globe?*
    Cambridge: Cambridge University Press.
Beck, U. (1992) *Risk Society*. London: Sage.
Bedford, K. (2011) 'Getting the bingo hall back again? Gambling law reform, economic regeneration and the gendered limits of "casino capitalism"', *Social and Legal Studies* 20(3): 369–388.

Bieler, A. (2006) *The Struggle for a Social Europe: Trade Union and EMU in Times of Global Restructuring.* Manchester: Manchester University Press.

Blyth, M. (2002) *Great Transformations.* Cambridge: Cambridge University Press.

Bratsis, P. (2006) *Everyday Life and the State.* Boulder: Paradigm Publishers.

Certeau, M. de (1984) *The Practice of Everyday Life.* Berkeley: University of California Press.

Chin, C. B. N. (1998) *In Service and Servitude: Female Domestic Workers and the Malaysian 'Modernity' Project.* New York: Columbia University Press.

(2013) *Cosmopolitan Sex Workers: Women and Migration in a Global City.* Oxford: Oxford University Press.

Cox, R. W. (1986) 'Social forces, states and world orders: beyond international relations theory', in R. O. Keohane (ed.) *Neorealism and its Critics.* New York: Columbia University Press, pp. 204–254.

Davies, M. (2005) 'The public spheres of unprotected workers?', *Global Society* 19(2): 131–154.

Davies, M. and Neimann, M. (2002) 'The everyday spaces of global politics: work, leisure, family', *New Political Science* 24(4): 557–577.

Dunn, K. C. and Shaw, T. M. (eds.) (2002) *Africa's Challenge to International Relations Theory.* Basingstoke: Palgrave MacMillan.

Enloe, C. (2013) *Seriously! Investigating Crashes and Crises as if Women Mattered.* Berkley: University of California Press.

Elias, J. (2004) *Fashioning Inequality: The Multinational Firm and Gendered Employment in a Globalising World.* Aldershot: Ashgate.

Elias, N. (1996) *The Germans.* New York: Columbia University Press.

Finnemore, M. (1996) *National Interests in International Society.* Ithaca: Cornell University Press.

Foucault, M. (ed.) (1980) *Power/Knowledge: Selected Interviews and Other Writings*, trans. C. Gordon. Brighton: Harvester Press.

Franklin M. I. (2005) *Postcolonial Politics, the Internet and Everyday Life: Pacific Traversals Online.* London: Routledge.

Gilpin, R. (1987) *The Political Economy of International Relations.* Princeton: Princeton University Press.

Hay, C. (2004) 'Ideas, interests and institutions in the comparative political economy of great transformations', *Review of International Political Economy* 11(1): 204–226.

Hobson, J. M. (2004) *The Eastern Origins of Western Civilisation.* Cambridge: Cambridge University Press.

(2007a) 'Is critical theory always for the white west and for Western imperialism? Beyond Westphilian, towards a post-racist, critical international relations', *Review of International Studies* 33(S1): 91–116.

(2007b) 'Eastern agents of globalisation: oriental globalisation in the rise of Western capitalism', in J. M. Hobson and L. Seabrooke (eds.) *Everyday Politics of the World Economy.* Cambridge: Cambridge University Press, pp. 141–159.

(2012) *The Eurocentric Conception of World Politics: Western International Theory, 1760–2010.* Cambridge: Cambridge University Press.

(2013a) 'Part 1 – Revealing the eurocentric foundations of IPE: a critical historiography of the discipline from the classical to the modern era', *Review of International Political Economy* 20(5): 1024–1054.

(2013b) 'Part 2 – Reconstructing the non-eurocentric foundations of IPE: from eurocentric "open economy politics" to inter-civilizational political economy', *Review of International Political Economy* 20(5): 1055–1081.

Hobson, J. M. and Seabrooke, L. (eds.) (2007a) *Everyday Politics of the World Economy.* Cambridge: Cambridge University Press.

(2007b) 'Everyday IPE: revealing everyday forms of change in the world economy', in J. M. Hobson and L. Seabrooke (eds.) *Everyday Politics of the World Economy.* Cambridge: Cambridge University Press, pp. 1–23.

(2007c) 'Conclusion: everyday IPE puzzle sets, teaching and policy agendas', in J. M. Hobson and L. Seabrooke (eds.) *Everyday Politics of the World Economy.* Cambridge: Cambridge University Press, pp. 196–213.

Jayasuriya, K. and Rodan, G. (2007) 'Beyond hybrid regimes: more participation, less contestation in Southeast Asia', *Democratization* 14(5): 773–794.

Keohane, R. O. (1984) *After Hegemony.* Princeton: Princeton University Press.

Kerkvliet, B. J. T. (1990) *Everyday Politics in the Philippines.* Berkeley: University of California Press.

(2005) *The Power of Everyday Politics.* Ithaca: Cornell University Press.

Langley, P. (2007) 'Everyday investor subjects and global financial change: the rise of Anglo-American mass investment', in J. M. Hobson and L. Seabrooke (eds.) *Everyday Politics of the World Economy.* Cambridge: Cambridge University Press, pp. 103–119.

(2008) *The Everyday Life of Global Finance.* Oxford: Oxford University Press.

Lefebvre, H. (1971) *Everyday Life in the Modern World.* New York: Harper and Row.

(1991) *Critique of Everyday Life.* London: Verso.

McCracken, A. B. (2014) *The Beauty Trade: Youth, Gender and Fashion Globalization.* Oxford: Oxford University Press.

Morton, A. D. (2007) 'Peasants as subaltern agents in Latin America: neoliberalism, resistance and the power of the powerless', in J. M. Hobson and L. Seabrooke (eds.) *Everyday Politics of the World Economy.* Cambridge: Cambridge University Press, pp. 120–138.

Overbeek, H. (1990) *Global Capitalism and National Decline.* London: Routledge.

Paterson, M. (2007) *Automobile Politics: Ecology and Cultural Political Economy.* Cambridge: Cambridge University Press.

Peterson, V. S. (2003) *A Critical Rewriting of Global Political Economy.* London: Routledge.

Phillips, N. (ed.) (2005) *Globalizing International Political Economy.* Basingstoke: Palgrave MacMillan.

Rupert, M. (2000) *Ideologies of Globalisation: Contending Visions of a New World Order.* London: Routledge.

Scott, J. C. (1976) *The Moral Economy of the Peasant.* New Haven: Yale University Press.

(1985) *Weapons of the Weak.* New Haven: Yale University Press.

(1990) *Domination and the Arts of Resistance.* New Haven: Yale University Press.

Scheper-Hughes, N. (1993) *Death without Weeping: The Violence of Everyday Life in Brazil.* Berkley: University of California Press.

Seabrooke, L. (2007) 'The everyday social sources of economic crises: from "great frustrations" to "great revelations" in interwar Britain', *International Studies Quarterly* 51(4): 795–810.

Smith, N. J. (2012) 'Body issues: the political economy of male sex work', *Sexualities* 15(5): 586–603.

Tétreault, M. A. and Lipschutz, R. D. (2005) *Global Politics as if People Mattered.* Lanham: Rowman and Littlefield.

Tickner, A. B. (2003) 'Seeing IR differently: notes from the third world', *Millennium* 32(2): 295–324.

True, J. (2012) *The Political Economy of Violence Against Women.* Oxford: Oxford University Press.

Wallerstein, I. (1974) *The Modern World System.* London: Academic Press.

Watson, M. (2005) *Foundations of International Political Economy.* Houndmills: Palgrave Macmillan.

    (2013) 'The eighteenth-century historiographic tradition and contemporary "everyday IPE"', *Review of International Studies* 39(1): 1–23.

Weber, H. (2010) 'Politics of global social relations: organising "everyday lived experiences" of development and destitution', *Australian Journal of International Affairs* 64(1): 105–122.

Wendt, A. (1999) *Social Theory of International Relations.* Cambridge: Cambridge University Press.

Widmaier, W. W., Blyth, M. and Seabrooke, L. (2007) 'Exogenous shocks or endogenous constructions? The meanings of wars and crises', *International Studies Quarterly* 51(4): 747–759.

Worth, O. (2008) 'The poverty and potential of Gramscian thought in International Relations', *International Politics* 45(6): 633–649.

Index

Lightning Source UK Ltd.
Milton Keynes UK
UKOW06n0749080816

280114UK00010B/81/P